"AVE ROMA IMMORTALIS"
Equestrian statue of Marcus Aurelius

ROME

BY

EDWARD HUTTON

Haec est in gremium victos quae sola recepit,
Humanumque genus communi nomine fovit,
Matris, non dominae, ritu : civesque vocavit
Quos domuit, nexuque pio longinqua revinxit.

LONDON
HOLLIS & CARTER
1950

First published 1911
Seventh edition, revised and enlarged, 1950

DG
806
H85
1950

MADE AND PRINTED IN GREAT BRITAIN
BY THE BURLEIGH PRESS, LEWINS MEAD, BRISTOL
FOR HOLLIS & CARTER, LTD., 25 ASHLEY PLACE,
LONDON, S.W.1

TO
CHARLOTTE MY WIFE
BELOVED COMPANION
OF ITALIAN YESTERDAYS

TE SPECTEM SUPREMA MIHI CUM VENERIT HORA
TE TENEAM MORIENS DEFICIENTE MANU.

PREFACE TO THE SEVENTH EDITION

IT is the times which change. When this book was first written there was a King in Italy and three mighty Empires dominated Europe. The Pope was a prisoner in the Vatican. Nothing of this remains. Italy is now a Republic. The Pope is again the Sovereign of an independent State—the Vatican City. He is seen to wield a formidable power and to be in fact the spiritual head and front of the defence of civilisation.

Very great changes, too, have befallen Rome. Rome has suffered a transformation beyond that of any other ancient city in Christendom. Whole quarters have been overthrown and excavated to reveal the ruins of the Imperial age : others, where an immemorial silence reigned, have been developed and built up. The time-honoured approach to St. Peter's has been swept away and replaced by a broad boulevard, and the majestic solitude of the Campagna has been invaded by the aerodrome and the modern suburb. In fact, Rome like the rest of the world has been engulfed in the Mass Age.

Yet she seems to possess a mysterious continuity which no disaster, no vandalism, not even the lapse of time can interrupt, or change or diminish her divine character. *Tempora mutantur nos et mutamur in illis.* It is the times which change and we too change with them. But our hearts ? In Rome as of old we may still find delight and wander through the centuries.

That is why I have re-written this book.

E. H.
1950.

CONTENTS

APPENDICES

LIST OF ILLUSTRATIONS

Plate

xi

LIST OF ILLUSTRATIONS

For permission to reproduce the photographs in this book, the publishers' grateful thanks are due to the following : to V. and H. Hankey (nos. 1, 2, and 32) ; to Francis Pollen (nos. 4 and 14) ; to the *Ministero della Pubblica Istruzione* (nos. 7 and 9) ; to W. F. Mansell, Ltd. (nos. 5 and 30) ; to Messrs. Anderson (nos. 6, 19, 22, 25, 27, and 28) ; to the Associated Press (no. 17) ; and to Messrs. Alinari for the remainder.

ROME

I

AVE ROMA IMMORTALIS

ONE April evening as I stood on the vast bastion of the Janiculum in the sudden silence of the hour after the sunset—Rome was looking terrible as a crater under the conflagration of the sky—I seemed to realise for the first time the true aspect of a place so augustly familiar, which, as Dante has perceived, Nature herself has formed for universal dominion —*ad universaliter principandum*—and out of which has risen all Europe and our Faith, all that is really worth having in the world.

An incredible majesty had descended upon the City and the hills. Little by little that far horizon, glorious with mountains, was hidden in the grey evening ; the desert of the Campagna was changed into a vast shadow ; like a snake of sullen gold the Tiber crept through the twilight into the darkness and the sea ; only the Dome loomed out of the night like some mysterious and lovely symbol, a visible gesture of the infinite, decisive and affirmative, never to be recalled or modified.

The material world, that close, impassable prison, seemed just then to be dissolving before my eyes, and it was as though in the silence I had heard again those words, so full of assurance and all gladness : *Sed confidite, Ego vici mundum :* Be of good cheer, I have overcome the world.

And so, *Ave Roma Immortalis* is for me no longer merely a greeting of love, but the expression of a fact that, little by little, has impressed itself upon me till I recognise it at every turn of the road, at every moment of the day. I feel the eternity of Rome as I feel the brief sweetness of every passing moment there : she seems to me as eternal and persistent as life, as strangely various, as mysteriously secret. In her name is married domination and love, ROMA-AMOR, which none may ever divide or separate ; they smile at me everywhere, in-dissolubly one, confounded in her, yes, even in the Forum, where in a ruined temple of the Empire there is a ruined church of the Middle Age cheek by jowl with a Renaissance or Baroque building amid the wildflowers of our spring.

Nor is it only in the stones of the City that old and new are confounded in her life. Consider then what she has made, after all so finely, of Christianity. Call to mind what you have seen in S. Maria in Aracoeli, in S. Teodoro, in S. Agostino. No, it is the ages that pass away ; Rome remains.

And was she not ever Cosmopolis ? That babel you hear in the Piazza Colonna any spring morning, Horace heard it too, and Aurelius, and S. Austin. It might seem, if you can but bear to think it, that Rome was never so true to herself as she is to-day. Her very excesses confound her with her past. That strange desire and eagerness to destroy and to build, how damnable it seems, yet what is it after all but the old necessity of Empire and Papacy to impress the people, to touch the imagination of the crowd, in whom they lived and moved and had their being ?

And the destruction ? But she lives by it ; it is her oldest secret. The vandalism of the Caesars became the vandalism of the Popes and was the vandalism of the modern kingdom. You think the monument of Victor Emmanuel merely the result of the vulgarity and insolence of our times ? Even so, I am with you. But it is the successor of Nero's Golden House and of S. Peter's church, nor, though its victims have been so many and so precious, may they compare with what those demanded ; and since it is the least beautiful of the three, it need not be the most lasting. For Rome is never perfected, but is always in transformation. Her life is as various as our own, responding, if you can but see it, to every mood of the heart. It is thus that she is the most human of cities— not the city of the soul, perhaps, as Shelley called her, but certainly the city of man who persists and lives by destruction and is never satisfied.

Who can tell her age, or prophesy when she shall be no more ? For the advent of Romulus was not her natal day, nor the death of Augustulus her funeral. She was before Evander came, and has outlived the Romans by more than a millennium. As her beginning is hidden from us, so is her end.

In this, too, is her eternity, that men have always longed for her as for a beloved mistress.   She, what she stands for, is the hope of the world and its despair : her life is a consuming fire that none may quench.   Yet it is this which, like true idolaters, we have thought to find in the Forum among her discarded stocks and stones, disturbing even the profoundest sleep to discover the secret of her immortality.   O foolishness ! we have questioned the dead, and in the unbreakable silence have heard only the falling of dust on dust ; but she is not there, she is risen, and her hands are clasped in ours.

II

THE CAPITOL

TO climb up to the Capitol to-day by the steps of
1536, between the statues of the Dioscuri into the
Piazza built at the suggestion of Michelangelo, as a
great and splendid chamber, one might think, for the equestrian statue of Marcus Aurelius, is to come into a world of
ghosts, of ghosts which have always ruled the world. In
spite of its fame, perhaps even because of it, the Capitol has
kept nothing of its antiquity—nothing but the rumour of its
eternity as in the lovely verses of Horace :

> . . . dum Capitolium
> scandet cum tacita virgine pontifex . . .

Before you is the Palazzo del Senatore, the Novum
Palatium of 1150, which in the hands of Michelangelo and
Sixtus V became the modern building we now see. To the
left is the Capitoline Museum built for the most part under
Innocent X, after a design by Michelangelo, while to the right
is the Palazzo dei Conservatori, a foundation of Nicholas V,
rebuilt, again in the manner of Michelangelo, under Pius IV
in 1564. Nothing at all remains of the time of the Republic
or the Empire ; only in the midst of the Piazza formed by these
three palaces rides the philosophic Emperor as though in
stoic contemplation, a ghost in the midst of ghosts, as it were
an exile in his own city. The most famous spot in the world
you might think has become nothing but a vast museum.

It is the same with the hills that on either hand tower over
the Piazza, the true Capitolium to the right, the dwelling-
place of Jupiter Capitolinus, which has returned to something
of its primitive wildness of which Virgil speaks :

> Aurea nunc, olim silvestribus horrida dumis

4

and to the left the Arx, the sacred citadel of Rome, beside which stood the temple of Juno Moneta—Juno of warning, where Christianity has built a shrine to the Madonna. And yet in spite of the absence of any building of the Rome of antiquity, it is chiefly of her you think amid the work of the Middle Age, of the Renaissance, of the world of to-day, that so strangely, it seems, at first at any rate, everywhere confronts you there on the caput and citadel of the world. Little by little, however, as you linger there you come to understand that, as everywhere in Rome, you cannot divide the old from the new, nor Antiquity from the Middle Age, nor either from the modern world. In her immortal life the one has proceeded from the other, and was not made nor created anew. They were moods, as it were, of the City : nor can we say of anything eternal that it was young and grows old. For as a melody is lost in a melody so in her everliving soul antiquity passed into mediaevalism, into modernity, each following other in perfect and lovely sequence ; and the last is there because of the first, the new because of the old.

And since this is the life of Rome, we shall find it perfectly expressed on the Capitol which has always, as it were, summed up the City and served for the whole world as a symbol of it. Because it was here that Curtius died for the people, that Tiberius Gracchus fell in their cause, and Marcus Brutus, after the death of Caesar, spoke in defence of the Republic and his crime, therefore in the Middle Age it was on the Capitol that Arnold of Brescia, Stefaneschi of Trastevere, Cola di Rienzo and Stefano Porcari would have proclaimed the Republic ; and because of all these things it is there Italy has to-day set up her monument to unity and freedom.

It is true that the mere material continuity in brass and stone is not so manifest. Yet the bare fact that over and over again everything that has been built here has been swept away is indicative at least of the passionate love that has always surged around this hill. If in the Middle Age the home of the Senator was set here, it was not by chance ; for the Capitol has always been the citadel of the Republicanism of the people, that, smouldering all through the Middle Age and the Renaissance, has now again appeared. In some sort the

B

Senator may still be said to dwell here on the Capitol, and the Palazzo dei Conservatori is even yet the meeting-place of the ancients of Rome. While in the Capitoline Museum opposite to it, the Romans have for ages placed their most precious possessions, those statues in marble and bronze carved or cast by their ancestors which of old adorned the Forum or the Palaces of the Caesars.

It was Michelangelo, himself a passionate Republican and always so unwillingly the servant of princes, who brought hither the most priceless treasure of the City, that equestrian statue of Marcus Aurelius, in gilded bronze, creating for it a magnificent chamber, fairer far, we may believe, than that we see, which was contrived out of his design by his disciples. The statue is indeed a stranger here where it seems so perfectly in place, for of old it stood before the Arch of Septimius Severus in the Forum, till Sergius III, struck by its beauty perhaps, and looking for a champion, thinking it was Constantine, placed it in front of the Lateran Palace. That was in the first years of the tenth century. Then towards the end of the same century, when there seemed to all but a reprieve of less than forty years before the Day of Judgment, the end of the world, the Emperor Otho the Great set John XIII on the Throne of the Fisherman against the popular will. The Barons, as always, ready for any excuse, roused the City, the Captains of the Regions, led by the Prior Peter the Prefect, followed them, and seizing Pope John out of the Lateran threw him into Castel S. Angelo, driving him at last to exile in Campania, till Conte Goffredo, the head and front of the mischief, being murdered, they set the Pope at liberty, who returned to Rome. Then came the Emperor at Christmas time to do justice on the Roman people. And he took the Captains of the Regions and hanged twelve of them, and Peter the Prefect he bound naked on an ass and set an earthen jar on his head and had him flogged through the City. And when he was dead he hung his body—what was left of it — by the hair to the head of the great bronze horse, on which, as he thought, Constantine rode before the Lateran, that all might see his justice on his enemies.

Called by the pilgrims Theodoric, by the people Quintus

Curtius, and by the clergy Constantine, it stood for more than five hundred years before the Lateran after it had served Otho for a gallows. It was ever held in veneration by all, and in the wild joy of the Tribunate of Rienzo the people filled the bronze belly of the horse with wine and water, so that water flowed from one of its nostrils and wine from the other. So greatly was it held in honour that though Michelangelo and the Pope had long wished to remove it from before the Lateran to its present position here on the Capitol, the Canons in whose care it was were only won to consent in 1538, demanding in acknowledgment of their rights payment from the Senators. So every year a bunch of flowers was and is still presented by the City to the Chapter : a custodian " Custode del Cavallo " being appointed with a salary of ten scudi annually to guard it. And so well did Michelangelo understand the ever-living City that he was not ashamed to make the pedestal out of one of the pillars of the Temple of the Dioscuri.

It is not, however, in the Piazza—that valley between the true Capitol and the Arx—that alone or even chiefly perhaps, we meet those ghosts which, haunting indeed the whole City, here more than elsewhere press upon us insistently, company by company. Climbing up past the Piazza dei Conservatori to the Tarpeian rock, *Capitoli immobile saxum,* we come upon that spot which for Virgil was the holiest in the City.

" *Hoc nemus, hunc," inquit " frondoso vertice collem*
(quis deus incertum est) habitat deus : Arcades ipsum
credunt se vidisse Iovem, cum saepe nigrantem
aegida concuteret dextra nimbosque cieret.
Haec duo praeterea disiectis oppida muris,
reliquias veterumque vides monimenta virorum.
Hanc Ianus pater, hanc Saturnus condidit arcem :
Ianiculum huic, illi fuerat Saturnia nomen." [1]

So Evander tells Aeneas, showing him the City. And indeed it was here that Saturn himself reigned in the Golden Age,

---

[1] " This grove," he cries, " this hill with its leafy crown, though we know not what god, a god inhabits ; the Arcadians believe they have seen Jove himself, while often his right hand shoots the darkening aegis and summons the storm clouds. Moreover in these two towns with walls thrown down thou seest the relics and memorials of men of old. This arx Father Janus built, that Saturn ; this Ianiculum was called, that Saturnia." Saturnia = Capitolium.

before the Titans broke out of the custody of Orcus, and, piling Pelion on Ossa, scaled Olympus. When the corn was sown and reaped on the hillside and there was a plenty for all, before war was born or any man thought to go armed, was it not up this hill they would pass, those fortunate folk singing at evening ? Till one day Evander came from the Palatine across the marsh with Aeneas and showed him Saturnia in ruin. The Golden Age was over : but the hill bore the name Saturnus till the time of the Tarquins.

And after Aeneas was dead Romulus came hither, and, finding the place a forest of ilex, hoping for men, established there a refuge for slaves who were fugitive, and after the rape of the Sabine girls he built there a Temple, not to peaceful Saturn, but to the God of spoils, Jupiter Feretrius. Not much later the Sabines in revenge for the rape, under their king Titus Tatius, seized the fortress on the other height, not by valour, but by the wiles of a woman, Tarpeia, who loved the gold on the arms of the Sabine youths and felt too soon the weight of it.

Dimly from very far off, sometimes when I have waited there alone in that lonely place the coming of twilight, I have seemed to see her still, Tarpeia, priestess of Vesta, daughter of Spurius the Captain, as she came at sunset, straight and slim as a reed, singing too, down the steep way to the valley, the earthen jar on her black head, to bring spring water for the evening sacrifice. Unharmed for all the war and vengeance, for she served the Goddess who had no statue but was living fire, who was served with bare feet, she came slowly, dreamily down the hillside in the sunset, and found Titus Tatius beside the fountain. It was the golden bracelet on his arm that she desired, as he saw doubtless in a moment. He gave it her, and shyly she took it.

" Is it for me," she said, desire in her eyes, " this that you wear on your left arm ? " for she knew not the name of gold. And he answered, " Give me the fortress to-night ; and not only I but all of us will give you . . . what we wear on our left arms." Well, if she were a traitor, he lied : yet it was she paid for all.

And it was so. For that night the Sabines went up stealthily to the gate, and Tatius led them. Then she who had forsworn her people opened to them—the gate was on the height above the arch of Septimius Severus—and Tatius as he passed struck her down under the weight of that which he bore on his left arm, but it was a shield ; and as they entered each did likewise. " So perish all traitors ! " said they doubtless. And when they had taken the city, they buried her at dawn under the rock that bears her name. But as they tell you, imprisoned in the hill, she sits there weeping to this day. And when Tatius was dead Romulus once more seized the Capitol and there Numa Pompilius, his successor, who founded the Roman religion, built a Temple to Fides Publica.

It was Tarquinius Superbus, the last king of Rome, who about 535 B.C. built the great Temple his father had vowed to Jupiter on the Capitol. He began it with the spoil of the Volscian war, and it was in digging the foundation, as it is said, that that sign was found which named the hill and promised, as was foretold by the Augurs, the lordship of Italy to Rome—a human head, still bloody. The proud king, however, did not live to see the dedication of the Temple he had built, for it was carried out by the first consuls of the Republic : who set up there the rude earthen image of Jupiter arrayed in splendid robes. For hundreds of years this Temple was the holiest shrine in Rome. Thither the greatest generals of the Republic, the heroes of the Punic wars among them, came in Triumph. And then as though to symbolise the approaching fall of the Republic, which had consecrated it, in the time of Marius it was burned to the ground. Sulla rebuilt this Temple, but it too was destroyed and so was that which Vespasian set there to replace it ; while the last and most splendid building of all was looted and spoiled by Genseric who carried off the statues to his African Palace and stole away the tiles of gilded bronze.

As it is with the southern height, so it is with the northern, where of old stood the Arx and the temple where the geese wakened Manlius on that wonderful night when the Gauls were already scaling the citadel. No fragment remains of that temple which Juno yielded to Madonna Mary, nor a single stone of the sacred Arx of Rome. And, indeed, one is like to forget them altogether as one wanders in that lofty brown church of the Friars which, as though moved by the *genius loci*, seems still to guard and keep the City.   Set on so sheer a height, the temple of old was only to be approached from the Forum, but in the fourteenth century of Christ, when the church of S. Maria in Aracoeli was rebuilt by the Franciscans, the towering flight of steps from the Temple of the Sun on the Quirinal Hill was brought hither and set up to bridge the precipice before the west front of the church, so that one might climb to it, though hardly, from the Piazza Aracoeli.

Those old precious buildings, the very citadel of Rome and the temples round about it, might seem to have no part in the church of S. Maria in Aracoeli.   And yet since it has been the courtesy of the Catholic Church, here in Rome at any rate, to preserve for her own use and our joy, all or almost all, that was best in Paganism, it is not without delight we learn that the title of Aracoeli is not of Christian origin.   For it seems that it was here Augustus set up an altar to the Son of God, prophesied by the oracle, that Sibyl to whom the Church still appeals in the marvellous Sequence of the Mass for the Dead :

> *Dies irae, dies illa,*
> *Solvet saeclum in favilla,*
> *Teste David cum Sibylla.*

Restless, it seems, with thoughts of the future of that Empire he had founded with so much craft and patience, Augustus, growing old, as it is said, demanded of Apollo : " After me who will rule the world ? " But the God was dumb.   Twice he asked the same question, but still Apollo was silent.   Then when again he besought him a third time he was answered in these strange words by the priestess : " A Hebrew child, a God Himself and stronger than all the Gods, bids me leave Heaven to give Him place.   Invoke me then no more ; for it is in Hades now that I shall dwell in sadness."   And for this cause the Emperor set up an altar to the Divine Child, with the inscription, *Ara filii Dei*.   So the place was called the Altar of Heaven, and there they built S. Mary a church.   And so it happens, as though in memory of the oracle, that the birth of the Son of God is still celebrated here as nowhere else in

Rome : and the children hold here their festival in honour of the Jesus Parvulus, but not, for us, at any rate, without some reminder too of the old honour due to Juno, who presided over the marriage of all women even as Mary does now, and was the especial protectress of children.

Some say that the church of S. Maria was founded by Constantine, but the Benedictine chroniclers assure us that it was built by Gregory I in 581. However that may be, in the eighth century certainly the church was known as Sancta Maria de Campitolio, which reminds us that all this part of Rome, the tenth Region, that included the Capitol, the Forum, the Colosseum and the Palatine Hill, was called Campitelli.

Those Benedictines who served the church, and, certainly by the year 882, had built their monastery beside it, gradually possessed themselves of the whole Capitol, which at that time must have been wild and savage enough to please even S. Benedict. In 1015 we find their Abbot signing himself, *Ego Dominicus Abbas Capitolii* ; and Anacletus II, Antipope, more than a hundred years later, in 1130, confirms them in their possession of it. Then in 1250 Innocent IV expelled the monks and gave their heritage to the Franciscans, who still serve the church though their convent has been destroyed, with so many other precious things, to make way for the Vittoriano monument. Meanwhile the Capitol had become the focus, as it were, of the undying Republicanism of the Roman people, which, smouldering always, burst out at times in those great flames of anger which so often nearly consumed both Pope and Barons. The most glorious and the most renowned place in the ancient City became indeed the " consulto " of the people, and was confirmed to them as such by Eugenius IV in 1445, two years after his return to Rome, whence he had been ignominiously chased in 1434

S. Maria in Aracoeli is now mainly a building of the fourteenth century, when it was largely restored and reconstructed, and the great flight of steps before the west doors was built in gratitude for the escape of Rome from the Plague of 1348. Later restorations by Cardinal Caraffa in 1464, by Pius IV, who destroyed the old choir, and by Gregory XIII, who restored the splendid roof, have, however, left their mark upon it.

Within, the church is one of the most impressive in Rome. Divided into a nave and two aisles upheld by twenty-two ancient columns from many different buildings, it is at once austere and simple. Here we seem really to have come upon a place that has always been dedicated to God. And this is so in spite of the furniture and decoration that too often spoil the chapels : not that, however, which we come to first, on the right, in the south aisle beside the west door. Lost though it is in an almost complete darkness, on some fortunate day, just before sunset, you may descry without too much weariness the work of Pinturicchio, those frescoes of the life of S. Bernardino which he painted for Ludovico Buffalini, advocate to the Papal Consistory, who died, as an inscription on a stone in the pavement tells us, in 1506. It seems that a deadly feud had for many years raged between the Buffalini and the Baglioni of Perugia, which S. Bernardino had contrived to extinguish. It was to celebrate this strange peace that Pinturicchio was commissioned to decorate the chapel. Concealed for long by a wooden panelling, these frescoes were only discovered in the end of the eighteenth century, which may account for their excellent preservation.

The tiny Gothic chapel, lighted only by a small window, is " architecturally decorated " in monochrome, the walls being divided by painted pilasters, hung with masses of fruits, caught in with ribbons.

But it is on the eastern wall, and above the altar, that Pinturicchio has done really his best ; and indeed those frescoes are among the finest of his works. In the arches above the wall on the left is S. Bernardino in sackcloth, almost naked, leaving his gay home and fair comrades in Siena to go " into the wilderness." And all that fantastic city is come out to see him, though he marks them not, nor those flowers, hyacinths and anemones and the lilies of the field, that " proud pied April " has spread under his feet ; nor the pleasant voice of the stream singing to itself as he passes, nor the fair towers of Siena which he is leaving behind him. It is as though he had taken " Our sister the Death of the Body " as a Bride. And indeed, beneath, Pinturicchio has painted his Funeral Procession. The lines of the marble pavement stretch away between the cloisters and the colonnades to a temple and those country places which are certainly not to be found in any earthly city. It is a place in that imaginative country, that romantic landscape of which Perugino his master was almost the creator, full of every delicate fancy, strange fruits and frail flowers and fantastic palaces in a world to which he had the key. In the foreground they bear away the saint, already in the embrace of his bride, to burial, and there follow after him sorrowfully all that gay or wretched company he had served so well : the beggars he so loved, the friars who were his brethren, the women who sought him out, the children upon whom he had compassion. And there, too, out of the long and beautiful loggia on the left comes Messer Avvocato Lodovico Buffalini, whom he had reconciled with his enemy. At the saint's feet two babies dance and sing, unconscious of our loss, and there beside them, wrapped in swaddling clothes, is the Bambino Gesù Himself, or that miraculous image of Him— is it ?—which is the most precious possession of this very church.

Only less lovely, though still full of that " light that never was on sea or land," the nimble air of a heavenly country, is the Glorification of the Saint over the altar. Christ in the heaven of this heaven, which has not forgone the sun as was told us, stands on a cloud in a mandorla of cherubim, while six angels there sing and play the songs of Paradise, and at His feet two seraphs, crowned with light and bearing each the Lily of Annunciation, hold aloft for S. Bernardino the crown of glory which fadeth not away. He stands as it were on a hillock, lifting his right hand in blessing, a little anxious about us even yet : and on either side S. Louis of Toulouse, the patron of Lodovico Buffalini, and S. Antonio of Padua are busy with Litanies.

Leaving so delicate a dream, the rest of the chapels, in this south aisle, at least, seem almost consciously half-hearted in their welcome. And it is not indeed till we come to the Savelli chapel in the south transept that we find anything to interest us at all. But there we have a witness to the early fame of Aracoeli. The Savelli were one of the first Roman families, and in the thirteenth century they built themselves a chapel here, and buried there Pope Honorius IV of their house in

1266 in what has proved to be the first papal monument that has come down to us in its completeness. Beside him lie Randolfo and Andrea his daughter, in a pagan sarcophagus decorated with reliefs of fruit and flowers. In the same tomb with the Pope lies his mother, Vanna Aldobrandesca. In the great choir another Savelli, a cardinal who died in 1498, lies in a tomb by Andrea Bregno.

Passing before the high altar we come upon those two Ambones from which the Epistle and Gospel are sung. The work of the Cosmati, they are exquisite examples of thirteenth-century work in mosaic, as is the wonderful if ruined pavement of the great church.

Not far away towards the north transept the little Tempio, the Cappella Santa di S. Elena marks the site of the altar Primogeniti Dei, and there lies in a porphyry bath Saint Helena, while close by sleeps another Queen, Catherine of Bosnia, who died in 1478.

In the north transept is a fine monument to Cardinal Matteo di Acquasparta, the General of the Franciscans in 1302 whom Dante praised and Boniface VIII sent to face the Florentines. It is a work of the Cosmati, possibly by Johannes Cosma himself. On the lid of the tomb the Cardinal lies in his pontifical robes, while angels lift the curtains that shelter him ; above, S. Francis presents the deceased to the Madonna and Child, while close by stands S. John the Evangelist. On the keystone of the arch, which, like the columns, is covered with mosaic patterns, is a painted bust of our Lord.

It is the second chapel in the left aisle that at Christmas time is the shrine at which all worship, for there the Bambino of Aracoeli, that little wooden figure which, as they say, was carved by a friar in Jerusalem and finished by an angel, lies amid the hay, the chapel being transformed into a stable, while the careful ox and the ass that will soon bear Madonna and Him into Egypt stand by, and Mary and Joseph receive how gladly the shepherds and the three kings. It was S. Francis who invented the Presepio, and here, in Aracoeli, it is of a peculiar splendour, not only for the sake of S. Francis but because the church possesses in the figure of the Bambino the most famous miracle-working image in Rome, covered with jewels and clothes of rich stuffs. The ducal house of Torlonia still, it seems, or at least till within the last few years, lends its great coach and its servants in livery when it is borne to the sick, who are not only poor or ignorant persons, but even Princes of the Church. But how amusing it is to watch the children who between the Feast of the Nativity and Twelfth Night recite verses in honour of the little Prince of Life, and without self-consciousness or any fear at all speak of one, little like themselves, whom they have loved. And, it seems to me, that, after the great Madonna of S. Agostino, is the most Roman sight in Rome.

III

THE FORUM

IF the Capitol was the citadel of Rome, the true *Caput*
of the world, the symbol, as it were, of the domination of
the City, on coming into the Forum we realise at once that
this was its heart, the focus of that wonderfully catholic,
religious, political, and economic life, the very centre of its
being. Always the true Piazza of Rome, since the day when
(according to Dionysius of Halicarnassus) Romulus and
Tatius, the one from the Capitol, the other from the Quirinale,
descended into the valley to make friends, it served alike as
market-place, court of justice, and public promenade. Nor
did it lose its pre-eminence when in the course of ages the Fora
multiplied themselves, and other market-places were built for
the sale of cattle, or of fish, or of vegetables.[1] And if this was
so during the years of the Republic, when the Empire rose it
was not less the meeting-place of the City, bridging as it did
the gulf between the Capitol and the Palatine Hill. When
Julius Caesar wished to impress the people, he built there, and
all the ambition of the Emperors but served to make more
splendid that which had always been pre-eminently the Forum
Romanum. Nor with the conversion of Constantine did it
fall into decay. Indeed it remained almost perfect until the
seventh century when, as the column erected by a decayed
Senate to the tyrant Phocas bears witness, it was still considered the greatest honour in the world to be remembered
there. If, after that time, it fell into ever greater ruin, it was
yet here from the heart of Rome that the Popes took the
treasures which adorned their newer city, so that the Forum
became a quarry, and thus out of the very heart of the ancient
city was hewn the Rome of the modern world. While the
Renaissance did not stay the vandalism of the Church, it yet
filled the hearts of men with an old remembrance ; and

[1] *Forum Boarium, Forum Piscarium, Forum Olitorium.*

therefore Pope Paul III, when in 1536 Charles V returned from Tunis, thinking to do him the highest honour, decreed him a Triumph along the old Via Sacra, under the arch of Titus, through the Forum, to the Capitol. It is from this time, however, that the Forum began to be transformed into the Campo Vaccino, that beautiful vale which Poussin and Claude and Turner so loved. Paul III had ruthlessly destroyed houses and churches to make that Triumphal Way for the enigmatic Emperor. Some fifty years later Sixtus V began to throw into the morass of ruins his predecessor had made, the débris of the buildings he too in his turn had destroyed in planning the Rome which, for the most part, we now see. Thus in the centuries that followed was formed the beautiful graveyard of the Campo Vaccino.

It was to impress the Roman people, to found their government more firmly on the wonder and awe of the Plebs that the Republic had made the Forum so splendid, that Augustus adorned it, that the Emperors built there those Triumphal Arches which are still the wonder of the world. For a like reason the Popes destroyed it all and built too after their fashion. And now modern Italy, with an enormous and learned patience, has uncovered once more the ruins of its ancestors if so be it may gather from that ancient splendour some new glory for itself.

And indeed as you walk to-day along the Sacred Way, certainly not without regret for the lost beauty of the Campo Vaccino, you are reconciled at last, not by the discoveries of the indefatigable Giacomo Boni, but by Nature herself which has already re-established her kingdom and sown even among the stones the wildflowers of the spring. Yes, the Forum is still green with bays and grey with olive. Are there not laurels —ah like bronze—among the ruins of Caesar's Temple ; do not the lilacs, purple and white, still spread their shadow on the stones and fill the Via Nova with their perfume ? It is Nature herself which has come in triumph along the Sacred Way, while the very stones have cried out *Io, Triumphe.* Long and long ago the cruel trumpets have been silent, the slave behind the victor no longer utters the slave's warning, for Scipio is not more dead than Caesar, and all the tears of their prisoners have been dried, therefore the flowers are come as though to assure us that there is no Triumph that shall endure but the triumph of love. Here, where the masters of the world have passed at last to the Capitol, and Emperor after Emperor has striven to outdo the dead in glory, where the greatest names in the world echo, how faintly after all, beside the most despicable, and all are mixed in a mere rumour of oblivion, we pass, softly, softly, looking for the flowers.

And certainly it emphasises the meaning we may find perhaps in their frail beauty, our distrust, too, of all that cruel glory, to learn how wide even here, even in the greatest matters, is the kingdom of forgetfulness. For it seems that the mere direction, the precise route certainly, of the most famous road in the world has been really unknown for ages, was more than doubtful even in antiquity, since both Varro and Festus tell us that the people were always uncertain which was indeed the Sacred Way, for no street bore then any written name.

Beginning, as these writers seem to suggest, in the neighbourhood of the temple of the Lares, of the Colosseum, the Via Sacra, in the highest part of the Forum, by the Arch of Titus which was later built across it, turned immediately to the right, and passing before the portico of the Temple of Venus and Rome, wound thence to the left, and, passing the Temple of Vesta and the Regia, proceeded straight to the foot of the Capitol, leading thence by a winding way to the Temple of Jupiter Capitolinus.

The Sacred Way thus marks for us very happily the true character of the Forum, which, as it suggests, was the centre of the life of the city, surrounded on all sides by temples, law courts, banks, and shops, and there, too, were to be found the Rostra and the Comitium, while the Capitol closed it in on the west, the Palatine on the south.

That the temples which so closely surrounded the Forum should have been so many and of such magnificence bears witness, one may think, to the significance that religion has always had in the public life of Rome, in antiquity as in our own time. And here too we may discern something of that continuity of life, of custom, of tradition which is the eternity of Rome, for if to-day she venerates with enthusiasm and joy Mary Madonna, of old it was another Virgo Veneranda who guarded the City and was adored in every household where the family was gathered together at the hearth.

The most important, and certainly the most venerated of all the Roman deities, was Vesta. For since man has always felt the necessity of worship, he has expressed it from time to time as well as he could, not least adequately or without a very real beauty in the worship of Vesta, which summed up in itself the divinity, the holiness of the hearth, and all that it means in the life of the family, of the household, that little city within a city ; so that every dwelling would be in some sort a Temple of Vesta, and round the sacred hearth each day the whole family would assemble for their common meal and, thus united, their very union became an act of worship, and the meal a sacrifice to her and to the Penates.

She had not any graven image in marble, or in ivory and gold, but showed herself only in the Sacred Flame that burned continually there in her temple, which was, as it were, the universal hearth of Rome, uniting all the citizens of the State, yes, in spirit, into one family. And as the hearth stood in the midst of the old Roman house, so the Temple of Vesta stood in the midst of the Forum.

It was Numa, the second king of Rome, who, so the Romans liked to believe, was the author of their whole religious system. It was he, they said, who had founded the Temple of Vesta midway between the Palatine and the Capitoline Hills, building it in his own fashion of circular form with a conical roof, just one of those rustic dwellings of the earliest Latin peoples. And throughout its history it preserved its primitive form, its smallness and simplicity, as though to remind even that Eternal City of her humble origin. Burnt many times under the Republic, rebuilt last of all by Julia Domna, the wife of Septimius Severus, it too fell with the ruin of the gods ; and with them was found again by the Renaissance during the last year of Paul III in 1549, only to be utterly destroyed ; even the foundations being dug up to provide material for new buildings. Then the excavations were filled up and the destruction hidden, not, however, before a design of the ruins had been made which we still possess.

Beside the temple stands the *Domus Virginum Vestalium*, the House of the Vestal Virgins, those priestesses who guarded the Palladium on which the safety of the City depended, and tended the Sacred Fire. Chosen by lot from among the daughters of twenty patrician houses named by the Pontifex Maximus, for thirty years they swore to devote themselves as maidens to the service of Vesta, and though at first they numbered but four they were later increased to seven. The whole City held them in the highest honour. Not only did a Lictor precede them in the streets, but the first places were reserved for them at the Public Games and Festivals ; while even the Consuls gave them precedence. Indeed they can have had little in common with the daughters of S. Benedict or the nuns of S. Teresa. It is true they had promised both a severe chastity and an absolute service, but these vows were rather material than spiritual. Nor did they give themselves to any heavenly bridegroom, but served indeed the goddess and the City, not for ever or even for their whole lives, but for thirty years, after which they might marry and bear children and in all ways conform to the reasonable life of the City, from which they had never thought for a moment of withdrawing their allegiance. Even during the period of their sacred service they were absolutely free to dispose of their property as they would, and they gave evidence too in the Courts, but without the customary oath. So honourable, indeed, was the character of their service that it was usual to entrust to them important wills and public treaties ; while to meet them by chance saved the worst criminal on his way to death. And as a crowning mark of the love and reverence with which they were regarded, the City conferred upon the Order the right of burial in the Forum, the highest honour she had to give.

Their dwelling seems to have been splendid and luxurious, and indeed, passing there to-day, in spite of its ruin we may gather some idea of its magnificence. There were baths, gardens, and fountains in abundance ; fair statues,[1] of which

---

[1] One of especial beauty is now in the Museo Nazionale.

THE BASILICA OF CONSTANTINE
(Forum Romanum)

TEMPLES OF SATURN AND VESPASIAN AND ARCH OF SEPTIMIUS SEVERUS
(Forum Romanum.)

many fragments remain, surrounded their courtyard, statues
of the noblest of their company. But while their life was thus
one of ease, honour, and splendour, the penalties for breaking
their vows were terrible ; for after being publicly whipped with
rods, they were buried alive. Very few, however—not more
than twenty—during the many centuries in which they were
the pride and honour of the City, deserved these penalties.
The most famous trial, that in which Domitian charged one of
them with incest, falsely as it would appear, is regarded by
Pliny certainly as a mad freak of that tyrant's cruelty.

" It seems," he says in a letter to Cornelius Minicianus,
who had already heard that Valerius Licinianus had been
accused of seducing Cornelia, the chief of the Vestals, " it
seems that Valerius is teaching rhetoric in Sicily. Had you
heard it ? I do not think you can have done so, for the news
is quite fresh. . . . You will say that it is all very sad and
pitiful, but that a man who defiled his profession of letters
by the crime of incest deserves to suffer. Well, it is true
he confessed his guilt, but it is an open question whether he
did so because he was guilty or because he feared even
heavier punishment if he denied it. For Domitian was in a
great rage and boiling over with fury because his witnesses
had left him in the lurch. His mind was set on burying
Cornelia alive,[1] for he thought to make his age memorable
by such an example of severity, and, using his authority as
Pontifex Maximus, or rather exercising the cruelty of a
tyrant and the wanton caprice of a despot, he summoned
the rest of the pontiffs not to the palace, but to his villa at
Alba. There, with a wickedness just as monstrous as the
crime which he pretended to be punishing, he declared
Cornelia guilty without summoning her before him or giving
her a hearing, though he himself had not only committed
incest with his brother's daughter, but had even caused her
death, for she died of abortion during her widowhood. He
immediately sent some of the pontiffs to see that his victim
was buried alive and thus put to death. Cornelia invoked
in turn the aid of Vesta and the rest of the gods, and amid
her cries, which were many, this was repeated most frequently : ' How can Caesar think me guilty when he has
conquered and triumphed after my hands have performed

[1] Such was the punishment. The Pontifex Maximus — Domitian himself
in this case—had her whipped, and then carried on a bier to the Campus Sclera-
tus near the Colline Gate (near the Acqua Felice) where she was buried alive.

the sacred rites ? ' It is not known whether her purpose was
to soften Caesar's heart or to deride him, whether she spoke
the words to show her confidence in herself or her contempt
of the Emperor. Yet she continued to utter them until she
was led to the place of execution, and whether she were
innocent or not, she certainly appeared to be so. Nay, even
when she was being led down into the dreadful pit and her
dress caught as she was being lowered, she turned and re-
adjusted it, and when the executioner offered her his hand
she declined it and drew back as though she put away from
her with horror the idea of her chaste and pure body being
defiled by his loathsome touch. Thus she preserved her
sanctity to the last, and displayed all the tokens of a chaste
woman, like Hecuba truly, ' taking care that she might
fall in seemly wise.' "

The Pontifex Maximus, who had thus so great a power over
the Vestals and was in some sort their governor, had his
official dwelling, the Regia, on the other side of the temple
beside the Sacred Way. Scarcely anything remains of the
house in which Julius Caesar spent the last months of his life.
He had chosen to occupy the Regia rather than to build or
buy a house on the Palatine as Augustus did later, true to his
habit of living always among the people, and indeed it was
from the Regia he set out to go to the Senate on that fatal
March morning in the year 44 B.C. Some hours later, his
body, covered with no less than twenty-three wounds, was
borne back hither through the Forum. " Many of the conspirators," says Plutarch, " wounded each other as they were
aiming blows at him." As is well known, he died on the
pedestal of Pompey's statue, " so that Pompey seemed to
preside over the work of vengeance." That murder shook the
world, and in fact accomplished what Brutus professed most
to dread, the establishment of a tyranny. " Brutus and his
conspirators," says Plutarch again, " yet warm from the
slaughter "—Brutus himself had struck Caesar in the groin—
" marched in a body with their bloody swords in their hands
from the Senate House to the Capitol, not like men that fled
but with an air of gaiety and confidence, calling the people to
liberty, and stopping to talk with every man of consequence
whom they met." The Senate passed a general amnesty, and

to reconcile all the factions decreed Caesar divine honours. Next day, however, the body was exposed before the Rostra, though whether those not far from the Arch of Septimius Severus or those which Caesar had himself established beside the temple of Castor and Pollux is doubtful. Wherever it may have been, there Antony harangued the people :—

> But yesterday the word of Caesar might
> Have stood against the world ; now lies he there,
> And none so poor to do him reverence.

Then he put them in possession of Caesar's Will, when it was found that he had left every Roman " a considerable legacy " :—

> To every Roman citizen he gives,
> To every several man, seventy-five drachmas. . . .
> Moreover, he hath left you all his walks,
> His private arbours and new-planted orchards,
> On this side Tiber ; he hath left them you
> And to your heirs for ever, common pleasures,
> To walk abroad, and recreate yourselves.
> Here was a Caesar ! when comes such another ?

The Plebs could no longer be kept within bounds. " They stopped the funeral procession," says Plutarch, " and tearing up the benches, with the doors and tables, heaped them into a pile and burned the body there "—" in the sacred place," as Shakespeare has it—the Via Sacra. Then snatching flaming brands from the pyre, some ran to burn the houses of the assassins, while others ranged the city to find the conspirators themselves and tear them in pieces ; but they had taken such care to secure themselves that the people could not find one of them. There followed Philippi, Actium and the Empire.

We meet Caesar again in the hour of his triumph before the Temple of Saturn, which after the Temple of Vesta was the most ancient and perhaps the most important religious building in the Forum. In the shadow of the Capitol, on the Sacred Way, it was built perhaps by the Tarquins, and consecrated by the Consuls Sempronius and Minucius in 497 B.C. Restored at the very beginning of the Empire in the first years of Augustus, and again after the great fire of A.D. 283 as the inscription tells us : S.P.Q.R. INCENDIO CONSUMPTUM RESTITUIT, eight of its columns are still standing. It was the State Treasury, and it is before its doors that we meet Caesar.

Having reduced all Italy in sixty days without spilling a drop of blood he returned to Rome. The City was, it seems, quieter than he had expected and, as was his way, for the greatest man in the world was one of the gentlest, he was kind and gracious to all. Metellus the Tribune, however, had the courage to oppose him when he would have taken money from the Treasury, here in the Temple of Saturn, alleging certain laws against it. But Caesar answered : " Arms and laws do not flourish together. If you object to what I am doing you have only to withdraw. War, as I say, will not allow of much speech. And even when I tell you this I am departing from my own right, for you and all whom I have found exciting a spirit of faction against me are in my hands." Yet still the Tribune opposed him manfully ; but Caesar, raising his voice, threatened to put him to death. " And, young man," said he, " you are not ignorant that this is so much harder for me to say than to do." Metellus, afraid at last, retired, and " ever after," Plutarch tells us, " Caesar was easily and readily supplied with everything neccessary."

After the Temples of Vesta and Saturn, the most ancient shrine in the Forum is that of the Dioscuri that stands beside the Fountain of the Dioscuri close to the House of the Vestal Virgins. Founded about 484 B.C. in honour of the great twin brethren who had led Rome to that victory over the Latins at the battle of Lake Regillus, it was built beside the Lacus Juturnae where, after the fight, those heroes, Castor and Pollux, as was believed, riding into Rome, watered their horses. So here in the Vicus Tuscus, close to the most sacred Temple of the Hearth, their shrine was built beside a spring of water. The ruins we see, the three beautiful columns of Parian marble, date, however, from the time of Augustus, when this temple which had suffered very grievously in the civil wars was rebuilt. It was indeed part of the policy of Augustus to establish the gods more firmly and more splendidly in the remembrance of the people. The shrine of the Dioscuri was not the only temple he rebuilt, before he established as the crown alike of his arms and his diplomacy, the Temple of Concord—Templum Concordiae Augustae—on the site of the ancient shrine which, built in 366 B.C., commemorated the peace between the Patricians and the Plebs. The Golden Age seemed for a moment to have come back again.

Such other temples as there are about the Forum are foundations of the Empire :—the Temple of Vespasian beside the Temple of Concord, built by Domitian and restored by Septimius Severus ; the Temple of Antoninus and Faustina, with its ten beautiful columns of cipollino above the Sacred Way, dedicated by Antoninus to his dead wife, the elder Faustina, in which to-day stands the church of S. Lorenzo in Miranda ; the Temple of Romulus, built by the Emperor Maxentius to the memory of his son ; the Temple of the Urbs Sacra, built by Vespasian, in the midst of which to-day rises the church of SS. Cosma and Damiano ; the Temple of Venus and Rome at the end of the Forum towards the Colosseum, in the Sacred Way, which Hadrian built from his own plan in A.D. 135 and which Maxentius restored in 307. Just there we come upon what must have been one of the most splendid buildings in Rome, indeed two temples in one, set back to back, as it were, and facing, the one towards the Colosseum, the other towards the Capitol. It possessed, we read, more than two hundred columns of precious marbles ; the colonnade surrounding it was one hundred and eighty yards long and one hundred and ten yards wide, consisting of one hundred and fifty columns. And there Venus was worshipped as the Mother of Rome.

There were other temples too—the Templum Divi Julii, of the Divine Julius, for instance, of which nothing or almost nothing now remains. Yet the Forum was not only the religious centre of the City, but the political centre also. And in spite of the changes and havoc of centuries, it is there, best of all, we may still reconstruct for ourselves, as it were, that ancient political life which the very form and shape of the Forum serves to endorse.

At the foot of the Capitol under the citadel to the north, a series of terraces rose one above another from this valley in which the Plebs were used to assemble ; and there the Rostra were built.   Above, on the first terrace stood the Comitium where the Patricians gathered, really little more than a square vestibule of the Curia,[1] which stood on the terrace above, where the Senate most often met.   In the time of the Republic the Comitium must have stood, as it seems, before the Lapis Niger, that mysterious black stone which has been thought to close the tomb of Romulus.

Thus the Curia and the Comitium rising over the tomb of the Founder of the City dominated it, the symbol and sign, as it were, of that aristocratic government which conserved the national spirit and traditions, and, in Rome not less than in England, built up with infinite persistence and wisdom the greatness of the State.

That part of the plain which lies immediately under the Comitium was the Forum proper, and there the Plebs assembled before the Rostra, which, standing as they did almost under the Comitium at the head of the Forum, enabled both Patricians and Plebs to hear the orators.   The centuries of struggle between them seem to pass there to-day almost before our eyes.

But the Rostra, as we now see them, are not in their original place, which was nearer to the Comitium ; for since the orator spoke in the open air, it was necessary, if all were to hear him, that the space should be small between the Comitium filled with Patricians and the Rostra about which the Plebs were gathered.   No doubt among a southern people, gesture, that marvellous language of gesture, which we may see to-day in any street in Naples, counted for much, while the many temples and buildings crowded round about in what after all is a narrow space helped to make the harangue audible. And yet one might think that amid the howls of the Plebs, the noise of a fight, the continual inarticulate interruptions, it must often have been difficult for any one speaking there to be perfectly heard in the Comitium.

And then in the general collapse of aristocratic government

[1] Cf. Livy, xlv, 24.

that helped Caesar to his mastery and that he encouraged by
every means at his disposal, we find that he did not hesitate
to remove the Rostra yet further from the Comitium so that
the Plebs were flattered and the Patricians in some sort divorced
from public life. It was but one sign more that the strong and
free government which had made Rome so great was at an end
for ever.

The Rostra, as we see them to-day, are but a fragment :
yet that fragment may well have heard some of the noblest
and some of the most brutal words that have been uttered in
the world. It was there that the oration of Cicero against
Antony—the first Philippic—was pronounced, and there the
head of the great orator and patriot was exposed after his unspeakable murder by the assassins of the Triumvirate. The
old man had fled to his villa at Formiae, but was overtaken on
the way as he was borne along in his litter. With a courage
which had seldom distinguished him he put his head out
between the curtains and bade his murderers strike. They
needed no second invitation. He died in 43 B.C. in his sixty-
third year.

It was under Trajan that the Rostra of Julius Caesar were
restored, the two balustrades which are to-day among the best
preserved fragments in the Forum being added at that time.
There we see Italy, just a mother, bringing a child to the
Emperor who on the left proclaims his edict from the Rostra,
establishing thus the famous institution for poor children.
In the background are a Triumphal Arch, the Basilica Aemilia,
the Sacred Fig-tree and the statue of Marsyas which stood near
the Temple of the Dioscuri. It was possibly this relief which
induced Pope Gregory to pray for the soul of the dead Emperor,
till he was assured of his salvation.[1]

The other relief represents again the clemency of Trajan
who is burning the records of certain taxes. In the background are the buildings on the western side of the Forum :
the Temple of Saturn, the Temple of Concord, the Basilica
Julia, and once more the Marsyas and the Fig-tree. On the
inner side of the balustrades which have been wrongly set up,

[1] See pp. 61 et seq.

for what is now the inner was of old the outer side, we see
carved in relief the victims at the public celebrations of the
Suovetaurilia, when a boar, a ram and a bull were sacrificed.
How different is this hard and realistic Roman art from the
work of the Greeks in the frieze of the Parthenon ! There,
with a perfect feeling for animals, Pheidias has carved the bull
led to sacrifice, the victim of the Gods, amid the chanting
of the priests, the songs of the people ; but the Roman artist
seems to have understood nothing and to have seen after all
only with his bodily eyes. It is before such work as this
that we seem to realise the limitations of Rome, the immense
gulf that separates her from Greece. Her artists lacked a
certain delicacy and clairvoyance and were without spirituality
or finesse. They seem, here at least, to have been copyists
of nature without insight or sensibility. We seem to understand at last, before such work as this, how even Aurelius
could sit through all the brutality of the amphitheatre, and
drag, even he, in his Triumph along the Sacred Way, that
little German family, the father and mother in chains, their
child crying in her arms, on the threshold of a home brought
bodily over the mountains " to make a Roman holiday," for
the enjoyment of the Roman people. Yes, that explains too
the failure of Rome. To the heart which would refuse to
look on just that with indifference—that and the rest—the
future belonged. But remembering the brutalities of the
modern world we shall do well not to flatter ourselves before
the Romans.

The Forum which we have seen thus, cursorily enough, as
the centre of the religious and political life of the City, was not
less, it seems, the centre of justice also. For there, beside the
Temples and the Rostra, stood the Basilicas, the law courts.
Those great rectangular buildings, divided into three aisles by
two lines of columns and ending in a semicircular apse,
were open on all sides, and were indeed like great arcades
beside the way, so that the law was literally administered in
public. Later, however, they were walled in and became the
model for the great Christian churches.

The earliest of these buildings was the Basilica Porcia, named
after the famous M. Porcius Cato, Censorius, who built it in

184 B.C., probably on the model of the Stoa Basileios at Athens. This building stood to the west of the Curia, where is now the church of SS. Martina and Luca.

Then to the right of the Curia in 179 B.C. the Censors Aemilius Lepidus and M. Fulvius Nobilior built the Basilica Aemilia which was so often restored by the Aemilian House, for the last time in the reign of Tiberius. Ten years after this foundation, the Basilica Sempronia was founded in 169 B.C.

Later Julius Caesar built the Basilica that still bears his name to the south of the Forum beside the Temple of Saturn. This was scarcely finished when it was burned to the ground. Augustus, however, rebuilt it and added to it. Only the foundations remain to-day.

It is, however, in the Basilica of Constantine at the far end of the Forum towards the Colosseum that we have the most perfect ancient example of what we understand by a Basilica. Begun by Maxentius and only finished by Constantine whose name it bears, it consisted of three aisles ending in three apses, covered by a vast vaulting as wide as that of S. Pietro in Vaticano. It was 300 feet long and 270 feet wide and 114 feet high. Before it stood eighty mighty Corinthian columns of white marble, only one of which has come down to us ; but it stands to-day before the church of S. Maria Maggiore where Paul V set it up in 1613. The entrance which faced the Sacred Way was once upheld by columns of purple porphyry, some of the broken shafts of which have been re-erected. They add to the splendour of those enormous ruins which seem even more impressive, more likely to touch the imagination, than the Colosseum itself. And this splendid ruin is indeed the herald not of the end, but of that tremendous change which turned the Pagan into the Christian world. It was built between two disasters ; founded by an Emperor about to be defeated, it was finished by him who deserted Rome.

There is one splendour in the Forum which might seem to sum up, as it were, the whole significance of the place, I mean the Triumphal Arches. Of these there were certainly four, but nothing, or almost nothing, remains of those built to Augustus and Tiberius. Of the two which are left to us the

Arch of Titus is the earlier. Set up in his honour by the Senate, to commemorate the fall of Jerusalem in A.D. 70, it was finished as that inscription proves—S.P.Q.R. DIVO TITO DIVI VESPASIANI FILIO VESPASIANO AUGUSTO—under Domitian, his successor, the last of the twelve Caesars. It stands not far from the Temple of Venus and Rome at the highest point of the Sacred Way across which it was built. Consisting of a single arch supported by composite pillars, it is decorated with fine reliefs. In the *tympana* are set winged Victories bearing palms and crowns, while beneath the inscription is carved a sacrificial procession as a frieze. Within, under the arch, are two marble reliefs in which we see Titus crowned by Victory proceeding along the Sacred Way to the Capitol in a chariot driven by Roma. Opposite is another relief of a Triumphal procession with the captives and the spoils : the table with the shew-bread, and the seven-branched candlestick from the Temple at Jerusalem ; while in the vault the divine Emperor is borne to heaven by the bird of Jove. Carved some twenty years before the balustrades of the Rostra, these reliefs have much of their character and as little feeling or sense of beauty as they. The work of those who were always the victors, they celebrate a strength and persistence which have suffered neither a love of beauty nor a love of truth to cheat them of reality. Rome was already incapable of any sort of expression save that of government. For her, life no longer had illusions or promises ; one not only died at the word of command, one lived by it also.

It was nearly a hundred and fifty years later that the Arch of Septimius Severus, at the other end of the Forum within the shadow of the Capitol, was erected by the Senate, in honour of that Emperor and his sons, Caracalla and Geta, to commemorate their victories over the Parthians in the year A.D. 203. Of old it was crowned by a bronze chariot drawn by six horses, in which the Emperor stood crowned by Victory. Four disengaged columns adorn the façade ; they add to the architectural beauty of the monument a certain charm, and it might seem that without them the Arch would be too dull and too heavy. But victory has here already destroyed the victors. All the ruins of Rome seem to cry *Vae Victoribus*, as though there were but one thing more disastrous than defeat

and that should be victory.   And if the reliefs of the Arch of
Titus carved in the year A.D. 81 move us little, what can we
say of those a hundred and fifty years later?   They are
scarcely art at all, but a sort of craftsmanship, a true cemetery
decoration.

Not far from the Forum, towards the Colosseum, at the
foot of the Coelian Hill, stands another Triumphal Arch,
better preserved than either of those in the Forum, built in
A.D. 312 to celebrate the victory of Constantine over Maxentius.
The decadence of insatiable victory has proceeded how far
in less than a hundred years.   For here, as we see in a moment,
the architecture is grandiose and exaggerated, and in every
way inferior to that of the arch of Septimius Severus.   As for
sculpture, it was apparently no longer practised, for the work
here has been stolen from a building of Trajan, though not
apparently from his Triumphal Arch.   Some of it is very
beautiful, especially the reliefs : Trajan's Triumph ; the Battle
with Dacians ;   the Prisoners beseeching Mercy, where we
see a Dacian village in the background ;   and the medallions
of Hunting, and the Sacrificial Scenes :   but we must think
of it as work of the second century, and not as sculpture of
the time of Constantine.   If we wish to judge of what his
age was capable, we must confine our attention to the small
reliefs beneath the medallions and to the statues of Victories
and Captives on the pedestals of the columns.

The inscription is interesting : IMP. CAES. FL. CONSTANTINO
MAXIMO PIO FELICI AUGUSTO S.P.Q.R. QUOD INSTINCTU DIVINI-
TATIS MENTIS. . . . " *To the Emperor Caesar Flavius Constantine
. . . who by the inspiration of Divinity has freed the Republic from
Tyranny.* . . ." One may well ask who was this Divinity ?
Was it the Prince of Life or Jupiter Capitolinus ?   Who was
the God of Constantine ?   It would be hard to say.   Beside
that arch we seem to stand on the threshold of a new world, in
the twilight of the gods.

But to-day, as I walk through the Forum among the flowers,
it is not after all of any divinity, Pagan or Christian, that I
think, but of the mortal life of man, eternally the same,
whether in the time of Jupiter or under the gentle dominion

of Gesù Cristo. It was but seldom, after all, that the Victor was accorded a Triumph, that Caesar after Caesar was acclaimed by the Senate and the populace ; but our brothers passed by all day long. And it is of those things which continually befall us all in such a place that one of them—not the least beloved—has told us in verse, how much more lasting than the temples of his gods !

I have said that the Forum was the true Piazza of Rome, the public promenade, and it is as just that Horace shows it to us, as no one else perhaps could do, as no one else has done, certainly.

"I happened to be walking," he tells us, "along the Via Sacra as is my custom—*Ibam forte Via Sacra sicut meus est mos* —I was thinking of some trifle or another, was indeed quite lost in it, when a man ran up to me whom I only knew by name, and seizing my hand, said he, ' How do you do, my dearest friend ? '

" ' Pretty well,' said I, ' as times go, and am quite at your service.' As he kept sticking close to me I anticipated him by saying. ' Have you any further commands ? '

" But he answered : ' You must know me. I am a scholar.'

" Then said I : ' On that account I shall esteem you more.'

" In truth I was wretchedly anxious to get away from him ; so at one moment I quickened my pace, at another I came to a standstill, I whispered in my servant's ear, whilst the sweat trickled down to my very ankles. ' O Bolanus ! ' said I to myself, ' how I envy you your hot temper.'

" Meanwhile he went on chattering about anything, praising the streets, the city. As I did not answer him a word he said : ' You are dying to get away, I have seen it from the first ; but it's no good, I shall stick to you and accompany you all the way you are going.'

" Then said I : ' There is no need for you to take so long a round. I want to visit some one you do not know ; . . . it is across the Tiber . . . a long way off and . . . he is ill in bed . . . it is near Caesar's gardens.'

" ' I have nothing particular to do,' said he, ' and I am a good walker. I will go with you all the way.'

" Down went my ears like those of a sulky donkey when it feels the weight too heavy for its back. Then he began :

" ' Unless I deceive myself, you would not esteem Viscus or Varius as friends more than me ; for who is a better or readier poet than I am ? Who can dance with more grace than I ? Hermogenes himself might envy my singing.'

" Here it seemed to me was an opportunity for putting in a word. ' Is your mother alive ? ' said I. ' Have you any relations to whom your life and health are important ? '

" ' No,' said he, ' no, I have no one ; *I have laid them all to rest.*'

" ' Happy people ! ' said I. ' Now I am left ; so despatch me at once ; for my sad fate is now at hand predicted to me when I was a boy by an old Sabine woman after she had shaken her consulting urn : " This boy," said she, " neither poison, nor the sword of an enemy, nor pleurisy, nor cold, nor gout will destroy, but one day a chatterbox will end his life, wherefore let him avoid all great talkers as soon as he grows to be a man." '

" We had now come to the Temple of Vesta, and a fourth part of the day was gone, and as it happened he was bound to appear in court to answer to one to whom he had given bail. If he failed to appear he lost his case.

" ' If you love me,' said he, ' give me your aid in court.'

" ' May I perish,' said I, ' if I can appear before a Praetor or know anything of common law, besides, I am in a hurry to get you know where.'

" ' I am doubtful,' said he, ' what to do—to leave you or my case.'

" ' Me, I pray,' said I.

" ' No, I won't,' said he. So he went on before, and I— for it is hard to contend with one's conqueror—even followed. Then he began again.

" ' On what terms are you with Maecenas ? He is careful in his friendship and a man of sense—no one ever made a more adroit use of his fortune. You would have a powerful backer in me, one able to play the second part—if you would but introduce me. May I utterly perish, if you would not make a clear stage for yourself.'

" I answered : ' We do not live on the terms that you imagine. There is not a house more honest than that, or more free from intrigues. It never annoys me if another richer or more learned than I is there. Each has his own position.'

" ' What you tell me,' said he, ' is wonderful, almost incredible.'

" ' But,' said I, ' it is truth.'

" ' Well,' said he, ' you increase my desire for his intimacy.'

" ' You have only to wish for it,' I answered, ' such is your virtue you will take him by storm ; he is one that may be won, and this is the reason why he is so hard to approach at first.'

" ' I will not be wanting to myself,' said he. ' I will bribe the servants. If the door be shut in my face to-day, I will not give in ; I will watch my chance. I will meet him at the corners of the streets. I will attend him to his home. Nothing is gained in this life but by toil.'

" While he was thus busy Fuscus Aristius came towards us—a dear friend of mine, who knew the man right well. We stopped, we exchanged salutations. I began to pull and pinch his arms, but they might have been dead. I nodded and winked to him to deliver me. The wretch laughed, pretending not to know what I meant. I began to get angry. ' Surely,' said I, ' you said you had some private matter to speak to me about.'

" ' Yes,' said he, ' yes, I remember well, but I will talk to you of it at a more convenient time. To-day is the thirtieth Sabbath ; you would not surely scandalise the circumcised Jews ? '

" ' Oh,' said I, '-I have no such scruples ! '

" ' But I have,' said he. ' I am one of the weaker brethren —one of the many, so pardon me. I will speak to you another time.'

" ' Alas ! ' said I, ' Oh, this day, how black it has risen for me ! '

" Off he went, leaving me like a victim with the knife at my throat. But by chance the plaintiff meets my man face to face, and in a loud voice shouts to him, ' Whither, thou basest of men ? ' then to me, ' May I make you a witness ? ' I gave my ear to be touched. He hurried my man off to the trial. . . .

" So I was saved, by Apollo."

Just there that strenuous and eager world later to become so disastrous is figured for us, not in any of those great and noble personages who have raised one upon another in stone or marble the temples and law courts we see, but, best of all, perhaps, in that unimpassioned poet, who was really so indifferent, so rarely, so fortunately a man of the world. We see him often in those poems of his, really a sort of autobiography, as the envied friend of Maecenas, the companion of Virgil, the so human lover of Pyrrha, joyful too, as a townsman always is in the country, at his Sabine farm—*Satis beatus unicis Sabinis.* But it is something lighter, more elegant and superficial than even those slight and perfect odes, more human too, where all are so full of humanity, that figures the age for us and brings it home to us, as we say, in a casual experience that might have happened to any of us—yes, here in London. For in him the ages are all equal, and we, too, are of his company.

IV

THE PALATINE HILL

TO leave the Forum for the Palatine Hill is to pass, not so much from the period of the Republic to that of the Empire, for the Forum itself is full of Imperial buildings, as from the Rome of the people to the Rome of the Emperors. And yet, though it is impossible to think of anything amid these ruins but the tragedy of the Caesars, the splendour and havoc of imperial Rome, it was here after all, on what is still the most mysterious and the most beautiful of the Roman hills, that Evander welcomed Aeneas, not with any great magnificence though he was a king, but modestly withal, in honourable poverty, giving him a bed of leaves and the hide of a Libyan bear for pillow :

> *Dixit et angusti subter fastigia tecti*
> *ingentem Aenean duxit, stratisque locavit*
> *effultum foliis et pelle Libystidis ursae.*
> Aenid, viii, 366.[1]

And indeed this Hill, just a vast ruin now, was not only the leafy cradle of Rome, but for long the very City herself. Here Romulus, calling about him all his comrades, according to the Etruscan rites yoked the oxen together to the plough and drove them round the Hill, tracing the line of the walls with the ploughshare, lifting it wherever the gates were to be set. The furrow thus traced was the sacred girdle of the City, which might never be broken, within which none might introduce the dead or the gods of strangers.

So *Roma Quadrata*—foursquare Rome—was founded according to the shape of the Hill on which it stood, an image as it were of an ideal *Templum* as the Augurs had decreed.

The story of Romulus and Remus, a mere legend, as the

---

[1] He spoke and beneath the roof of his humble dwelling led mighty Aeneas and laid him on a bed of strewn leaves and the skin of a Libyan bear.

Germans have so often insisted, thus becomes at least true as a parable ; and then, as though to confirm us in our scepticism of " history as a science," as though a thing so concerned with humanity could be anything but an art, that legend has suddenly been proved to be, well, the mere truth, by the irrefutable witness of the earth, those stones and tufa walls which have so lately been found beneath the Palaces of the Caesars ; the foundations even of the great gate Porta Mugonia having been laid bare, where Romulus first lifted the plough-share, and whence at dawn his oxen went forth to pasture in the meadows of the Forum. Nor, it seems, is this all. For to the right of the Gate stands a huge pile of stones, in which one may almost certainly recognise the foundations of a temple—the Temple of Jupiter Stator, which, as Livy tells us, [1] Romulus built in honour of Jove, who had inspired him to build the City, later giving him victory, after defeat at the hands of the Sabines. Close by, in that grove of ilex on the western height of the Hill, is the Temple of the *Magna Mater*, founded in 191 B.C., which came almost untouched through the worst years of the Empire.

So we see the Palatine, later the grave of the Empire, its Palaces crushed under the too great weight of the world, as the cradle of Rome, the home of its founder, the throne of its first kings. And so it became the hill of the Patricians ; through all the years of the Republic it was there they pre-ferred to dwell, till, with the advent of the Emperors, they were expelled. Catullus, we read, made his home there, and there the orator Hortensius lived, whose house Augustus bought later. There, too, lived Cicero beside his victim Catiline, his rival Clodius and his assassin Antony. If, among its famous inhabitants, we do not find the name of Julius Caesar, it is because for a political end he preferred to live among the Plebs in the Suburra until as Pontifex Maximus he went into residence at the Regia. This fact in itself goes to prove how patrician the quarter of the Palatine had always been. Augustus was born there, and, while still Triumvir, went to live in the house there he had bought from Hortensius and enlarged, but which still remained merely a private mansion.

[1] Livy, lib. i, cap. 2. See also Ovid, *Trist.*, iii, i.

Nor did he much increase it after he became Emperor. The simplicity of his life was one of his weapons ; and indeed the display and luxury that came later would have been repugnant to the severity of his taste. It was not till the accession of Tiberius that the Palatine Hill came into the hands of the Emperor.

It is Suetonius who has left us a description of the house of Augustus. "It was remarkable," he says, "neither for size nor splendour. The porticoes were but small and were sustained, too, by pillars of the common stone of the Alban Hills. In the rooms there was neither marble nor mosaic. During all the forty years he lived there, he occupied the same apartment in summer as in winter. . . . He wore, you must know, only such clothes as his sister or his wife or his daughter made for him. He ate but little, and that consisted of a coarse bread with cheese, fish, or green figs. He drank very little wine. . . ."

The Domus Augustiana stood on the south side of the Hill looking over the Circus Maximus. The ruins we now see belong for the most part to the time of Domitian who built there ; the remains of the original house are merely state apartments, the private rooms of Augustus lying still beneath the Villa Mills.

We may, however, understand something of the simplicity which surrounded the Emperor if we explore the dower-house of his wife Livia. The Domus Liviae is the only building of the kind that remains on the Palatine. Descending by a flight of steps to the level of the Hill in early imperial times, one finds oneself in the *Vestibulum* paved with mosaic, whence one enters the *Atrium*, a quadrangular court, once partly covered, out of which three tiny rooms open whose only luxury is the frescoes which even yet may be traced on the walls. In those paintings, once so fine, you see certain classic tales, Io guarded by Argus about to be released by Mercury, Polyphemus and Galatea and two small sacrificial scenes that might pass almost for easel pictures or rather veritable triptychs.

Another room is decorated with frescoes of fruits and masks and flowers ; while still another is simply painted in panels,

over which are set certain winged figures on a white ground.
But what has struck you chiefly after all is the smallness of
everything, a smallness that would make any great ceremony
impossible.

Beyond the white room is the *Triclinium*, the dining-room,
painted in panels of clear crimson, and decorated with two
frescoes of landscapes and certain vases and fruits. How
light and delicate is this work which gives to so small a place a
certain airiness and grace ! It seems to prove certainly the
good taste of that time which allowed nothing heavy or sombre
or even too serious to hang there always on the walls. It is
as though these people had preferred the delicate landscapes
and etchings of Canaletto or Tiepolo for instance, to live with
at least, before the " Mona Lisa " of Da Vinci, or the sombre
canvases of Rembrandt, the too eager and insistent work of
Velasquez.

Here, doubtless, Livia passed the years of her widowhood
devoted, as we know, rather to the memory of Augustus, to
marry whom she had, as we remind ourselves, divorced her
first husband, than to the cause of her son Tiberius of whom she
was so unaccountably jealous.

The policy of Augustus had combined a personal simplicity, that was certainly not ingenuous, with a public display
that whatever its object, finding Rome of brick, as he said,
left it a city of marble. Among the many monuments that he
had thus given the Romans in exchange for their liberty, not
the least splendid was the Temple he built, on the eastern
height of the Palatine towards the Arch of Constantine,
to Apollo, Actian Apollo, as Virgil calls him, who, as was
thought, had interfered on his behalf at the battle of Actium ;[1]
and this was his reward. If his own house contained " neither
marble nor mosaic " it was not so he built this temple which,
surrounded by a magnificent portico, with a library on either
side, was upheld by columns of marble, walled with jasper
and ivory, paved with porphyry and crowded with statues,
among them the finest works of the Greeks.[2]

[1] *Aeneid*, viii, 704.
[2] Propertius, *El.*, ii, 31 ; Ovid, *Trist.*, iii, i, 59-61 ; Horace, *Ep.*, i, 3-16.

The tradition of Augustus, that simplicity on which he had
so prided himself, lingered on into the reign of his stepson
Tiberius who, however, found the Domus Augustiana too
strait for him.   The palace he built, the Domus Tiberiana,
stood to the north of the Palatine above the Clivus Victoriae.
Covered as it still is with gardens and a great grove of cypresses
—and may it be long before they are destroyed to disclose after
all another brickfield—certainly, the ruins we may now see
are not of much interest ; and in fact Tiberius lived there but
little.   Really a great soldier, the better part of his life had been
spent in the field, and when at last in A.D. 14, already fifty-
six years old, he succeeded to Augustus, the passionate indis-
cretions of youth must have been almost forgotten.   And then
he had long been used to an absolute or nearly absolute command in the Provinces, which he seems never to have forgotten
or ceased to think of really with affection.   Suetonius, often a
gossip, and sometimes we may suspect a malicious one, tells
us that the first eight years of Tiberius' reign were marked by a
just government and personal frugality.   And though the
following six years were less happy—more than a hundred
persons suffering death on suspicion of conspiracy—it was not
till he was sixty-eight that he suddenly left Rome, going first
into Campania, then the garden of Italy, and later to Capri,
as we are asked to believe, to indulge himself in the most brutal
sensuality.   It might seem that however unwise it was to
leave Rome in the power of Sejanus, the tragedies that had
befallen his house, the murder of Agrippa Postumus, the
mysterious death of Germanicus in the East, the poisoning of
his son Drusus, the exile of Agrippina, were sufficient to excuse
a disgust of that world of sycophants and traitors which
always surrounded the imperial throne ; so that Tiberius may
well have fled away to the meadows of Campania, the sea of
Capri, rather in weariness than in love of a world in which,
soldier as he was, he must ever have been something of a
stranger.   Certainly the almost insane gloom which descended upon him in his last years when he had struck down
Sejanus for dreaming of the purple, and put a worse monster in
his place, suggests a certain despair of the world which may well
have crept into his heart in that city of little men.   The

crimes of Macro seem neither to have surprised him nor to have moved him, for he had fallen into a kind of lethargy, such as often comes to those who, having spent all their lives in the field, or on the sea, or among the mountains, are suddenly caught, in old age perhaps, between the walls of a city, so that he scarcely resisted those who came to suffocate him at the order of Macro in March A.D. 37.

Tiberius might well have despaired of the future of the world had he known the true character of his successor, that Caius Caesar, the son of Germanicus and Agrippina, whom the army called Caligula. It is to him we owe the enormous and picturesque ruins facing the Capitol which are all that is left of the magnificent additions he made to the Domus Tiberiana. Always lavishly generous, he lived the life of a mad egotist, from the first indulging himself in every far-fetched vice, both of soul and body, which he could contrive or hear of. Weakened by his vast excesses his mind seems to have tottered under the weight of that dream which was the Empire. Dizzy with the thought of his own eminence he conceived of himself as a god, ordained his own worship in Rome, and in an insane hour decreed that his horse should be both priest and Consul.

The enormous palace, whose foundations might seem to be the work of Titans, which to-day astonishes us beyond anything else on the Palatine Hill, was the scene of his madness and his death. The conspiracy, as it seems, was conceived almost on the spur of the moment by Cassius Chaerea, Tribune of a Praetorian Cohort. It was, doubtless, but one among countless plots that had failed to rid that cynical Roman world of a tyrant of whom it was weary at last. On January 24th, A.D. 41, the Emperor had presided at the Games all the morning, and at midday, wishing to return to his palace, he had taken the secret way, leaving his German guard to follow the road. Almost alone he entered the Cryptoporticus, that underground gallery, a great part of which has been excavated, which led from palace to palace about the Hill. There the conspirators, as is supposed, awaited him. It was Chaerea himself who struck him down, ridding the world of a monster terrible as a universal disease. His wife and his daughter were also put to death.

It is not, however, of Caligula alone that we think as we follow to-day the windings of that subterranean path among the foundations of the Domus Tiberiana. By this way, too, came Messalina, the wife of the pedantic Claudius, on her way to the brothels of the Suburra. Like a scarlet shadow, even yet she seems to pass along this labyrinth at sunset, a pallid tongue of fire trembling with her inscrutable desires.

Nero, the successor of Claudius, has left no mark at all on the Palatine. That formidable pupil of Seneca doubtless found no room there for the gardens he built at last at the foot of the Coelian Hill, nor for that Golden House which he contrived on the Esquiline—beautiful things, doubtless, that were so soon swept away.

The election of Vespasian, however, showed how weary Rome had at last become of the excesses of Caligula and Nero. The Flavian House came at last, in the person of Domitian, to build much on the Palatine, but both Vespasian and his more cultured son Titus, the conqueror of the Jews, imitated the simplicity of Augustus, only building, lavishly as he had done, those public monuments, Baths, Amphitheatres and Basilicas, which dazzled the people of his time not less than they astonish us to-day. Their greatest monument was the Colosseum, which Vespasian began on the site of the ruined gardens of Nero, and which Titus finished in A.D. 80.

> *Hic ubi conspicui venerabilis amphitheatri*
> *Erigitur moles, stagna Neronis erant. . . .*
> *Reddita Roma sibi est ; et sunt te praeside, Caesar,*
> *Deliciae populi, quae fuerant domini.*
>
> Martial, *De Spec.*, Ep. ii, 5.

In truth, as Martial sang, Rome had become herself again, and, thanks to Caesar, that which had served as the pleasure of one man was now offered for the enjoyment of all.

On the Palatine, however, it is the name of Domitian we remember before that of his father Vespasian or his brother

Titus. He alone of the Flavian House seems to have been touched with the madness of Caligula. He, too, proclaimed himself to be divine ; and the Terror that reigned in Rome under his predecessor befell again in his own latter years. He was unfortunate and unhappy. All his campaigns came to nothing, and both Tacitus and Juvenal have told us in words that cannot die of his misery and his shame. Yet it is rather of his splendour we think when to-day we look upon the ruins of the Stadium or the *débris* of that Palace which he built to outshine every other, even, according to the verses of Statius, " losing itself in its loftiness, among the stars, rising above the clouds in the full splendour of the sun, exciting the jealousy of Jove himself."

Standing, as it does, on the most splendid site on the Palatine, overlooking the Forum and the Via Sacra on one side and the Circus Maximus on the other, the grandeur of its proportions alone might excuse the name the poets of the time bestowed upon it—the sanctuary of the Emperor—for certainly no temple was more splendid. On the east, towards the Forum, it was approached by a magnificent portico or vestibule, which stretched across the entire façade. Entering by the great doorway one came into the *Tablinum*, the *Aula Regia*—the Throne Room, as we should say. Here the Emperor gave audience. Spanned by one tremendous arch, the Hall was lighted from above, and its walls, lined with statues, were panelled with precious marbles. To the left of the *Tablinum* one entered the *Lararium*, the private chapel, where stood a statue of Minerva, whom Domitian looked upon as his especial patroness. To the right of the Throne Room one entered the *Basilica*, the Hall of Justice in which S. Lorenzo was condemned. Behind the *Tablinum* and entered from it was the great central court of the palace, the *Peristylium*, which was open to the sky but surrounded on all sides by an arcade, so that it was a veritable cloister. Beyond this one came into the *Triclinium* or Banqueting Hall, a marvellous chamber encrusted with wonderful marbles and paved with *opus sectile*. On either side opened the *Nymphaea*—withdrawing rooms, each with a fountain adorned with statues of marble and bronze.

Dion tells us very graphically of one of those strange orgies

which must often have taken place here in the time of
Domitian ; but the one he describes is rather horrible than
voluptuous.

"Domitian," he says, "once made a great feast for the
citizens, proposing to finish it with a fine entertainment to a
few of the highest nobility. To this end he caused an apartment to be decorated in complete mourning. The ceiling
was black, the walls were black, the pavement was black, and
the stone seats for the guests were black also. They were
introduced at night, alone, and at the head of each couch was
placed a column like a tombstone, on which the name of the
guest who sat there was graven, while above was hung a little
lamp such as is hung in tombs. By and by there entered troops
of naked boys, blackened, and these danced with horrid move-
ments, and then, halting each before a guest, offered him such
fragments of food as are commonly presented to the dead.
Paralysed with fear, expecting each moment to be put to death,
they sat in absolute silence, not knowing whether their neigh-
bour was yet alive, while the Emperor spoke of those things
which only pertain to the state of the departed." This, however, proved to be but a bad jest. Presently, with a laugh,
Domitian sent them off, not indeed quite reassured, for they
still expected the worst, but yet safe and sound ; presenting to
each the silver cup and platter in which the strange supper
had been served and, along with these, the slave who had served
it.

It was in this palace, where he had so often practised on the
fear of others, that he himself faced the dagger of the assassin,
and fell, slain like a beast by the knife of a slave. The victim
of every sort of superstition, he dreamed that Minerva, his
guardian, had withdrawn her protection from him at the
bidding of Jove, the guardian of the Empire. This might
seem likely enough. It was even said that he had knowledge
of the very day he should die and of the sword which should
kill him. Extraordinary precautions were taken ; no one was
allowed to approach him save after a rigorous search, and the
corridor where he walked was by his own order lined with a
marvellously polished marble, so that it might reflect the
image of any one approaching silently from behind. With a

fatuous lunacy, worthy alone of Caligula, he suddenly exclaimed one day as he walked there : " Something is about to
happen which men will talk of all the world over." Then
drawing a drop of blood from a pimple on his forehead :
" May this be all ! " said he. But he was right ; " all the
world over " men had had enough of this madman. Not
long after, as he walked in his mirrored corridor, some slave,
we know not by whose order, struck him in the belly with a
knife. The Emperor staggered and tried to draw his weapon,
but some one had already plucked it away. Clutching at
the knife of his assassin, which cut his fingers to the bone, in a
last desperate attempt to save himself he " thrust his bloody
talons into the eyes of his assailant, beat his head with a golden
goblet, shrieking for help." Then Parthenius Maximus and
others rushed in and killed him as he lay on the pavement.

Not much more than a hundred years lie between the murder
of Julius Caesar and the murder of Domitian, yet almost all
the great buildings on the Palatine whose ruins we now see
were contrived and established within that time. In the
century which followed, comprising the reigns of Nerva,
Trajan, Hadrian, Antoninus Pius and Marcus Aurelius,
nothing, or almost nothing, was added to the palaces that had
made this Hill the most splendid throne in the world and, one
might almost say, the only one. Indeed, there was room for
nothing more. Septimius Severus, however, that African
under whom the Empire tottered into dotage—he stands almost
midway between Julius Caesar and the end of the Empire of
the west (A.D. 476)—did not think so. He proposed to outshine all his predecessors, and when he found that there was no
space sufficient for his dream on the Palatine itself, he built,
as it were, a hill of brick beside it, in the valley towards the
Coelian Hill, rearing his enormous palace on high beside the
Stadium on the tremendous foundations and substructures
we see to-day ; while he built too the Septizonium with its
many stories to improve the view from the Appian Way,
which, as it seems, ended there.

With Septimius Severus the history of the buildings on the

Palatine may be said to come to an end ; but the Hill itself, its palaces and ruins, remained at least the theoretic seat of government for more than a thousand years.   We see them pass, these pale ghosts of buried Caesars, who through all the Middle Age tried to save or pillage the Eternal City : Goths and Vandals who came half in wonder to spoil the glory of the world ; Odoacer and the great Theodoric, the Greek Officials, the Dux of Rome, the Exarch of Ravenna, the great Autocrator, Charlemagne, King of the Franks, the Barbarians of the Holy Roman Empire, and last of all, Napoleon III, Emperor of the French, who, having won and lost everything, stripped himself last of all of " the Palaces of the Caesars," which he sold to the City of Rome during his exile in England.   And those palaces had become a garden, a garden of wildflowers, under whose fleeting beauty nature has hidden both Caesar and Caesar's House ; the glory and the shame of the dead.

V

THE COLOSSEUM

A LMOST all the beauty which had till the time of our grandfathers made of the Colosseum the most mysterious and most astounding ruin in Rome, contriving out of its mere size something monstrous, spellbound, has departed from it, perhaps for ever, since it has come within the radius of action, so unfortunately wide, of the improver and the restorer of ruins.   With the destruction of those trees that grew along the broken arches, waving " dark in the blue midnight," and with the passing of the flowers, the Flavian Amphitheatre has become almost absurd in its rueful nakedness ; a sort of inadequate monstrosity, a mighty heap of patched and ordered débris on the verge of the brickfield of the Fora and the lower slopes of the Esquiline Hill.   Stripped and ashamed, with all its wounds exposed, to say nothing of the horrible patchwork of the archaeologists, it is now just a vast and empty shell, that indeed scarcely impresses us, mere size being after all but a poor claim upon our notice.   Yet of old it seems to have been the most wonderful thing in the City. *Quamdiu stet Colysaeus, stet et Roma,* sang the pilgrims.—While stands the Colosseum Rome shall stand, when falls the Colosseum Rome shall fall, and when Rome falls—the world.   And yet something of its original splendour, if not of its medieval mystery, has been restored to it with the driving of the Via dell'Impero from the Forum of Trajan and the foot of the Capitol to the Colosseum which now closes a magnificent vista.   But look at any picture of it as it was even so recently as the seventeenth and eighteenth centuries and you will realise at once what we have lost.

Begun by Vespasian, in the gardens of the Golden House, on the site of the lake in which, like Narcissus, the son of Agrippina had adored his own beauty, it was finished by Titus, and is really, like the Pyramids, the work of the Jews, whose lives here

too were " bitter with hard bondage in mortar and in brick " ;
for since the whole structure was completed within three
years, doubtless " all their service, wherein they made them
serve, was with rigour." Who the architect may have been
we know not ; but his work was finished in the year 80, and
the Flavian Amphitheatre, as it was called, opened with a
great spectacle.

An amphitheatre, that at Capua as this in Rome, was
generally an oval building surrounding an ellipse covered with
a floor of planks resting on deep subterranean walls among
which the machinery and the cages of the beasts were placed.
Within, the walls were lined with seats tier above tier, and
without were arcades one above another, the lowest admitting
to a corridor which ran round the building and from which
a staircase led up to the different rows of seats. Here, in the
Colosseum, there were four arcades—the first of Doric, the
second of Ionic and the third of Corinthian columns, while the
fourth was a wall decorated with Corinthian pilasters and
pierced with windows. Within, immediately round the arena,
a high and massive wall was built, within which were caves
and vaults for animals. Above this, and protected by it, was
the *podium*, where the seats of honour were placed for the
Emperor and his family, for the Vestal Virgins and the great
officers of the State. Above the *podium*, rose, in terrace after
terrace, the seats for the Senators, for the magistrates and
military knights, and then for the male citizens, while the
women sat in the highest part of the building under a colonnade, parts of which, we are told, were portioned off for the
common people. The whole of this vast space, capable, it is
said, of seating more than seventy thousand persons,[1] was
sheltered from sun and rain by an awning supported on masts
set in corbels of stone that jutted out from the wall that on
high surrounded the building, while an ingenious contrivance
allowed the arena to be flooded with water for those *naumachiae*
or naval fights to which Julius Caesar had first accustomed the
Romans in the Circus Maximus in 46 B.C.

The theatre thus completed in A.D. 80 was certainly the most

---

[1] The estimates differ very greatly. The bull ring at Valencia—the largest
in Spain—will accommodate 70,000 people.

tremendous stage the world has ever seen, nor did it stand alone in mere size, for the spectacle there provided remains the most monstrous of which any word has come down to us. Splendid and even marvellous in the harmony, largeness, and grace of its construction, the Flavian Amphitheatre is altogether lost sight of as a building in its tremendous moral significance. For more than two thousand years its true name has been lost, in that of the Colosseum ; and this marks not merely a physical fact obvious to the most superficial observer, but a spiritual truth also, of rarer significance. It was this monstrous colossus that overthrew Paganism and the Empire and served as the stage on which Christianity was at last to meet them both in combat and defeat them.

It might seem that no people save the Romans, no European people at any rate, have made of agony and death a spectacle to amuse the populace. They alone were ignorant of pity. The clemency that seemed to them so strange and even wonderful in Julius Caesar is but a proof of the hardness, even the brutality, of the national manners. They seem, and their art continually proves what their manners have led us to expect, to have been lacking in imagination ; not in force or in that mental grasp of the things of the great world which was an instinct almost unconscious and perhaps ineradicable ; but in imagination, a kind of reverie, or shall I say a clair- voyance, which would have made such a thing as the Flavian Amphitheatre and all that it stood for impossible, a nightmare haunting the moral consciousness—the soul. Beginning, perhaps, with a genuine indifference to suffering, a certain hardness that was part of their strength, little by little this insensibility to suffering—for which no shame or horror was really intolerable, so that the father would, without too in- tolerable a pain, condemn his son to death and even himself be his executioner, while such a punishment as that to which the faithless Vestal was condemned seems to have revolted no one—encroached on the soul, till cruelty, a kind of joy in speculating on the endurance of others, less indifferent cer- tainly, put to the most dreadful of tests, came to be with them a kind of delight, which, secretly at first, but altogether openly at last, involved all their pleasures, their public entertainments

in its marvellous horror. From the enjoyment of watching the skill of two trained gladiators, or of a gladiator, in
dealing with a wild beast, there was but a step, it seems, to
the breathless delight of seeing the appalled antics of some
wretched criminal in the power of the lion or the bear, to the
stripping of women and children at the mercy of a host of
animals, to the long expectancy, with as much sport as might
be in the interval, of the inevitable death of the helpless at the
hands—yes, it came to just that—of that most brutal populace
which was Rome.

At first the gladiatorial combat had been but private
sport offered amid the pomp of a funeral perhaps in memory
of the Homeric Games ;[1] but already in the last years of the
Republic these had come to be the favourite spectacles of the
Roman people. Caesar used them to gain the love of the
Plebs ; but it was only under Augustus that they became, as
it were, a national institution. That wily politician, intent
on keeping Rome quiet, was able to boast in his last years
that he had offered the people eight combats in which 10,000
gladiators had taken part. Little by little this lust for slaughter
grew upon them until, under Domitian, the public shows,
which of old came but twice in the year, were declared
obligatory on ten days at least. But even this, in the light of
what came later, seems but a beginning, for Trajan after his
Dacian victories gave a contest which lasted 123 days and
employed 10,000 gladiators, as many indeed as Augustus had
used in twenty years. When at last the professional gladiators
no longer sufficed to appease the passion of the people, recourse was had to the lowest criminals and to prisoners from
every part of the Empire.[2] The thing became a sort of trade
in which the tribunals acted as purveyors, and a regular service
of caravans was run along the great roads from Gaul and
Pannonia. But since many of these wretches gave but poor

[1] The custom seems to have come from Etruria, where it was a survival of the
human sacrifices formerly used at funerals.

[2] Originally Roman citizens could not be sentenced to the arena, but later this
punishment was extended to criminals of low condition. Sometimes they were
prisoners of war, or slaves, or even volunteers, for the arena was often the last
recourse of a ruined man. Such were called Auctorati. Troops of gladiators
were often kept by the rich, or as a speculation by trusts. The emperors kep
schools of gladiators under procuratores of equestrian rank. In Domitian's
time there were four such schools in Rome.

sport when matched either with one another or with a trained gladiator, they were most often reserved for the fight with beasts on the occasion of a triumph. In that vast space resounding with terrible cries, we have stood beside our brothers, Germans from the far away Rhine, Bretons and Gauls, Dacians, Alains and Ethiopians, and those too, who were to avenge us, the Goths whose children under Alaric, only six years after the last combat, that which celebrated the victories of Stilicho under Honorius, thundered at the gates of the Eternal City. It was there in the awful din and horror, under the cruel eyes of those who had failed to understand, that our soul was born, that soul which was to make such a spectacle as that for ever impossible. And amid the bravery, the unspeakable courage and devotion of our friends who, a new love in their hearts, stood beside us, we, too, bewildered in the glaring sunshine did not disgrace the dream in our hearts. One day we read that thirty Saxons, as they were about to be led into the Circus, strangled themselves in their prison.

All the fate of the world was decided in the arena of the Flavian Amphitheatre. It was Rome who stood there at the tribunal of humanity and heard the universal verdict—guilty.

Yes ; it was on the bloody floor of the Colosseum that Rome contrived her own slavery and our freedom. It was there that Christianity met the world and overcame it, there the martyrs won for Christ His Kingdom in the hearts of men —and certain poor folk, almost nameless, men, women and children, weak too, weeping and afraid, overthrew for ever the despotism of Rome.

So the Colosseum, that monument of our love, fallen into ruin, for it is the privilege of Love to forget the unforgettable, came in the Middle Age to be the most fabulous thing in Rome, and to serve rather than the Capitol even, differently too, as a symbol of the City : so that we sang to ourselves as we passed by, the old song of the English pilgrims :—

Quamdiu stet Colysaeus
Stet et Roma :
Quando cadet Colysaeus
Cadet et Roma :
Quando cadet Roma
Cadet et Mundus.

And no one any longer remembered the cruelty of the Roman people.

Yet dimly some memory of evil hung about it. " It is the old Temple of the Sun," we would tell one another, as passing from church to church we climbed toward our mother S. Giovanni in Laterano ; till a rumour ran through the crowded, straggling ranks of the pilgrims, coming, it seemed, from one who was a clerk and had learning. And ever after we told ourselves that that vast ruin, dark with trees to its very summit, was the work of a magician, one Virgil, wise at his business, who in a song of passing sweetness had prophesied the joy of Our Lady and the birth of Christ. And thinking of this we passed on and on to the shrine of the Apostle.

The Romans, however, cursed with hatred, had no such illusion, or, if they had, it profited them nothing. For, magical or no, the barons Frangipani and Annibaldi turned it into a fortress for civil war, till in 1312 the Emperor Henry VII took it from them and restored it to the Senate and the people. And as might have been expected, they used it, as well as they could, in the old fashion, organising there bull fights and such. Incorrigible Rome ! It was only after the return of the Holy See from Avignon that these spectacles were put an end to, and the Colosseum, already in ruins, became a quarry for the Popes. From the earliest years of the Renaissance to its last moments under Paul III the walls were destroyed daily to furnish stone for the new buildings, till, deserted at last, it became the lair of wolves, which Julius II proscribed in 1512, setting a price on their heads. Again in the eighteenth century it was used for material till—was it only to prevent further damage, or may we see in it one of those acts of imagination on the part of the papacy, not so rare after all ?—Benedict XIV consecrated it to " The Passion of Jesus Christ," Who in the place where so many martyrs confessed His Name and assured Him the victory, speaks neither of anger nor of punishment, but seems to remind us, there surely more than anywhere else in the world, of that " new commandment " " . . . that ye also love one another."

THE COLOSSEUM

THE PANTHEON OF AGRIPPA

THE PANTHEON

THE continuity of the life, of the political life of the City that is so well expressed by the Capitol is found too, in its religious aspect certainly, in the Pantheon, which, since the time of its foundation, has always been sacred to the gods, to the saints, those Divi—Divinities, as both Pagans and Christians have agreed to call them. If we need, then, a witness to the continuity of the religious life of the City, of the slow and after all so gentle passing of Paganism into Christianity, in the hearts of men, at any rate, with many a strange and beautiful conservation of old things, old customs, old ways of thinking, we shall find it best, perhaps, in the Pantheon.

" There is nothing," says Horace, " that the earth has hidden, but Time shall bring it forth into the sunshine " :—

Quicquid sub terra est in apricum proferet aetas ;
defodiet condetque nitentia.

" and how many things now glittering it will bury and hide away." Though we may never see Agrippa's colonnade[1] of which he speaks, the Pantheon, which he built in 27 B.C., remains the most perfect ancient building in Rome, the only one, indeed, whose walls and arches have been completely preserved. Born in 63 B.C. and dead in 12 B.C. Agrippa was the friend and later the son-in-law of Augustus, as well as his general and minister. And as it seems, for the original purpose of the building is unknown, it was to the Julian House, the divine Caesar, that he built the Pantheon, that all-divine place which was one of the greatest monuments of the ancient City, built with all the solidity, boldness and splendour of the Roman genius, and remains one of the wonders of the world. A circular structure, 142 feet and 6 inches in height and diameter, its beautiful portico, formed by sixteen Corinthian columns 47 feet high, was 103 feet long. Of the columns,

---

[1] This colonnade was built by Agrippa's sister, Polla, and called Porticus Pollae. It was there that Augustus caused to be engraved in marble the circular map of the world which Agrippa had made.

eight support a massive pediment, behind which rises another, still higher, set against the blind loggia which connects the portico with the dome. The other columns separate and divide the portico itself into three parts that of old were covered by vaults, and there beside the entrance are the two niches which once held the colossal statues of Augustus and Agrippa, the emperor and his friend. The tremendous walls of the *rotunda*, a perfect circle, are divided into two stories by ring courses, while above them springs the most wonderful thing in Rome, that cupola of concrete, of old covered over with tiles of gilded bronze, which was once the greatest dome in the world. The diameter is indeed the same as that of the building itself, the walls which support it being 19 feet in thickness. Divided into five circles of deeply sunk panels, twenty-eight in each circle, diminishing in size as they ascend, it is crowned with a crown of light 27 feet in diameter, which floods the whole sanctuary with its marvellous glory. Within, the temple was lined with precious marbles, while in the seven niches that were set in its circumference stood, as we may suppose, the images of the gods, though only those of Mars and Venus, the deities of the Julian House, are known to have been there. The whole place was so spacious and wonderful that even in antiquity it was supposed to derive its name from heaven itself, lighted as it was by the sun or the moon, while round about the statues of gods were set those seven planets which ruled the destinies of men. It is no wonder that the applause which greeted Agrippa passed almost into a proverb, so that Horace would warn us against hoping for such praise :—

> . . . *scilicet ut plausus quos fert Agrippa feras tu,*
> *astuta ingenuum vulpes imitata leonem.*

The Roman, save exceptionally, was not, one may think, a highly-cultured man ; like the modern Englishman, he rather distrusted and despised the things of the mind, and left them to Greeks. Cicero makes Cato say that one of his great Romans, C. Flaminius, I think, *multae etiam ut in homine Romano litterae. Litterae* was, of course, Greek literature and philosophy, of which he had " much for a Roman."

There must have been, indeed there was, far more in Roman religion than one discerns on the surface, especially after its contact with Greek religion. For the very powerful influence of Greek thought is evident, not only in Roman religion but in Roman culture generally. In things of the mind, Rome was a province of Athens ; but whence did Virgil draw his deep religious sense, and how is it that Cicero so firmly, and even passionately, defends the belief in life after death and the immortality of the soul ? No one in antiquity, save S. Paul, has more eagerly defended a belief in a life hereafter. He even makes Cato greet the day of his death with : *O praeclarum diem* . . . and says that this belief of his is the reason he can bear the greatest of misfortunes, the death of a beloved son, because he will certainly find him again after death.

And then there is the famous Roman *pietas*. What, then, did the Roman mean by *pietas, religio, fatum* ? These words, with *gravitas* and *simplicitas*, might almost be said to express the Roman's conception of himself. It is difficult for us to appreciate a religion which had no creed, and was without a serious theology. *Religio*, however, according to Cicero, was a fundamental Roman characteristic, and means " attention ", a careful attention to, a being bound by, a manifestation of the divine. Its antithesis is *neglegentia*. Roman religion, at first just that attention, came perhaps to be a body of usages or ritual, not so much an attitude of mind as a rule of manners, before in the decline it fell into outrageous superstition. Yet the men who built Rome, and even those who built the Empire, must have been of a Puritan sort, one thinks, *durum genus*, but continually attentive, all the same, to any suggestions of nature, from the stars to the flight of a bird, or the entrails of a sacrificial victim.

And to-day the Pantheon is like a sudden revelation, as though in an unexpected moment we had come upon a legion of Caesar's army, or in the quiet sunlight, amid the ruins of the Forum, had heard the persistent voice of Cato in the Senate House : *Delenda est Carthago.* Yet it has suffered much from restoration, even in antiquity. It was first altered by Domitian, and then, struck by lightning in the time of Trajan, it was restored by Hadrian, who, it seems, left only the portico altogether unchanged, and indeed it is to him rather than to Agrippa that we owe the whole of the present *rotunda* and the beautiful dome. Then in A.D. 202

Septimius Severus and Caracalla had their way with it.   So
it remained in some sort a Temple of the Gods—of all the gods,
it seems, for the misunderstanding which has turned this
" all-divine " place into a temple " of All the Gods " began
early—till Phocas the tyrant, in the exile of the gods, presented
it to Pope Boniface IV, who on May 13, 609, consecrated it,
placing it under the protection of S. Mary of the Martyrs.

So the Pantheon became S. Maria ad Martyres, and to
ensure its sanctity the Pope caused to be buried there twenty-
eight wagon-loads of the bones of the martyrs brought hither
from the catacombs.   Then began the spoliation : as though
after all one were not sure that the gods had indeed been
turned out.   So Constans II, in 655, did not scruple to steal
those precious tiles of gilded bronze for his palace in Constantinople.   It was only with lead that Pope Gregory III
covered the church some eighty years later, for the gods were
humbler than of old, and, instead of our most precious possessions, demanded now but an humble and contrite heart.
But it still kept about it some shadow of its ancient wonder and
holiness, so that we find in the thirteenth century that every
Senator was obliged to take an oath to defend it and preserve
it for the Pope.   Yet it was the Pope himself who did his best
to destroy it, for Urban VIII took the brazen tubes on which
the roof of the vestibule rested, to convert them into the
twisted columns of the baldacchino of S. Peter—*Quod non
fecerunt Barbari, fecerunt Barberini*.   And if of old it excited
the wonder and awe of the City, and in the Middle Age
guarded the dust of the Martyrs, certainly then, more precious
than silver or gold, it became the very model of the greatest
buildings of that and a later time.   The Baptistery of Florence
was certainly meant to be as like it as might be ; it inspired the
dome of S. Maria del Fiore, and Michelangelo swore to build
it, as it were aloft, over S. Peter's, an oath which he contrived to
keep ; while it was there that Raphael preferred to lie, with his be-
trothed beside him and his disciples at his feet, pursuing the dream
of beauty which, as was said, had ravished him from our world.

And yesterday, too, it was there that Italy laid her kings—
him who came down with gifts from Piedmont and him who
fell by the dagger of Monza.

VII

THE FORUM AND COLUMN OF TRAJAN

OF the many Fora which under the Empire sprang up in the neighbourhood of the Forum Romanum, the Forum Pacis of Vespasian that lay close to the Basilica of Constantine behind the Basilica Aemilia, the Forum Nervae that joined it on the west and led again into the Forum Augusti, which in its turn led under a Triumphal Arch into the Forum Trajani, the last and most splendid of all reminds us of the Greek Apollodorus who built here with so much magnificence the Basilica Ulpia, the two libraries, the Temple *Divi Trajani*, the Triumphal Arch, the two hemi-cycles and the Column which occupied or surrounded the Forum of Trajan. Of all these great and splendid things but one has come down to us practically intact—the Column in which, closed in a golden urn, the ashes of the Emperor were destined to lie till Alaric and his Goths spoiled it of its treasure.

By good fortune, the last of the historians of ancient Rome, Ammianus Marcellinus has left us a vivid description of the Eternal City on the morrow of the removal of the seat of Empire by Constantine from Rome to Byzantium, while it was still in all its glory, its unapproached magnificence unspoiled, its classic architecture, its treasures of sculpture and every art, its forums and baths and palaces still perfect and intact, in all the splendour of their unsullied beauty.

The occasion of his most graphic record was the visit and triumphal entry of the Emperor Constantius, in April, 357. He was received by the magistrates and Senate. The streets were lined with an innumerable multitude, so that the Emperor is said to have affected surprise that the human race should thus suddenly be collected on the same spot. He was lodged in the ancient palace of Augustine, he presided in the Senate

House and harangued the people from the tribunal which Cicero had so often ascended. He was present at the games of the circus, and accepted the crown of gold prepared for the ceremony.

His short visit—no Emperor had been present in Rome for thirty-two years—was employed in viewing the monuments of the Eternal City. In his company was a Persian prince who had taken refuge in his train. Together they visited the Forum, and together were overwhelmed and astonished by the marvellous beauty of the City. They admired the many centuried Capitol, beheld with wonder the mighty Baths of Caracalla and Diocletian, which in their vast extent resembled provinces, " the massy greatness of the amphitheatre of Titus " (the Colosseum), the Pantheon like the whole quarter of a city, rounded smoothly, and fair with lofty columns and arches, the pillars bearing the figures of former princes, the wonderful Theatre of Pompey, the noble Temple of Peace. But above all they were amazed by the Forum of Trajan with its Column, " a work unique under the whole heavens, wonderful, worthy as we consider of the approval of the gods." So much did they admire this incomparable structure that Constantius thought to mark his advent by imitating the equestrian and colossal statue he had seen there, till the subtlety of his Persian guest remarked that he must first command such a stable to be made if he could. And with the malice of his race he added that one thing only had pleased him : to find that men died at Rome as well as elsewhere.

It was, it seems, a Greek custom to set up sometimes a single column as a memorial to some great or noble personage or in commemoration of a victory. In erecting the *Columna Rostrata* in the Forum Romanum, adorned with the beaks of ships, in memory of the naval victory of Duilius over the Carthaginians in 261 B.C., the Romans, after all, were but following a precedent. It was thus nothing new that Trajan did when, in A.D. 113, he erected, in the midst of the Forum he had built, a column to commemorate his Dacian victories, to be imitated by Marcus Aurelius whose great Column we admire still in Piazza Colonna. The astonishment lay doubtless in the continuous episode carved about it and in the magnificence of the work rather than in the memorial itself. For the shaft standing on the tomb of the Emperor, a four-sided pediment adorned with trophies of war, rises a hundred and twenty-four feet into the air. Tapering very slightly, it has a diameter of ten feet at the base while, within, a spiral staircase of a hundred and eighty-five steps leads to the summit where stood the gilded statue of Trajan, which in 1587 was replaced by a bronze figure of S. Peter. The shaft itself, formed of twenty-three drums of marble, is covered with a series of reliefs three feet and three inches high, a great procession of two thousand five hundred figures, animals and engines of war, mounting, as it were, on a winding way twenty-three times round the column to the top, to the very feet of the Emperor who stood there. And what is so surprising, so astonishing and new in this, perhaps the most beautiful of all Roman works that have come down to us, is just that continuous episode, the whole campaign told us in chapter after chapter realistically, as an historian might tell it, with a sincere insistence upon just facts, on the natural difficulties of that Dacian country, of the crossing of the great river, and yet with a marvellous idealism, an idealism of form, at any rate, so that it is by no means impossible to think of these reliefs beside those of the frieze of the Parthenon. And yet the intention here is, how different from that of the Greek who has conceived an " idealised state," a whole people lifted out of itself into a world perfect, as we might say, in communion for a moment with the gods. Here, on the column of Trajan, we have after all Roman work, Roman work at its best, expressing Roman thoughts and ideas so perfectly that, as has rightly been said, these sculptures are the splendid counterpart of the historic prose of Rome. Even the form, that continuous episode, was Roman, as we may see if we examine the wall-painting dating from about 200 B.C., divided into four zones, now preserved in the Palazzo dei Conservatori. And the artists are unknown. It was Rome herself who thus expressed just herself, her idea of war, of victory, of the business of the Emperor, of that shadowy divinity which fell upon him on the day he mounted the throne of Augustus.

To describe these sculptures in any detail would require not a short chapter, but a book. I must content myself with referring the reader to the work of Petersen and of Mrs. Arthur Strong, whose excellent work on Roman Sculpture has made us acquainted in our own tongue with a subject unaccountably obscure and neglected. What is so striking in this marvellous and heroic history, so profoundly Roman, is the continual presence of Trajan. The Emperor, idealised certainly, the true father of his country, of the Empire, is always present, full of counsel, of authority, of encouragement, not disdaining menial tasks such as scouting and bridge-building, but at all times and everywhere proving the soul of the army, the soul of Rome, before whom the Barbarian falls on his face, and in whom literally is victory.

Who was this man, half divine with the shadowy divinity that had fallen first on Julius Caesar, from which even the worst of the Europeans could not escape, who was thus able to sum up and to express the very dreams and characteristics of Rome, in whom she seemed to see, as it were, her own image ? Marcus Ulpius Trajanus was born at Italica near to Seville in September, A.D. 52. His youth was devoted to arms, and he seems to have served with real distinction both in Germany and in the East. Consul in 91, he was at the close of 97 adopted by the Emperor Nerva, whom he succeeded in the following year under the title of Imperator Caesar Nerva Trajanus Augustus. Nor did he disappoint the promise of his youth. He heard of Nerva's death in Cologne, and returning slowly along the great roads he entered Rome on foot at last with his wife Pompeia Plotina, amid the shouting of the people. Almost at once the first Dacian war broke out, to be followed in 104 by the second against Decebalus, who, as was said, had broken the treaty. So Dacia was reduced to a Roman province ; and Trajan, the idol of the people, was accorded a Triumph, which he celebrated by public games that lasted a hundred and twenty-three days. But his wars were not yet done with. In 114 he broke the Armenians and, spending the winter at Antioch, fell in the next year on the Parthians. In the course of two campaigns, attended by the most brilliant success, he reduced the Parthian Empire and took the capital

Ctesiphon. Then he descended the Tigris and came into the Persian Gulf. He died on his way back to Rome in 117.

A life thus devoted to war, to victory, might seem to have afforded but little time for the more generous achievements of peace, and yet, in spite of the splendid praise of the reliefs of the Column, as it were a plainsong winding its way upward to the feet of the divine Emperor, it is rather of his generosity, his clemency in devising those Agrarian laws celebrated on the balustrades of the Rostra that we think in remembering him, than of his successful wars, so much more strong is peace than victory. And indeed a kind of immortality, awarded to none other of all those who sat in the seat of Augustus, which even Marcus Aurelius—a Christian, as one might think, without knowing it—has failed to win, has been given to him in accordance with the general wish of mankind, expressed, as it is said, by Pope Gregory the Great. Trajan alone has been welcomed into the Paradise of the Christians, from which, as we know, even Virgil was excluded. It is there Dante sees him led by Beatrice in the midst of the sixth heaven. No victory, howsoever glorious, would have sufficed to bring him there, where David reigns, but a victory of Love, that Pity of which the Romans seem to have known so little, from which even Marcus Aurelius has excused himself, preferring to endure all things rather than to weep.

It is one of the most curious legends of an age of legends which finds Trajan thus the one Pagan who, in the words of the Church, has found salvation ; an unique salvation, it seems, without precedent or sequence. For, as it is said, while S. Gregory was one day walking in the Forum he stayed by chance beside that bas-relief where Italia is represented as thanking the Emperor for those generous measures of the year A.D. 101, for the protection and support of poor children.[1] This measure was an attempt to check the depopulation of the countryside and to encourage Italian agriculture. The Pope, knowing nothing of the occasion, went away sorrowful. Could it be, he asked himself, that a prince so virtuous as to listen to the appeal of the widow and orphan was indeed

---

[1] Others say (and Dante seems to agree with them) that it was another bas-relief, now lost, of the poor widow who asked for justice.

damned past hope to the company of the wicked, to the everlasting absence of Him who had said, Suffer little children
to come unto Me and forbid them not ?   *Oravit et flevit*, says
his biographer—he prayed and he wept.   And his prayer was
heard.   " Be consoled," our Lord told him, " I will pardon
your Trajan.   But be careful in future to intercede no more
for the wicked."

So Trajan was saved, but hardly ; and even concerning
him many theologians have, it seems, the gravest doubts,
for such is their business.   How can a Pagan be saved ?
they ask, with irresistible logic.   How can a Pagan be saved,
since without baptism there is no salvation ?   But we who are
rather human than theological may well reply that Trajan
was saved, as were Peter and John indeed without baptism,
by the infinite grace of God.   For a logician and legalist,
such an excuse from a dogma which would make even S. Paul
a prisoner is inexplicable and absurd, but to S. Gregory, as
to us, it seems but in the nature of things, the delightful nature
of things wholly divine.   Yet for S. Thomas Aquinas a miracle
yet more wonderful was necessary to explain the astonishment of this ; and we find him solving the difficulty by a
suggestion that Trajan returned momentarily to the world,
was baptized by Gregory, and so passed into heaven.   This
subtle explanation of the Angelic Doctor's sufficed to convince
the scholastic world, which found it hard to conceive of
anything strong enough to break its laws.

Dante, however, theologian though he was, was yet a poet,
" intelligent in love."   In the tenth canto of the *Purgatorio*
he describes the story graven in the white marble of the
mountain of Purgatory :—

> I moved my feet from where I had been standing
> To examine near at hand another story. . . .
> There the high glory of the Roman Prince
> Was chronicled, whose great beneficence
> Moved Gregory to his great victory ;
> 'Tis of the Emperor Trajan I am speaking ;
> And a poor widow at his bridle stood
> In attitude of weeping and of grief.
> Around about him seemed it thronged and full
> Of courtiers, and the eagles in the gold
> Above them visibly in the wind were moving,

The wretched woman in the midst of these
Seemed to be saying : " Give me vengeance, Lord,
For my dead son, for whom my heart is breaking."
And he answers her : " Now wait until
I shall return." And she : " My Lord," like me
In whom grief is impatient, " shouldst thou not
Return ? " And he : " Who shall be where I am
Will give it thee." And she : " Good deed of others
What boots in thee, if thou neglect thine own ? "
Whence he : " Now comfort thee, for it behoves me
That I discharge my duty e'er I move ;
Justice so wills, and pity doth retain me."

Then in the sixth Paradise, in the iris of the Eagle's eye, whose pupil is David, Dante sees Trajan

Who the poor widow for her son consoled.
Now knoweth he how dearly it doth cost
Not following Christ, by the experience
Of this sweet life and of its opposite.

Is it strange that that goddess just come to our earth should have willed the salvation of the pitiful Emperor ? Saved by Pity, new born into the world in spite of all rules and dogmas, useful and right but by no means omnipotent, Trajan is greeted in heaven by the great poet of Christianity, on the eve of the Renaissance of man, in the morning of our resurrection.

VIII

THE BATHS OF CARACALLA

IT might seem that the two characteristics of the later Roman civilisation that came to such splendour under the Emperors, the two characteristics which mark it off from any other civilisation Europe has ever known, and impress us most to-day, were its indifference to death, to the spectacle of death, a thing so hard to understand, and its care for the body, for even the smaller material needs of life which, in a sort of reaction, Christianity was so eager to condemn. If the Colosseum stands even yet as a memorial of the one, we are most vividly reminded of the other by the immense ruins of the Baths of Caracalla, at the foot of the Aventine Hill on the verge of the Appian Way. The greatest building in Rome, greater even than the Colosseum, these Thermae, which Caracalla began and Elagabalus completed, were more than a mile in circumference, and could accommodate more than 1,600 persons at the same time. It is difficult to realise that such a building was only a Bath ; and indeed it was much more, for the Thermae had come to be a public meeting-place, a sort of club, and a gymnasium.

Among the Greeks, warm baths were for long only used for special purposes, to take them often being looked upon as a mark of effeminacy. And indeed the Athenians even, never attained in this matter certainly to the luxury of the Romans under the Empire.

It was after the Second Punic war that the Thermae began to multiply in Rome ; before that time men had been content to take a weekly bath merely in the *lavatrina* or wash-house, close to the kitchen. But about 200 B.C. Rome began to devote the hottest hour of the day, between two and three—the hour of the siesta—to the Bath, which with the Gymnastica gradually came to be the chief recreation, and therefore for a host of people the most important event of every-day life. The Baths were then placed under the superintendence of the aediles, a small fee, *balneaticum*, of a *quadrans*, about half a farthing, being charged for men, and rather more for women. Little by little the hours of bathing lengthened, as more and more it became the fashionable recreation, till, before the fall of the Republic, the Baths were open in the City from two o'clock till sunset, and in the suburbs were often lighted up and used long after nightfall.

It was, however, under the Empire that the daily bath grew really into the most absorbing function of life, among the wealthier people, at any rate : one bathed not once but many times a day. And if thus the Thermae became the great meeting-place of the City, full of luxuries, music, for instance, and statues, the splendour of the arrangements, especially in private houses, increased too with the number of Baths. It was not only for bathing that one went there, but for conversation and exercise, to hear music or the verses of a poet, to lounge through the day. Already numerous in the time of Augustus, Agrippa, when he was aedile, added a hundred and seventy Thermae to those already in existence, and the Emperors did likewise, so that by the middle of the fourth century their number within the City alone was not far short of a thousand.

Agrippa, the first great builder of baths, was the first too, it seems, to introduce the Thermae or hot baths, such as those which in southern Italy were already in use, attached to the Greek gymnasia. It was about this time then that the Baths began to be built with at least three chambers, each having separate parts for the use of women. The *Tepidarium* was a room heated with warm air in which one reclined after undressing. Thence one passed into the *Caldarium*, where the hot bath was taken in a tub, *solium*, or a basin, *piscina*. Passing again through the tepidarium, one entered at once the *Frigidarium*, where one took the final cold bath or douche. This being over, one entered a special apartment, or perhaps in one of the older baths the tepidarium, to have oneself scraped with the *strigilis*, rubbed down with a linen towel, and anointed with oil. Dressing-rooms, withdrawing-rooms, cloisters and halls for reading and conversation were, in the more luxurious baths, at any rate, everywhere provided. And indeed so

general was the luxury and so fond were the Romans of it,
that it was not uncommon for a rich man to bequeath a sum
of money to throw open the Bath to all for a day, or a week,
or even for ever.

The Baths of Agrippa, of Nero, of Vespasian and Titus had
already filled Rome with Thermae when Caracalla thought to
outdo all his predecessors by building in the Appian Way the
immense Baths whose ruins we now see. A mile in circumference, these enormous Baths were open at certain times
for the free use of every citizen, whether patrician or plebeian,
and could accommodate some sixteen hundred persons at one
time. The domes—the dome of the Laconian or hot-air
bath, for instance—were covered with mosaics, and the walls
were lined with precious marbles from Egypt and Numidia.
Even the pipes and taps and fittings generally were of silver
and bronze, while in the various halls and porticoes stood the
most celebrated statues of the City—the Farnese Bull, the
Venus of the Capitol, the Venus Callipyge, the Hercules and
the Flora of Naples, the Dionysus of the British Museum.

" Let us follow," says Lanciani in his *Ancient Rome,* " let
us follow one of those elegant youths into one of the great
Thermae. He is welcomed on his entrance by the *ostiarius*
or porter, a tall, majestic fellow with a sword at his side,
and by the *capsarius,* or wardrobe-keeper, who takes charge of
his wraps. Then follows a general salutation and kissing of
friends, exchange of the last topics and scandals of the day ;
reading of the newspapers or *acta diurna.* The visitor then
selects the kind of bath which may suit his particular case
—cold, tepid, shower, or perspiration bath. The bath over,
the real business begins, as for example taking a constitutional
up and down the beautiful grounds, indulging in athletic
sports or simply gymnastics to restore circulation and to
prepare himself for the delights of the table. The luxurious
meal finished, the gigantic club-house could supply him
with every kind of amusement : libraries, concerts, literary
entertainments, reading of the latest poems or novels, popular
shows, conversation with the nobles and most beautiful
women. Very often a second bath was taken to prepare
for the evening meal. All this could be done by three or
four thousand persons at the same time without confusion or
delay, because of the great number of servants and slaves
attached to the establishment."

Returning perhaps from the Campagna towards evening along the Appian Way and coming suddenly upon those enormous ruins smouldering in red and purple and gold in the sunset, one understands one of the secrets of Rome, her contempt of smallness, of perfection, of mere detail, the delicate proportion of the Greek artist, in which every stone was of importance, and in place for a special need and purpose of beauty. Rome has never cared for just that, which makes its appeal after all to the few and leaves the multitude not only indifferent but unaware. In her there remained always the universal rather than the absolute, that catholicism which is her birthright, and in which good and bad are mingled for the sake of life. She has never expressed herself in any divine beauty, but has believed always in vastness, a true magnificence, in weight and spaciousness. She has taken the world captive by mere strength and bigness ; without understanding the Greeks she has overwhelmed them by the universality of her appeal ; the cry of the multitude is in her voice, and she has found in her own heart every dream that has captured it. To her the Parthenon was a toy, a Gothic cathedral, a sort of barbarism—built altogether for the service of the gods they seemed to her, as it were, beside the point. For her there remained man, that enemy of perfection, to whom she, a sort of Titan after all, has brought gifts after his own heart. As it was in antiquity, so it is to-day. She is still the universal expression of the world. The Baths of Caracalla, the Colosseum, the Temples we know so well, will not bear comparison for a moment with any Greek work even of a poor period, and if in like manner we may compare things equally different in intention, we find the same failure in beauty, mystery and completeness when we enter S. Peter's, for instance, or S. Giovanni in Laterano and remember Amiens or Chartres. But in the midst of our disappointment even, we seem to understand. Here are space and light, two universal things, necessary too for a vast multitude, and Rome has always believed them the two most splendid and majestic things in the world.

Certainly those enormous Thermae, now so bare and almost, as one may think, without the sentiment of ruins, make to even

the least sensitive, the most superficial among us, that universal
appeal which is the secret of Rome.   They are like the débris of
a city beside which London in ruins would be just a brickfield, a mean desolation.   Even now, when we have stripped
them naked, when science has numbered the very bricks and
forbidden the flowers, they seem to be (in the twilight perhaps)
the most wonderful thing in the world.   What we have spoiled
for the sake of fools !   A traveller in the first years of the nineteenth century saw, or might have seen, so much more than
we may see.   " I passed," writes such an one, " through a
long succession of immense halls, open to the sky, whose pavements of costly marbles and rich mosaics, long since torn
away, have been supplied by the soft green turf that forms a
carpet more in unison with their deserted state.   The wind,
sighing through the branches of the aged trees that have
taken root in them without rivalling their loftiness, was the
only sound we heard ; and great birds bursting through the
thick ivy of the broken wall far above us were the only living
things we saw."

Well, one might think that a place so lonely, so deserted,
might have been left untouched in the beauty that time had
bestowed upon it.   It was the Italian Government, we learn,
that destroyed the evergreens and the flowers, men even being
" let down by ropes . . . to tear out any stray plant which
. . . found a resting-place in the sides of the walls."   Were
they seeking for the eternal life of the City, that secret continuity, which is insatiable and inexhaustible ?   If it be so,
they need not have destroyed a single flower to find it.   Yet
you might think this the last place in which to seek so elusive a
thing.   But the eternity of Rome manifests itself everywhere,
everywhere if you can but see.   " This poem," says Shelley in
the preface to the *Prometheus Unbound*, " was chiefly written
upon the mountainous ruins of the Baths of Caracalla, among
the flowery glades, and thickets of odoriferous blossoming
trees which are extended in ever-winding labyrinths upon its
immense platforms and dizzy arches suspended in the air."
Did he remember Horace ?   Did he remember that it was in
the Baths that the poets were wont to recite and try their
verses ?

CLOISTER by Paulus (SS. Quattro Coronati)

BASILICA OF ST. GEORGE, PROTECTOR OF ENGLAND (S. Giorgio in Velabro)

In medio qui
scripta foro recitent sunt multi quique lavantes :
suave locus voci resonat conclusus.

" Many recite their writings in the midst of the Forum or in the Bath ; they say the voice sounds sweetly in the enclosed place."

IX

VIA DELL' IMPERO—THE ROME OF MUSSOLINI

IT would be true to say that under Mussolini and his Fascist régime Rome was largely transformed. Mussolini called the result *Roma monumentale del XX secolo* and declared : "All that which is great and beautiful and venerable we will conserve ; not only that, we will add to it."[1] Well, the chief monument of his régime here in Rome would seem to be the Via dell' Impero, the wide processional way from Piazza Venezia, through the excavated Fora of the Empire to the Colosseum.

Other demolitions and excavations too have brought to light many ruined monuments of the ancient City : the Temples of the Zona Argentina, the excavations in the Circus Maximus, the isolation of the Capitol, the liberation of the Theatre of Marcellus and so forth. It might almost be said that Mussolini and the régime were ready to sacrifice buildings of the Middle Age, the Renaissance and the Baroque period in order to bring to light the ruined monuments of the Imperial City. No doubt their enterprise had a political as well as an archaeological purpose, yet they do not seem to have been more destructive than the new Kingdom was in the time before them.

But the transformation of the City was by no means confined to excavation and the re-erection of the columns of Temple and Basilica. The Coelian and Aventine Hills especially were opened up, wide boulevards were driven all over them and the half-deserted Via di San Gregorio between the Coelian and the Palatine became the Via dei Trionfi. Housing estates were developed and built up and presently

---

[1] He seems to have been especially proud of the two roads he built, the road to the Hills and the road to the Sea. In regard to the latter, which leaves Piazza Venezia on the right, he said : "One thing I am proud of, to have brought back the Romans to the sea. They had forgotten it. It is only twenty minutes distant by tram or automobile. I hope in time the virtues belonging to the sea will spring up in us again."

the electric tram destroyed an ancient silence and a peace which were immemorial there.

Nor was this all. The traditional approach to S. Peter's and the Vatican across Ponte Sant' Angelo and through the narrow Borgo Nuovo and Borgo Vecchio, which for ages had only at last disclosed to the pilgrim the glory and the majesty of the Piazza and the great church the goal of his journey, was also transformed, the narrow Borgo Nuovo overthrown and a wide new street was driven from the Bridge to the Piazza Rusticucci, so that all is now open and visible at once from the bridge-head.

Some of these things will perhaps delight us, others may distress us as they do me, but all are in the tradition of the City which has continually and ruthlessly transformed herself with every change of epoch and her fortunes : when the Republic became the Empire, when the Empire passed into the Papacy, when the Papacy was captured by the Renaissance and the Renaissance passed into the Baroque and at last into the vulgar commercial and mechanical age we now enjoy.

Undoubtedly the most dramatic, and in its own way the most successful, change has been achieved by driving the great processional way of the Via dell' Impero through the old quarters which hid the Imperial Fora, from the Piazza Venezia to the Colosseum. The vista alone along the whole length of the way, closed by the magnificence of the Colosseum, may perhaps be thought to justify the road : but to those who knew Trajan's Forum surrounded by old houses, it is is hard not to resent the blatant vulgarity of it all.

The Via dell' Impero issues out of the Piazza Venezia and crosses the Esedra Arboria, the trees of which were characteristically planted here fully grown, leaving the Victor Emmanuel Monument—the Vittoriano—on the right with the Imperial Fora on the left.

On the right we have the Clivus Argentarius which of old joined the Via Lata, the Corso, with the Via Sacra. The tomb of Caius Bibulus, an aedile of the plebs, to whom the Senate granted this burial place, tells us that this was outside the gate of the ancient City on the road that connected the Forum Romanum with the Campus Martius. Passing the Basilica

Argentaria, as it is conjectured, we come to the Forum of Julius Caesar in which stood the Temple of Venus Genetrix the remarkable ruins of which—the stylobate, columns and Corinthian capitals, pieces of architrave and cornice and parts of a finely sculptured frieze with Amorini have been set up. The Forum of Julius was the second after the Forum Romanum, and, like all the other Fora which came later, had its Temple, here aptly of Venus Genetrix, the mother of Aeneas and the ancestor therefore of Julius. To the south of the Forum rise the storied tabernae or shops.

After crossing the Fora of Nerva which is closed by the Basilica Aemilia, and of Peace which abuts on the Temple of the Penates, in which now stands the church of SS. Cosma and Damiano, the Via dell' Impero passes the Basilica of Constantine and the Temple of Venus and Rome within which is the church of S. Francesca Romana.

Turning now to the left of the Via dell' Impero where it leaves Piazza Venezia, we pass the site of the Basilica Ulpia and Library, the Forum of Trajan and the Mercato of that Emperor with its fine storied hemicycle and covered hall behind which rises the Torre delle Milizie and to the right again the charming Loggia of the Knights of Rhodes who were established here as Knights of S. John of Jerusalem in 1230. The Loggia dates from the fifteenth century.

Beyond the Forum of Trajan is the Forum of Augustus with its exedra, its Aula del Colosso and Aula Porticata and its Temple of Mars Ultor.

His Forum was inaugurated by Augustus in 2 B.C. and a notable festa marked the event in which 260 lions were slaughtered in the Circus Maximus. Here he built the great Temple of Mars the Avenger—the avenger at Philippi of murdered Julius. He adorned the Temple with many famous statues and works of art. The excavations under Mussolini have exposed the stylobate of the Temple with its flight of steps, parts of its Corinthian columns of which some have been re-erected, and the Arco de' Pantani—one of the entries to the Forum. One of the Corinthian columns here was copied for the Nelson Column in Trafalgar Square.

Beyond the Forum of Augustus, the Forum called of Nerva

stretches right across the Via dell' Impero. The two elegant
columns, now fully excavated, of old known as *le Colonnacce*,
supported the wall of the Forum and still retain aloft a high
relief of the goddess Minerva whose Temple was here.

The fourth of the Imperial Fora is that built by Vespasian
after the fall of Jerusalem. It too stretches across the Via
dell' Impero and included the Templum Pacis in the midst of
which was deposited the booty of Jerusalem, brought here by
Titus and pictured in sculpture on his Triumphal Arch.

The Via dell' Impero now drives through the ridge visible
to left and right, of the Velia which united the Palatine with
the Esquiline. On its summit to the right stands the afore-
said arch of Titus, built to commemorate his triumph over the
Jews in A.D. 70. Here on the right were upreared the mighty
vaults of the Basilica of Constantine or rather of Maxentius
and the platform and the ruins of the Temple of Venus and
Rome in which stands the church of S. Francesca Romana
with its lovely Roman Campanile of the thirteenth century.

In front at the end of the Via dell' Impero rises the majestic
ruin of the Colosseum.

The " isolation " of the Capitol has also radically altered
the quarter of Piazza Montanara, exposing the Forum Olitorium and the Theatre of Marcellus. In the Piazza a medieval
house has been revealed and restored.

As to the Largo Argentina, the four ancient Roman temples
brought to light by the demolition of a large block of buildings,
seem to belong to the Consular era, of which so little remains.
There are four temples in all, of which one is circular. Among
the débris a colossal statue has been discovered, with a body
formed of wood which was covered with plaster of gilded bronze
and with the nude parts of marble. It represents some female
divinity.

The region surrounding the Bocca della Verità about S.
Giorgio in Velabro has also been cleared and the Temples
renovated, the Temple of Fortuna Virile has been freed and
restored, and the Temples and Forum Boarium isolated.

These are perhaps the chief archæological achievements of
the régime. I say nothing of its immense social building and
development both within and more especially without the walls.

X

THE CATACOMBS

THE Catacomb—the place by the tombs, in which to the curious philologist every symbol of Christianity seems to lie hid, the cup of the Holy Grail, the ship of the Church, was indeed the very cradle of Christianity, of Catholicism, where she lay helpless, a little child, till she was strong enough to take the whole world into her arms. Born, as it were, in the desert, in the stony silence of Judea, Christianity, by an act of love, had at once solved the great mystery : it was in itself a denial of death, of the power of death, and as though to prove its sincerity, its belief in the assurance it alone had dared to offer mankind, it made its first home in the Catacombs, those cemeteries of the dead. They too are of our company, it seemed to say, for death is not death but a sleep[1]; and so it refused to be separated from them, waiting patiently beside their resting-place, really in communion with them who had slept and wakened. The Christian alone in Rome found hope in his heart. While the City amused herself at the Bath or grew weary with horror at the Circus, that little society, secret so reluctantly, driven underground, waited, not without songs—the songs of children mainly, we are told—beside the tombs, where alone it was safe, far from the Pagans, in those burial places which gradually grew, outside the City, about certain villas along the Appian Way or between it and the Via Ardeatina ; the villa of Lucina, for instance, or the house of Cecilia, places excavated by the householder and inviolable, as were all places of sepulture declared by their owners to be religious, to belong to their *cultus* or sect. There in the darkness, lighted only by occasional *luminaria*, they celebrated their mysteries, even in the time of the Apostles,

---

[1] Cf. Lucian : *Passing of Peregrinus* (Loeb, v, 15). "The poor wretches (i.e. the Christians) have convinced themselves first and foremost that they are going to be immortal, in consequence they despise death."

the Mass, the *Commendatio Animae*, the *Funeralia*, refusing always to speak of the departing brother or sister as dying, but rather as of one summoned or called away, *accersitus*, as the beautiful Roman inscription has it, *accersitus ab angelis*—summoned by angels.

These cemeteries, later to bear the names of saints, S. Calixto, S. Sebastiano, S. Balbina among the rest, excavated almost entirely in the volcanic soil, stretched really for miles outside the Walls on the left bank of the Tiber.[1] And beside them were the gardens—*horti*—those cemeteries in the open air: the *Hortus Hilariae* where S. Hilaria was buried, the *Hortus Justi* where lay S. Nicomedes, the *Hortus Theonis* beside the Via Ostia where they buried S. Timothy. These gardens were, however, comparatively few and were too public to be used for worship. It was in the Catacombs, so many of which still remain unexplored, that the Church spent her childhood, in those five especially which date from Apostolic times, and which were added to little by little, till in the third century we find some forty-five, only twenty of which were still in the hands of private owners, the rest being under the government of the *Ecclesia Fratrum*.[2] For with the growth of the Catacombs, their enlargement, till one led into another, the Church herself took command ; these places of sepulture which she attached each one to a parish church being indeed her first possession and remaining for ages the most holy shrines in the City. " The people of Rome," writes S. Jerome, " have left the ancient Temples covered with cobwebs and rust, the golden Capitol squalid with filth, while they pour out from the City and run to the Tombs of the Martyrs."

Serenity, a bold and confident gladness,[3] grave and yet by no means without its more joyful moments, would seem to have been the most striking characteristic of the life of the Catacombs, expressing itself in many a beautiful or graceful custom accommodated to the human heart, a little wistful perhaps after the years of persecution, in a strange power of

[1] De Rossi, *Roma Sotteranea*, III, 622.
[2] S. Cyprian, *De Unitate Ecclesiae*.
[3] Serenity in contradistinction to Pagan hopelessness and Jewish fussiness (τό ψοφοδεές). Cf. Glover, *Conflict of Religions*, 165. " They were the most essentially happy people of the day." Justin, *Apol.*, I, 14.

sweetness and patience and especially in a wonderful new music and poetry. With the inexplicable blindness of all the best minds of that old Pagan world, Tacitus, like Marcus Aurelius later, has failed to understand the joy in the heart of that new song, recording with a curious bitterness in A.D. 58 the conversion of Pomponia Grecina, the first Lucina, whom he thinks of ever after as leading a life *lugubre et maestum*, dejected and mournful, in a retirement little less complete than that of the grave. Yet as we know, even in those days of austere *ascêsis*, that element of profound serenity in the soul of her Founder was part of the very being of the Church, soon in the Minor Peace under the Antonines to come to its own—to involve her altogether in its beauty and sweetness. It was, as it were, the very soul of her song. Singing certainly, " though often it dared only be of the heart," there had been, from the first[1] the singing of children, as on the morrow of a great deliverance.[2] Was it only that song which Pliny heard,[3] caught it might seem, almost in spite of himself, by its freshness and blitheness, long a stranger in that complicated Roman world, was it only that morning or evening song— like the evening itself full of hope and fear, and yet with the stars there in the darkness after all—or, was it yes, something more eager, more mysterious even than that, which he heard as he passed in the early morning on his way to the City ?

> *Sursum corda.*
> *Habemus ad Dominum.*
> *Gratias agamus Domino Deo nostro.*
> *Dignum et justum est.*

The Mass indeed would seem to have been said always, even in the Apostolic age, and already in the Catacombs to have had the character of something ancient and venerable.[4] A ritual, altogether expressive and full of meaning, grew little by

---

[1] Cf. Glover, *op. cit.*, 185, " Over and over again there is a sound of singing." Renan, *Marc-Aurèle*, 525.

[2] Scenes of deliverance are represented in the Catacombs, among them Susanna and the Elders, Daniel in the lion's den, the Three Children, Isaac, Noah, Peter in prison, etc.

[3] Pliny's Letter to Trajan, *Ep.*, 96, 97 in Teubner (1898), 231.

[4] Renan, *op. cit.*, 507 ; Walter Pater, *Marius the Epicurean*, where we find perhaps the best modern picture of Mass in the Catacombs (founded on Renan), says : " The Mass emerges to general view already substantially complete."

little about it in those early times really for the sake of expressing some profound mystery that could only thus be made plain, which it was not lawful to speak. And for the Christians of the Minor Peace certainly, the ritual of the Mass, its action namely, was altogether indicative, not hiding but expressing the very " heart of the mystery," which for them, as for us, was often rather obscured than made plain by the words, then in the Greek language, the people answering in their own tongue, that colloquial or base Latin into which, the whole of the Liturgy has gradually passed : but not without leaving certain indications of its Greek origin, the mighty vocatives in the Mass of Good Friday for instance, the old plea for mercy of the *Kyrie eleison.*

There, certainly, in Lucina's house on the Via Appia, amid what we now call the Catacomb, the cemetery, of S. Calisto, the Mass was sung, already before the final triumph of the Church, substantially complete.[1] In the old Pagan worship, in its essence at any rate an act of worship, of appreciation of the beauty of the world, the warmth and splendour of the sunshine, the refreshment of the rain, the serenity of the blue sky, there might seem to have been little to satisfy the spirit. But in that earliest act of Christian worship, eloquent and yet reticent of so much, there was more than enough, a whole new world of thought revolving round a fact or series of facts known to every one, and, rightly understood, the very secret of the whole. " If we knew what the Mass was," one has said who loved it exceedingly, " we should die, yes, of joy and gratitude : for there, that which was the desire of the Patriarchs and was foreseen by the Prophets, of which the shepherds at Bethlehem, the Apostles at the Last Supper, Mary and the holy women on Calvary, and at the holy Sepulchre, the Disciples after the Resurrection, were witnesses, we see ourselves to-day." While Pope Innocent III tells us that " the order of the Mass is arranged on a plan so wonderful that everything done by Jesus Christ from His Incarnation to His Ascension is there contained in words and in actions wonderfully presented." And indeed amid those sacred readings, in silence at certain intervals, or

[1] Renan, *op. cit.*, 517 : " *C'était bien déja la messe, mais la messe complète.*"

again with bursts of chanted invocations, amid the many prayers and protests of love,[1] the complicated but expressive ritual of an act of sacrifice, little by little the drama, the dramatic narrative disengages itself till it appears with all the vividness of a picture, and we see that mournful Figure towards whom the whole act of worship is continually turned, who has, as it were, summed up in Himself all the impassioned hopes of man, as the hero, the central figure of a divine tragedy—the tragedy of the Life and Death of Jesus Christ.

It was, then, as a dramatic action, a tragic drama, as we might say, that the Mass from the earliest times presented itself to those who in the subterranean oratories of the Catacombs were gathered together not merely in a common act of worship to hear the words of life, to be made partakers with Christ of the Kingdom of Heaven, but in an act of sacrifice and to remind themselves of the great deliverance won for them by that Figure who passed before them in the words of the drama, the actions of the priest, from birth to death, to resurrection, into His Heaven.

Thus the story of the life and death of Christ, fading already from the memory of men, of men who had heard of it as the wonder of a far land, was caught up and made immortal by an art unconscious for the most part and highly dramatic, universal too in its appeal, as no Greek play or even the more human work of Shakespeare has ever really been.

That heroic Figure round whom the tragedy gathers is, you might think, inexplicably absent, is never represented there, the whole mystery, if such it be, centring indeed in the actions and words of one person, but not He, arrayed in beautiful vestments, and aided now and then by assistants, at an altar strangely like a tomb before which the whole drama passes like a great procession, to which it leads and from which it issues, ending so inexplicably in farewell.

For the acceptable soul certainly, acceptable always in proportion to what it can admire,[2] such a vision of the most wonderful act of worship the world has ever known is even

---

[1] Renan, *op. cit.*, 520.
[2] Renan, *op. cit.*, "*La valeur morale de l'homme est en proportion de sa faculté d'admiration.*"

to-day not too difficult, but for the Christian of the Minor Peace it might seem to have been just a matter of course.

We can picture such an one a little weary after a long night journey along the Appian Way, still at dawn some little distance from the City, arrested suddenly on his way by that singing Pliny heard, and knowing its import, turning out of the road through that narrow door in the vineyard wall of the old villa, and, following the path, coming to that " gap of blackness " in the grassy hill at the back of the house and so descending by devious, narrow ways, lined with the names of those already sleeping—his own friends perhaps—till he would come at last to the " Church in Lucina's House "[1] to remind himself once more in the early spring morning of that great deliverance.

And so one's first impression on entering one of those catacombs to-day is altogether of serenity and peace ; a kind of ecstatic happiness, temperate and still fresh with a hope that has never quite passed away. On the walls one reads words of quiet expectation, full of light, confidence, and repose : *Pax*, you read, *Pax tibi, in Pace Christi* or *Vivas in Deo* ; and then sometimes, as though to sum up all contentment, *Vivas in Christo, in Bono*. And the scenes painted there are serene and glad. In those days at any rate they do not seem to have been pre-occupied with the Crucifixion, the death of Christ ; they thought only of the resurrection. A certain Latin sanity and quietness are expressed in the work we find there ; and indeed there is no hatred or contempt at all of Pagan thought or religion, nor even a complete repudiation of it, for it remains, yes, a real thing, seen with new eyes, as we might say, seen really for the first time, and drawn gently into the service of Christ, so that Orpheus becomes as it were but a prophecy of Him there in S. Calixto, and the Good Shepherd bears the lamb on His shoulders precisely as Hermes had been wont to do, but with a new tenderness. The continuity of life, of art the most sensitive expression of life, was not to be interrupted even by that New Song, which, as Clement of

---

[1] De Rossi has identified the first Lucina with the Pompeia Grecina of Tacitus. She was the wife of Aulus Plautius, the conqueror of Britain and its first governor A.D. 43–47. The name of Lucina appears as that of the Mother of Roman Christianity from the minor up to the major peace of Constantine.

Alexandria tells us with reference not only to the story of
Orpheus and Eurydice but to Paganism generally, " has made
men out of stones and out of beasts so that those even who were
as dead, not being partakers of the true life, have indeed come
to life again, simply by being hearers of this song." The
picture of Christ is but seldom found, for already we seem to
feel the shadow of the coming controversy between Tertullian,
for instance, who continually reminded himself of the words of
Isaiah, " He hath no form nor comeliness," and his opponents
who found in the Prince of Life the fount of all beauty. But
when we do find a presentment of Him, He is represented as
young and bearded with a smile on His lips, splendid as Apollo,
who has forgotten everything but that He is a god and our
friend. Yet, it is a shadow, which hardly dims the serenity
of this world, that we are aware of, when we consider how rare
those presentments of Christ really are. For in that world of
the Catacombs surrounded by symbols of Hope one was content with the new Love born into the world which changed the
whole aspect of life, of death, of conduct, so marvellously,
and made things hitherto difficult and mysterious just a kind
of joy. It was indeed a new " state of soul," really a new
morality that one came upon suddenly in those dark obscure
ways, out of the boisterous cruel delight of the Colosseum or
the ennui of the Baths, a profound spiritual enthusiasm, an
eager need of love, of the redemption of just that. There, as it
were, after the agony of the arena, the new fraternity was born,
the new brotherhood of man.

Side by side they lay down to sleep, the rich beside the
poor, the bond by the free, all whom Christ had made equal,
to await in perfect confidence the promised resurrection.
They buried one another still by night, as they had been used
to do, but the rite was no longer a gloomy or even a sad one :
Exercitia sunt . . . non funera. And indeed the *Funeralia* of
the earliest times were quite unlike those of the Middle Age
even, less self-conscious, less self-reproachful. Then, as in our
day too, for the Church is not forgetful, the *commendatio
animae* was said over the dying, with its pitiful cry for mercy,
Kyrie eleison, its invocations and the marvellous prayer, *Libera,
Domine, animam servi tui, sicut liberasti Petrum et Paulum de*

carceribus ; ending, too, still with a song : *Requiem aeternam dona ei, Domine : et lux perpetua luceat ei.*

Nor have we added much, or even at all, to the rite itself. For the Christians even in the earliest days observed the customs of their ancestors, though in more seemly wise and with a new intention. The ancient rite of extreme unction was administered, the dying being literally anointed with aromatic oils and balsams, till in the fourth century the body was merely touched in various places with myrrh. Then, singing still, they swathed it in stuffs, often precious, the arms close to the body, the *Funeralia* beginning where death had taken place and coming to an end in the cemetery itself. The ceremony was almost exactly that of an Office for the dead, the same psalms were sung, but *cum omni gaudio* ; the sacrifice following, the sacrifice of the Eucharist, at the tomb itself. Sometimes, as though for comfort, the divine Species would be buried with the dead, but this was forbidden in the sixth century. There they laid them, one after another, thousand upon thousand in those subterranean galleries, closing the place carefully with cement and writing above *Dulcissima . . . in Pace. Vivas in Christo.* Often they would return to those silent resting-places through the long galleries often filled with a far-away sound of children's voices singing. And one such, heartbroken in spite of himself for all that new joy, without a single look, kiss, or even a clasping of hands these many days, has written there over and over again the name he loved, *Sofronia vivas . . . in Christo—Sofronia in Domino, Sofronia . . . dulcis, semper vivas in Deo. Sofronia. . . .*

XI

SAN CLEMENTE AND SANTI QUATTRO CORONATI

THE greatest figure, certainly, after the Apostles themselves, of those early years before the Minor Peace under Antoninus Pius, would seem to have been Clement, Pope and Martyr, as the canon of the Roman Mass calls him, " whose name," as S. Paul himself tells us, " is in the Book of Life." The son of Faustinus, a Roman by birth, but of Jewish extraction, Clement was converted, it seems, by S. Paul, whom he afterwards attended so closely that for S. Jerome he is himself an apostle speaking, in that extraordinarily farsighted Epistle to the Corinthians, for instance, with all the authority of one who had received the Faith from those who had in truth seen Jesus with their bodily eyes. He seems to have followed S. Paul not only to Philippi and on the long journeys with S. Luke and S. Timothy, but to Rome itself, where he found S. Peter preaching, and became indeed in some sort his disciple as S. Irenaeus and Pope Zosimus testify. It is Tertullian, however, who tells us that S. Peter ordained him Bishop, appointing him, as some have thought, his vicegerent in Rome during an absence on a mission. However that may be, he was certainly Pope before he died, martyred in the Crimea, as is supposed, under Domitian, or even as some have it, under Trajan. *Nominis ejus memoriam usque hodie Romae exstructa ecclesia custodit*, as Jerome, writing at the end of the fourth century, has it : " Even to this day the church built in Rome preserves the *Memoria* of his name."

The *Memoria* of Clement was his tomb or his dwelling, something certainly more tangible than his mere memory ; and as though to confirm us in such a belief, among the inscriptions published by Fabretti was one found on the bronze collar-plate of a slave, which spoke in unmistakable terms of the dwelling, the house of Clement. *Tene me quia fugi et*

revoca me Victori acolito ad Dominicum Clementis—" Hold me fast,
for I have run away, and bring me back to Victor the Acolyte
at the church in the house of Clement "—*dominicum* being
indeed, as S. Cyprian tells us, the place where Christians used
to assemble in the days of persecution—the church that was
in his house.

Any doubt, however, that we may have had as to whether
the church of San Clemente occupied the site of the dwelling
of S. Clement was set at rest by the discovery of the Irish
Dominican, the late Father Joseph Mullooly, who, as it seems,
loving the place, curious about it too, as who would not have
been, wandering one day in the crypt came upon a piece of old
wall-painting, and searching further, after many months of
labour, found for us the *Memoria* of S. Clement, beside the old
wall of the kings, the cave of Mithras, and the subterranean
basilica we now see.

These important discoveries help to assure us that the present
church was, as had been suspected, of the eleventh or ʰwelfth
century, while the walls of the subterranean basilica prove to
be of the age of Constantine, that is to say, of the first quarter of
the fourth century, the Mithraic cave of the third century, the
" Memoria " or small " stuccoed chamber " of the first, the
" titanic wall " taking us back to the days of the Tarquins or,
as some think, to those of Servius Tullius.

That " stuccoed chamber," so carefully preserved directly
under the apse of the old basilica, fills the place which in so
many other churches is occupied by the shrine of the saint,
under whose protection they are, and seems to confirm us in
our belief that this was already a place of Christian worship
in the first century. But if that be so, we may well ask ourselves how we are to explain the existence close beside this very
place, and indeed opening into it, of a cave of the third century,
sacred to a Pagan divinity.

The worship of Mithras, traces of which may be found at
Rome in the time of Tiberius, in the second century became of a
real importance, spreading under the Antonines through the
whole Roman Empire. The Persian god of created light, of
all earthly wisdom therefore, Mithras became identified with
the sun, Phoebus Apollo himself, who disperses the darkness

with its uncertainty and fear. Born from the rocks, he was generally worshipped in natural or artificial caverns; the immense number which have been discovered bearing witness to the universality of his worship. The cavern, so his religion taught, was the world into which the human soul must descend that it may be purified by many trials before it shall be worthy to pass on its way. And symbolically, the person initiated in his mysteries had first undergone a whole series of tests, as it were, some eighty in number, we are told, always of increasing difficulty, to prove himself at least capable of suffering hunger, thirst, scourging, and solitude without being subdued by agony, longing, or fear. Just there we seem to see the last effort of Paganism to meet Christianity, as it were, on its own ground, as it seemed to understand it, summing up really in the person of Mithras all the mythology of Olympus in order to defeat it. Little by little in the long fight which followed, by no means so sure in its result as it might appear—the Mithraic religion adopted certain Christian rites, but such names given to the sun god as " Lord and Creator of all things," " Father and source of all life " may well have owed nothing at all to Christianity.

It was not till the end of the fourth century that a Christian Emperor dared to interfere or suppress Pagan rites, and, indeed, in 395 we are told sacrifices at private expense were still permitted. Yet S. Jerome, writing in 392, tells us that " the *Memoria* of S. Clement is still preserved even to this day in the church built in Rome." It might seem then that the dwelling of Clement, that " stuccoed chamber," venerated and used as an oratory by the Christian Church of the first three centuries, was confiscated, as many such *loca religiosa* were, during the Diocletian persecution (284), and used by the followers of Mithras, not reluctantly, we may believe, for their worship, the larger chamber, the cavern itself, being altered and rebuilt and converted into the necessary *spelaeum*. Then in 312 in the Final Peace the Emperor Maxentius restored it to Pope Melchiades as having been originally Christian property. It was there, in the time of Constantine, that the old basilica was built above this shrine or memorial of S. Clement, and a hundred years later a Council sat there. Pope Zosimus,

writing to S. Augustine in 417 concerning the Pelagian Celes-
tius, says, " We sat in the Basilica of S. Clement, for he, imbued
with teaching of Blessed Peter the Apostle, had corrected
ancient errors with such authority, and had made such progress,
that the faith which he had learned and taught he also consecrated by his martyrdom."[1]   Indeed a fragment of fresco
preserved in the old basilica might well have represented this
Council.   From the time of its foundation the church seems
to have been continually embellished.   The beautiful marble
screen now in the upper basilica enclosing the *Schola Cantorum*,
the ambones and the great Paschal candlesticks, for instance,
seem to belong to the sixth century, if we may believe the
inscription found on one of the marble beams under the panels
west of the Gospel ambo, to the pontificate of Hormisdas which
lasted from 514 to 523.   S. Gregory, we read, would often
preach here, and took good note of the place, speaking very
eloquently in a sermon at S. Paolo fuori le Mura of S. Servulus,
the beggar who used to sit in the porch there, " rich in heavenly
treasures," while Pope Adrian I restored it, and his successor,
Leo III, presented the basilica in 796 with " a vestment of
crossed work, having its borders studded with gold, and a
silver corona of fifteen pounds' weight."

It was about this time that the basilica was painted in
fresco, though some fragments there are of earlier date, the
young Christ in a *tondo* and a Virgin and Child being work
certainly of the early part of the eighth century.   But in the
south-west corner of the nave there is a series of frescoes
painted in the time of Leo IV (847–855), as the inscription
there tells us—SANCTISSIMUS DOM. LEO QRT. PP. ROMANUS.
One of these represents the Assumption of the Blessed Virgin ;
and that is not surprising, since we learn that Leo IV ordered
the Octave of that Festa to be kept solemnly in the City, a
thing unknown till his day.   Among the rest we see the
Crucifixion, with S. Mary and S. John on either side, the
Maries with the Angel at the Sepulchre, Christ in Hades
drawing forth Adam and Eve, and a fragment of the Marriage
in Cana of Galilee.   The wall on which these frescoes are

---

[1] Cf. Constant., *Rom. Pont. Ep.*, p. 943, quoted by the Bishop of Clifton, *The
Basilica of San Clemente in Rome* (London, 1900), p. 26.

G

painted was an addition, built probably at the time to
strengthen the support of the roof, and then painted. We
find the same restoration on the other side of the nave, where
the strengthening wall is painted with frescoes of our Lord in
Benediction with S. Andrew and S. Clement on either side,
and S. Cyril and S. Methodius, " the Apostles of the Slavs,"
kneeling before Him, guarded by Archangels.

It was indeed S. Cyril and his brother S. Methodius who
discovered the tomb of S. Clement in the Crimea, or, as some
say, on an island, or again in the depths of the sea. For,
as Gregory of Tours has it, S. Clement was drowned, an anchor
tied to his neck, and the angels under the sea built a shrine for
him. Once every year, on his Festa, the sea itself, in adoration,
ebbed, as it were, some three miles that the faithful might visit
his shrine. But when S. Cyril came, whether in forgetfulness
or punishment, we know not, this had not happened for five
hundred years. S. Cyril, however, nothing doubting, began
to search, and soon found the shrine on a little island now,
given up by the sea. The holy relics he carried away, carefully taking them always with him on his wanderings, till
coming to Rome, Adrian II and his clergy going out to meet
him, he bore them with his own hands to the church of S.
Clement, where some of them remain, the rest being in the
great abbey of La Cava whither the Emperor Lewis Debonair
carried them in 872, a present from the Pope.

It might seem that the frescoes more or less illustrating these
events were painted not long after, and certainly they seem to
be the work of the ninth century. There we see S. Clement
enthroned by S. Peter, with S. Linus on one side and S.
Cletus on the other, spoiled by the floor of the upper church.
Below S. Clement is saying Mass when he is interrupted by
Sisinnius, first a persecutor of the Church and then a convert.
This fresco may well represent his conversion. In another
is set forth the life, death and recognition of S. Alexius, and
then the legend of the child miraculously saved and found in
the shrine of S. Clement under the sea. For it seems on one of
these Festas a woman had taken her little son to that marvellous
shrine built by the angels of the sea, and, as happened with
Mary Madonna, she lost the child, nor would her weeping

avail anything, for at the end of the day the sea returned, and
so, frantic with grief, she left the place.   And lo, returning
next year, there he was safe and sound in the shrine of the
angels in the sanctuary of S. Clement.

Last of all we see the translation of the relics of S. Clement
by S. Cyril, the Pope and the clergy.

The destruction which has for so long hidden this now
subterranean basilica came upon it, we may suppose, in 1084,
when Robert Guiscard and his Normans sacked it on their way
to deliver Pope Gregory VII, besieged by the penitent of
Canossa in Castel Sant' Angelo.   The old church seems to
have been literally buried under the havoc of those costly
saviours, so that Cardinal Anastasius, to whom the Episcopal
chair in the upper church points as the builder of the present
church—*hoc opus cepit, perfecit*—abandoned it altogether, and
decided to build on its ruins the great church we now
see.

There we have what is, substantially still, a church of the
eleventh century.   The nave with its flat ceiling is separated
from the aisles by sixteen antique columns : and the canopy
with its four columns of pavonazzetto is of the same period.
It is, however, to the mosaic of the apse we turn with the
greatest interest, since it may well have been a twelfth-century
copy, in which much of the old material was used, of the mosaic
of the lower church.   It is perhaps a little disappointing, less
remarkable certainly than that of S. Maria in Domnica, yet
with a marvellous gift of decoration after all—and indeed just
that is the chief quality of mosaic, which looks its best in old
age.   Among the tendrils of the vine Christ reigns on the Cross,
twelve doves about His head, and the Madonna and S. John
weeping at His feet.   Four fathers of the Church stand among
certain shepherds, goats, harts, sheep and birds, as it were,
beside the rivers of Paradise, where the Lamb reigns over the
beloved city and the new Jerusalem (Rev. xx. 9, and
xxi. i).

On the arch of the Tribune we see Isaiah, S. Lorenzo with
his gridiron, S. Paul as a sailor, S. Peter and S. Clement with
the anchor that drowned him, the sign of his martrydom.
Above is the head of Christ, the symbols of the four evangelists.

The beautiful pavement is a work of the Roman marble and mosaic masters—the Cosmati—of the twelfth and thirteenth centuries.

Little else calls for our attention—little else but the Cappella della Passione which the great Florentine Masolino painted in the fifteenth century for Cardinal Branda Castiglione. There on the arch over the entrance he has painted the Annunciation as though that were, as indeed it was, the beginning of our deliverance ; and at the side stands S. Christopher, as though to carry us safely over the river of Death, into the meadows of Paradise. The Crucifixion over the altar seems to have named the chapel : but the paintings on either side are concerned with the life of S. Catherine of Alexandria and the life of S. Clement, the latter being very much spoiled. After the frescoes of the lower church, the mosaic of the apse, this work seems a little sophisticated—a painting done to order amid much that was achieved hardly, in a sort of darkness, just for love.

Not far from San Clemente on the other side of the road on a height at the foot of the Coelian stands fortress-like the very old church of SS. Quattro Coronati which dates from the fourth century, was rebuilt by Honorius I in the seventh and enlarged by Leo IV in the ninth. Ruined by Guiscard's fire in 1084 it was rebuilt within the old shell by Paschal II in 1112, on a smaller scale, which spoiled its proportions, as we see. It was restored later in the fifteenth and sixteenth centuries when its fine roof was given it.

There are two atriums, or courts, now before it, the inner one having been part of the church which Paschal shortened. Eight granite columns divide nave and aisles and above small columns form galleries. The exceptional galleries in San Lorenzo and Sant' Agnes fuori le Mura were due to the level of these churches, sunk to bring them in contact with the tomb of the titular martyr. Here at SS. Quattro Coronati the explanation is different. The three aisles of the new church being crowded into the old central nave the galleries were necessary if the outer walls were to be used with their windows.[1]

---

[1] Cf. Fotheringham : *The Monuments of Christian Rome* (New York, 1908).

Paschal II's favourite builder was the artist who signs himself Paulus, he was the first of the *marmorari romani*, the architects, decorators, mosaicists and sculptors who built the beautiful Roman campanili and that masterpiece the Lateran Cloister. Here at the SS. Quattro Coronati Paulus not only made the mosaic pavement which still remains, but refashioned and decorated the whole church and built the lovely cloister about 1113. This is the earliest Roman cloister remaining now except that of S. Prassede which is of the end of the eleventh century. It is built of marble, the plan is oblong and between the corbels are mosaics of white and verde antico marble. The columns are coupled. which we do not find again till the thirteenth century in the Cloisters of San Cosimato.

The Campanile is curious and perhaps unique for it surmounts the centre of the portal leading into the court in front of the church. In the tribune are figures of the seventeenth century by Giovanni da San Giovanni. The roof of the church, that is the ceiling, is a fine work of the sixteenth century.

In the separate chapel of San Silvestro are frescoes which might seem to caricature the Byzantine style. In the midst is a curious representation of the Last Judgment surrounded by eight scenes from the legend of Constantine and Pope Sylvester—poor work.

As for the Quattro Coronati, the Four Crowned Holy Ones, they are the brothers SS. Severus, Severianus, Carpophorus and Victorinus, Roman officials who were scourged to death by order of Diocletian for attacking the worship of the gods. They were with five other martyrs originally buried outside the City on the Via Labicana but their relics were brought here by Leo IV in the ninth century together with the relics of five other martyrs, who, it seems, were sculptors or stone masons. For this reason the chapel of San Silvestro belonged to the Guild of *Scalpellini*. The church is served by the Capuchins.

XII

SANTA PUDENTIANA

IN the second Epistle to Timothy, written from Rome in the
time of Nero, the author, who has unconsciously con-
tributed more than any Council of any time to the con-
stitution of ecclesiastical discipline, sends greeting to his
correspondent from Pudens and Linus and Claudia, and all
the brethren. Legend tells us that the Senator Pudens listening, unwillingly at first certainly, to the prayers of his daughters
Praxedis and Pudentiana took S. Peter, at that time almost a
fugitive, into his palace on the Viminal Hill, where later an
oratory was built in the place where the Prince of the Apostles
had spent his last days. Pudentiana can have been but a
child when she persuaded her father to give refuge to S. Peter,
for later we hear of her, very definitely, herself mistress of that
palace on the Viminal Hill, having escaped the Neronian
persecution, as converting her whole household of some ninety-
six souls and bringing them—she must then, it might seem,
have been more than ninety years old—to Pope Pius I (140–
155) for Baptism. Under the Antonine law which forbade,
though not cruelly, at any rate, the public worship of Christ,
Pudentiana, we hear, received Pius with many Christians also
into her house where Mass was still said daily in spite of the
edict. " In these Christian offices of piety we hear she passed
out of this life," being buried on the " fourteenth kalends of
June beside the Via Salaria."

Two figures, indeed, seem to pass under the name of
Pudentiana, another daughter perhaps, the one comforting
in early youth the last days of S. Peter, the other in like fashion
supplying a refuge in time of trouble to Pope Pius I and his
fellows. However that may be, and the tradition is very
definite, it was S. Praxedis, we are told, who between the years
141 and 145 persuaded the Pope to dedicate a church on the

site of a palace where the Apostles themselves had taken refuge, and as was customary, this church went by the name of the mistress Pudentiana in whose house it was.

The church we see to-day, restored and spoiled though it be, is still substantially a building of the time of Constantine, of the renaissance which seems to have followed on the death of the first Christian Emperor. For, indeed, most of those early Christians, in Rome at any rate, far from being foes of the Empire, continually looked forward to the day of reconciliation, dreaming, though only in their hearts, of a Christian Empire which should hold the world for Christ. It seems to have been in the midst of the first expression of this hope, or vision rather, that the church of S. Pudentiana was rebuilt, built really for the first time, about the year 398 by those three presbyters who have left a record of their work in the inscription of the apse. But the church, thus a memorial of the first purely Christian art, has been restored again and again, in the eighth century, in the eleventh by Hildebrand, in the twelfth too and again in 1597 by Cardinal Caetani who gave it its present form, and even to-day.

Descending the steps from the Via Urbana, and ignoring the modern painting of the façade, one finds oneself in a great grey nave, divided from the aisles by fourteen antique columns. There is little in those chapels which now fill the aisle to interest us at all ; only in that to the left of the altar a well is shown where it is said the sisters S. Pudentiana and S. Praxedis collected the relics of more than three thousand martyrs who had suffered under Nero. What, however, really calls our attention after the first moment is the marvellously lovely mosaic of the apse, the most beautiful example in Rome of the work of that renaissance of Christian art which followed on the death of Constantine. And here, indeed, we see, not as in S. Maria Maggiore, a work half Judaic, still in its essence of the third century, but an art altogether Christian in its intention and scarcely less classical in form than that of two centuries before—scarcely less classical, but assuredly less articulate and less perfect.

There, in the largeness of the apse, we see the Cross around which shine the great baroque beasts of the Apocalypse, the symbols of the Four Evangelists against a sky of a delicate prismatic radiance, classical certainly in its inspiration. Beautiful as it is, something has been lost since the time of the mosaics of Santa Maria Maggiore.

In the centre, Christ as the Pantocrator, like some splendid Jupiter arrayed in azure and gold, is seated on a great throne under that marvellous jewelled Cross against the rosy sky of dawn, His right hand raised in blessing, in His left the Gospel. On either side His Throne two heroic figures seem to wait His word—the two Churches *ex circumcisione* and *ex gentibus* with victors' crowns, their hands raised aloft in prayer or praise.[1] Beside them stand S. Peter and S. Paul their representatives. For as Basil the Great wrote to the Emperor Julian " in conformance with a practice dating from Apostolic times, representations of S. Peter and S. Paul are to be found in all the churches." Beneath the throne are the figures of the Apostles, only ten of which remain. Above in the heavens appear the towers and porticoes of Rome—of the Heavenly Jerusalem.

Looking on that mosaic one seems to understand that already in the fourth century everything has been decided. The primacy of the Roman Church, already asserted there, sets a seal on its sovereignty, in the majesty of its traditions, in the power of Roman art.

[1] Some authorities suggest that these figures represent S. Pudentiana and S. Praxedis : cf. Crowe and Cavalcaselle, *A New History of Italian Painting* (Edit. Edward Hutton, 1908), vol. I, p. 10.

XIII

SANTI COSMA E DAMIANO

IF Roman art from the second to the fifth century is mag-
nificently represented by the mosaics of S. Maria Maggiore,
S. Pudentiana and S. Sabina on the Aventine Hill, the
wonderful mosaics of SS. Cosma and Damiano beside the
Forum reveal to us better than any other work of art in Rome
what the art of the sixth century had come to be in a City that
was already on the morrow of a great disaster. The Goths
and the Vandals had passed over her, the western Empire
had fallen.

Composed as it is of a single nave divided not into aisles
but into an upper and a lower church, the main part of the
building is really the old Temple of Peace built by Vespasian,
where, so we are told, the Archives of the City were kept.
Destroyed, or almost destroyed, in the fire of A.D. 198, it was
restored by Septimius Severus and Caracalla, who, placing
there the great plan of Rome, called it *Templum Sacrae Urbis*.
Then, after many years, came Maxentius, who in the fourth
century, certainly before the Final Peace of the Church,
built there a round temple to the memory of his son Romulus :
it was these two buildings which, about two centuries later,
Pope Felix IV (526–530) threw into one building, the Temple
of Romulus with its four beautiful columns forming the
vestibule of the church, towards the Forum, while the four-
sided Temple of the Sacred City became the church itself, a
new chamber being then added which later became the
sacristy, as it still is. The débris of time, the ruin of tumult
and disaster little by little had raised the ground about the
place, so that by 1623, when Urban VIII sat on the throne of
S. Peter, the church was almost subterranean. Thinking to
remedy this without much trouble he strangely divided the
church horizontally, building, indeed, a new floor halfway
up the old walls. By the greatest good fortune, for Urban

VIII was a Barberini, so much more to be dreaded, as we know, than the Barbarians themselves, he left the main part of the mosaics in the tribune, work of the time of Felix IV, untouched, destroying, however, no doubt without a thought, the lower part of the mosaic wherein the twenty-four elders threw down their crowns at the feet of the Prince of Life.

In the great vault of the tribune, in the very sky itself, Christ stands, a sublime and melancholy figure, majestical, and yet sweetly withal raising His right hand in blessing, while His left holds a scroll as it were of the fate of the City itself. Above, the hand of God the Father seems to guard Him, and at His feet, as it were, in a meadow of flowers S. Peter and S. Paul present S. Cosma and S. Damiano, those two barbarians, to Him. Beside them winds the river of crystal, and from the height of a palm-tree there, the phoenix, symbol, as Tertullian tells us, of the resurrection, takes its flight. Below, Pope Felix IV and S. Theodore wait in adoration.

Decoratively magnificent as this mosaic is—and indeed just that might seem to be the chief business of mosaic work generally—it has not the concentration or the power, the essential contact with life of the work in S. Maria Maggiore. And indeed those mosaics have, rightly understood, less affinity with this which followed them in perfect succession than with the reliefs of the time of Marcus Aurelius and Septimius Severus, the Roman busts of the second and third centuries, as it were, their ancestors.

Here, in the church of SS. Cosma and Damiano, those clouds of an almost terrible fire and shadow are wholly symbolical, or, as one may think, merely decorative, and because of their beauty, their unnatural beauty, it is interesting to compare with them the absolutely natural and realistic loveliness of the clouds in the Abraham and Melchizedek, for instance, in S. Maria Maggiore, where the artist, altogether classical as he is, has really felt the beauty of a real Roman sky at sunset, with its fiery clouds and air heavy with purple and gold, and has expressed it once for all as well as he could.

As one looks at that solemn and melancholy Christ towering there, mysterious and almost threatening even in His forgiveness, or considers those two Arab martyrs, so rude and full of energy and fanaticism, we seem to understand the very emotion and soul of the time. The invasions of the fifth century had ended in the fall of the western Empire, and in the midst of that awful confusion, to save herself from the northern hordes, Rome—Italy—had passed, as a mere province, once more into the universal Empire ; but the Emperor was a barbarian at Constantinople.

XIV

SANTA MARIA ANTIQUA
AND SANTA FRANCESCA ROMANA

THE subtle Byzantine spirit seems really to have over-whelmed the City in the sixth and seventh centuries, introducing a whole new world of thought and experience. It brought new customs too ; among the rest the custom of building a Christian church in a temple of the gods, as though a place once consecrated to divinity must needs be holy still, though as it were in a new service. The first of those pagan temples to give place to a Christian church was the Templum Sacrae Urbis, in which, about 526, rose the basilica of SS. Cosma and Damiano, dedicated certainly to no Roman saint. Less than a century later the Pantheon passed into the hands of Our Lady, and about the same time the Templum Divi Antonii et Divae Faustinae gave place to the church of S. Lorenzo in Miranda, while in the Curia of Honorius S. Adriano rose. It was a Byzantine custom.

It must have been in this period, and certainly not before the sixth century, that the church of S. Maria Antiqua in Foro was built in the precincts of the Templum Divi Augusti, probably in a part of the library, beside the Temple of the Dioscuri and the Temple of Vesta, the most sacred places of the ancient City. Its name—Old S. Mary's, as we might say —remains a mystery, for it certainly was not the first church to bear her name in Rome, S. Maria Maggiore having been placed under her protection in the fifth century (432–440). The name seems indeed to be inexplicable, and though we know that its chief benefactor, Pope John VII, calls himself the servant of Mary, that helps us but little to explain it. Probably the church was a shrine for one of the ancient Byzantine images that later became not uncommon in Italy, taking its name from it.

Though Pope John VII in the eighth century seems to have been the chief benefactor of the church, decorating it with frescoes, it was not bare before his time.   Three layers of frescoes have been discovered, a new series, replacing those of John, having been painted in various parts of the building in 741–767.   The history of the church, however, meagre as it is, is short, for in the time of Leo IV (847–855) S. Maria Antiqua was crushed by the fall of part of the Imperial buildings, which overhung it on the north-west edge of the Palatine.[1] This calamity probably happened during the earthquake of 847.   In consequence of it the diaconate was removed to S. Maria Nova, the church we now call S. Francesca Romana in the Temple of Venus and Rome.   The outer hall of S. Maria Antiqua, however, escaping destruction as it did, seems to have remained in use till a much later period, as is proved by the fragments of painting it contains.   The final destruction of the whole building, its burial under the débris, dates from the fire which devastated this part of Rome in 1084, when the Normans, under Robert Guiscard, came to deliver Gregory VII out of the hands of Henry IV.   Thus it remained, altogether hidden from sight and almost unsuspected, till it was discovered in 1900.

At the time of the foundation of S. Maria Antiqua, at the time of its decoration by Pope John, Rome was full of Greeks— Greek officials, Greek monks, Greek residents, as it were a whole Byzantine army of occupation.   Everywhere in the church we see Greek inscriptions, costumes, and saints, which serve to remind us that S. Maria Antiqua was, even structurally, connected with the Palatine, the seat of Byzantine government, that it was indeed on the edge of, if not within, the Greek quarter, whose centre was S. Maria in Cosmedin.   And just as Rome in the seventh and eighth centuries was dependent on Constantinople, but already struggling, and successfully, for independence, so in the wall-painting of S. Maria Antiqua we see a Byzantine art that has been transplanted to the west, that has acquired already something of a Roman character in consequence, in the use of a certain number of local saints, for

---

[1] Cf. Mr. G. M'N. Rushforth's masterly paper, ' S. Maria Antiqua,' in *Papers of the British School at Rome* (Macmillan, 1900), vol. i.

instance, in the alternating of Latin with Greek inscriptions,
and even in the general decorative treatment of the church.

S. Maria Antiqua is indeed a Byzantine church in process
of transformation, about to become Roman. The plan is
Byzantine, broken by Latin custom, the liturgical chambers on
either side the altar having, in one case certainly, become
chapels by the middle of the eighth century. Not important enough to be decorated with mosaics—all the more
valuable to us on that account, for mosaics alone are a little
meagre as evidence, and we already have more of them than
of anything else of the time—S. Maria Antiqua shows us in
what manner a whole church was decorated in that confused
age.

The wall paintings in their subjects fall into two classes,
namely, figures of saints and scenes illustrating a story. That
array of Eastern saints, people altogether unknown to us, shows
us very vividly how overwhelming the Byzantine influence
has become in Rome. Yet, little by little, amid this crowd of
aliens we see the figures we know so well appearing one by one
—S. Gregory the Great, for instance, and Pope Martin I,
the latter dead barely fifty years when he was painted there,
the champions of Roman independence, of the dominion of the
Roman Church in the West. There, too, we see S. Clement
who might seem to reconcile East and West under the
sovereignty of Rome ; but that figure certainly has been
painted under the growing western influence, for he alone,
against all Byzantine custom, appears with his emblem the
anchor, the instrument, so his legend tells us, of his martyrdom.

It is difficult, however, and perhaps impossible to draw
any really definite conclusions as to the state of Roman art
from the work here in S. Maria Antiqua. For we are ignorant
as to who the artists were, whether Greek monks or Greek
artists, merely settled, generation after generation perhaps, in
Rome, or Romans indeed who had passed under the Byzantine
yoke. That the paintings must be described as " Byzantine "
there can be no doubt, and though some few, especially in
the sanctuary, have an unmistakable affinity with classical
Roman art in types and the treatment of these types, in method,
and technique, yet there is little in that to help us. And

indeed, if the means of expression were the same in east and west, so, largely, was the subject-matter : it was the spirit that was different. There, amid those crowds of strangers, strangers only because they were far off maybe, we see just our friends—Joseph in Egypt, David and Goliath, the Prophets, the Madonna at Annunciation, the Magi, Jesus crucified, the Apostles, our Lord in glory. And then, like a vision almost, we come upon those two heads of so singular a beauty, to the right of the apse. Who can have painted them ? It is as though suddenly in them " this tyranny was overpast," and we stood already in the dawn of some forgotten renaissance.

When in the ninth century it became evident that S. Maria Antiqua was falling into decay and would have to be abandoned, Pope Leo IV founded a new church of S. Mary, S. Maria Nova at the eastern end of the Forum in the Temple of Venus and Rome. This church, or rather its successor, became S. Francesca Romana. The saint was buried in the crypt and was canonised by Paul V in 1608 : forty years later Bernini made a portrait of her for her tomb.

The church of Leo IV, S. Maria Nova, was destroyed by fire and rebuilt by Alexander III in the twelfth century when the Cosmati *marmorari romani* built the beautiful campanile which remains to us, one of the finest in Rome. The mosaic in the apse of the church opens a new epoch in which, instead of the sober vestments which we find for instance in SS. Nereo and Achilleo and in S. Maria in Cosmedin, here they shine with oriental splendour, the Virgin's crown flashes with gems, the throne is covered with gold and the sky is no longer of azure but of gold crusted with shining shells, and below an arcade of five arches, encrusted with jewels, surrounds Our Lady enthroned supported by saints. Above amid clouds and vases of flowers appears the hand of God the Father. For the first time the Divine Child stands on His Mother's knee and is not borne on her arm. Made about 1160, the tesserae of the mosaic are not of different shapes as in previous works but more or less regular and all of a shape. The figures are stiff and the work not very satisfactory in its effect. In the seventeenth century the church was given a Baroque frontispiece perhaps by Carlo Maderna, a most successful and a most restrained and tasteful work.

The tomb to the right of the apse has some interest. It is the tomb of Gregory XI, Pierre Roger de Beaufort, who was elected Pope at Avignon in 1370 while he was not yet a priest. He was a man of peace but was obliged to excommunicate Barnabò Visconti, Duke of Milan, who, when the legates brought him the Bull of excommunication, compelled them to eat the parchment on which it was written. Gregory then declared war on him and took into his service the English condottiere, Sir John Hawkwood. Bernabò was compelled to sue for peace. Not long after, S. Catherine of Siena persuaded Gregory to return to Rome. " Be a brave man," she told him, " and not a coward." The long exile of the Papacy was over. Gregory left Avignon September 13, 1376, boarded a ship at Marseilles on October 2 and by way of Genoa reached Tarquinia-Corneto on December 6th. In the new year he set out again and landed at Ostia on January 14, 1377, sailed up the Tiber to S. Paolo fuori le Mura, from where he made solemn entry into Rome on January 17. In this tomb in S. Francesca Romana lies the last Pope of the exile, the last Pope of French nationality. But only death prevented him from returning to Avignon.

XV

SANTA MARIA IN COSMEDIN
AND SAN GIORGIO IN VELABRO

OF that mysterious Greek world which during the sixth and seventh centuries had gradually overwhelmed the City, S. Maria in Cosmedin may well be said to have been the centre. Around it stood the Greek quarter, in which those Byzantine officials dwelt with others of their nation and Empire, forming indeed a world apart, really a sort of corporation or *Schola*.

Built, as was the custom of the Greeks, in the ruins of a pagan Temple, the Temple of Ceres, S. Maria in Schola Greca, as the church was then called, stood in what, till our fathers' time, was the most picturesque quarter of Rome, in the shadow of the cypresses of the Palatine, within sound of the Tiber, close to the Ponte Rotta beside S. Maria del Sole, that tiny round pagan shrine on the Ripa Greca, and S. Maria Egiziana, small too, in which some have thought to find the Temple of the *Mater Matuta* the goddess of dawn, Stella Maris —star of the sea.

The date of its foundation is unknown, but, as we have seen, it cannot have been earlier than the sixth century when, as we are told, it was numbered among the diaconatic churches of Rome. The Diaconia was the *domus* or residence of one of those seven deacons who presided over the seven ecclesiastical regions which divided the City. And, as though to remind us of its Greek origin, the street beside it still bears the name Via della Greca.

It was Adrian I (772–795) who rebuilt the church, which then seems to have been ruinous, Rome having, in the agony we know, thrown off the Byzantine yoke but a few years before. It was he who changed the name from S. Maria in Schola Greca to S. Maria in Cosmedin, still as is thought conserving there some memory of its Byzantine nationality, giving it a name which later came to fit it perfectly—S. Maria Splendida, as we might say Our Lady of Adorning—S. Maria κοσμίδιον. But the people then, as now, would not have it so, calling it instead in their own tongue Bocca della Verità, because of the great marble masque that we still see in the portico, and which in antiquity, as in the Middle Age, seems to have been used in matters concerning an oath ; the merchants of old resorting to the well which it adorned, sacred to Mercury, of which Ovid speaks, to cleanse themselves as it were of perjury ; while in the Middle Age, to prove they spoke truth, they thrust their hand in the mouth which might suddenly make them prisoner, it was said, if they spoke falsely.

In the ninth century S. Maria in Cosmedin was again restored and a papal residence built beside it. Then in the troubles which followed the death of Charlemagne we lose sight of it, till, nearly three hundred years later, in 1133, we hear of a new restoration and even a consecration which speaks certainly of some unrecorded ruin due, perhaps, to Arnulf and his Germans, to Henry IV after Canossa, or to Guiscard and his Normans. It is to this time, to the twelfth century, that so much of the beautiful work still remaining here belongs, the Cosmati mosaic pavement, for instance, spread like a rich carpet between the delicate columns, the high altar, the episcopal throne, work directed, with love and pride we may think, by Alfanus, Chamberlain to Calixtus II, since he has graven his name three times there within the church itself and is buried under the portico in a beautiful sarcophagus bearing this inscription : *Alfanus, cernens quod cuncta pereunt, hoc sibi sarcophagium statuit, ne totus obiret* : Alfanus, knowing that all perishes, has caused this sarcophagus to be made for him that he may not altogether die. Was this what Christianity had come to in just a thousand years after the assurance of the catacombs, the new hope of the Church ?

The beautiful, slender Campanile, the two marble ambones decorated with mosaic, the beautiful twisted candelabrum there, with that in the tribune, the lovely canopy over the high altar, the ciborium, these are work of the great family of

Cosmati, the last being said to be from the hand of Deodatus Cosma.

To the eighth century, certainly, though to the reign of John VII rather than of Adrian I, belongs that spoiled mosaic of the Adoration of the Magi now in the Sacristy. It belonged originally to the old Basilica of S. Pietro in Vaticano, is indeed just a fragment of the mosaics which adorned the oratory of John VII in old S. Peter's ; and though it has really nothing to do with S. Maria in Cosmedin it belongs as it were to one of her periods. For that eighth century too, we may claim, and with a far greater significance, the majestic picture of the Blessed Virgin in a little chapel leading out of the nave on the south-west. Θεοτόκῳ, ἀεὶ Παρθένῳ we read there in shining letters—To the Ever Virgin Mother of God. Well, that might seem just a confession of a truth implicit in the Catholic religion, as indeed it is, but in fact it is, as it were, a proclamation of the deliverance of Rome of the Latin world, of our world rightly understood, from the domination of Byzantium. About 750, as it seems, the Nestorian heresy had again raised its head. Constantine V, the Iconoclast, had again forbidden us to pray to the Virgin on pain, as it is said, of death or exile worse than death. The Patriarch of Constantinople, seeking a compromise, seemed to hesitate. It was Rome who spoke, restoring to us our gods of old ; our gods that we seemed for a moment to have lost for ever.

Close to S. Maria in Cosmedin stands the beautiful small basilica of S. Giorgio in Velabro. The Velabrum seems in antiquity to have been a market and to be alluded to by Horace :

> edicit, piscator uti, pomarius, auceps,
> unguentarius ac Tusci turba impia vici,
> cum scurris fartor, cum Velabro omne macellum
> mane domum veniant.[1]

The gate of the goldsmiths, the Arco degli Orefici, the ancient Arcus Argentariorum and the four-wayed Janus Quadrifrons

---

[1] He decreed that fishmonger, fruitseller, fowler, perfumer, the Tuscan street's vile throng, cooks and parasites, the whole market and Velabrum should come to him next morning. Horace : *Sat.* II, iii, 227 *et seq.*

of the time of Constantine stand beside the church which was
founded in the fourth century and originally bore the name
of Basilica Sempronia from the house of Titus Sempronius
which stood near by, but S. Leo II in the seventh century
restored it and dedicated it in honour of S. Sebastian. A
century later Pope Zachary, a Cappadocian, added S. George
as joint patron, for this part of the City, as we see with S.
Maria in Cosmedin, was then the Greek quarter.

The church itself is beautiful and very complete, with a fine
Portico with four antique columns and a Campanile, works of
the Cosmati, the Campanile heavier than is usual with
these lovely Roman towers, less graceful certainly than that of
S. Maria in Cosmedin.

Within, the church is austerely impressive, the arcade upheld by sixteen antique columns, and though restored in
1924 still possesses in part its beautiful mosaic pavement,
its ciborium and altar and confession adorned with mosaics,
all works of the Cosmati of the twelfth and thirteenth centuries.
Nothing could be more attractive, especially as the church is
generally quiet and deserted. Englishmen should not fail to
visit it, for S. George is the Protector of the Kingdom and the
church possesses a major relic of the Saint, to wit his head, as
well as the spear with which he killed the dragon and a part of
his standard, which we have made our own.

The apse of the church, higher than the nave, is reached by a
flight of five steps on either side the confession and the altar.
It was once decorated with frescoes executed to the order of
Cardinal Gaetano Stefaneschi in 1295, by the Roman master
Pietro Cavallini or, as some have it, Giotto, but restoration has
left us nothing or very little from either hand—perhaps the
design. There we see Our Lord seated on the globe with Our
Lady, S. Peter, S. George with his white horse and S. Sebastian
on either side. The lovely ciborium towers up beneath
with its double tier of little marble columns supporting its
roof, a work of the Cosmati.

The sunlight pours from column to column and in the
silence there one's thoughts conjure up the pathetic figure of
Petrarch's friend, Cola di Rienzo, who in 1347 on the fifth day
of Lent erected here his provocative proclamation : *In breve*

tempore Romani torneranno al loro antico buon stato. A day or two later he bore the banner of S. George preserved in this church in procession to the Capitol, dreaming of the unity of Italy and the domination of Rome and there he was crowned Tribune April 15, 1347. Seven years later after incredible fortunes he was murdered by the Roman populace.

XVI

SANTA PRASSEDE

THE church of S. Prassede on the Esquiline Hill, not far from S. Maria Maggiore, was one of the most ancient "titular churches" in Rome. Said to have been built on the site of the house of S. Praxedis, the sister of S. Pudentiana, it would seem to have been founded really in Apostolic times, and we hear of it more than once before the end of the fifth century. In the beginning of the ninth century, however, it was in ruin—" The church of the Blessed Martyr of Christ Praxedis which was built in the first times was now," we read in the ninth century, " altogether ruinous from age ; so that Pope Paschal I, for the sake of his great reverence for that holy martyr of Christ, determined to rebuild it." The church he built was, for the most part it seems, merely a replica of the ancient building, but he adorned it with mosaics very splendidly, and added three chapels—those of S. John Baptist, S. Zeno and S. Agnese, with a monastery for a "holy congregation of Greeks." The chapel of S. Agnese has in the course of centuries disappeared, and the monastery, after passing under Innocent III into the hands of the Vallombrosan Order, is now a barracks, though it still houses a few monks with the soldiers. Nor has the church itself escaped the spoliation of the restorer. Restored in the sixteenth century by S. Carlo Borromeo with much lack of taste, it became what we now see, only the mosaics and the beautiful campanile of the ninth century escaping the unfortunate enthusiasm of the author of the *Catechismus Romanus*. It is not, however, with the work of one altogether devoid of a sense of beauty that, happily, we are concerned, but with the work of the ninth century which he permitted to remain.

These mosaics might seem almost to imitate tapestry, to be as contentedly just a decoration as though they were a rich carpet of figured stuff mysteriously closing the apse and hiding the mere stone of the great double arch of the tribune. Just a decoration without a sense of life, they would seem to look behind the art of Rome to some vague antiquity and to have brought hither still heavy with incense some vague hierarchical splendour from Byzantium.

The mosaic of the apse, where we see a mournful Christ, His right hand raised in blessing, while on one side stands S. Paul with S. Prassede and S. Zeno, and on the other S. Peter with S. Pudentiana and Pope Paschal, is really but a copy of the great mosaic of SS. Cosma and Damiano, an adaptation of it accomplished without enthusiasm or emotion, just a church decoration without any but the feeblest purpose. Not for another three hundred years would Rome dare to look back behind all her disasters to the art of antiquity and, as it were, hand in hand with an old beauty, return, yes, to Nature, in communion with which she was to recreate the art of Italy in the work of the Cosmati and of Cavallini of the twelfth and thirteenth centuries. The mosaic on the face of the arch of the apsis, where the Lamb on the altar between the seven candlesticks is surrounded by angels and the symbols of the Evangelists, while beneath, in ever diminishing rows, we see the four-and-twenty elders of the Apocalypse, clad in flowing robes and bearing crowns in their veiled hands is also copied from SS. Cosma and Damiano. The mosaic of the triumphal arch is like a religious poem. There, as in some mysterious tapestry, we see the New Jerusalem in the midst of which Christ stands, guarded by angels, to receive the homage of the Elders, while at the gates the saints invite certain chosen ones to enter in. Just as later some Norman artist is to tell the story of the Conquest in the tapestries of Bayeux, so here the story of the heavenly vision in the Apocalypse is told really as one might chant a canticle or a prose by heart, after many years, without enthusiasm : " And I saw a new heaven and a new earth, for the first heaven and the first earth were passed away ; and there was no more sea. And I, John, saw the holy city, new Jerusalem, coming down from God out of heaven pre-pared as a bride adorned for her husband : . . . and her light was like unto a stone most precious, even like a jasper stone, clear as crystal. . . ." It is into a world as mysterious as that, as unreal as that, we are come when we look on these mosaics of the ninth century in S. Prassede.

There remains that obscure and mysterious chapel of S. Zeno, built by Pope Paschal I in memory of the saint, to receive the dust of his mother. *Orto del Paradiso* the Romans call the chapel where amid an astonishing profusion of gold and splendid colour, not without wonder, we see those pale and burning figures shining there like ghosts, as amorphous certainly and with as little real relation to this world. In the arched window above the door is a double border of medallions, eight busts of saints, Christ in Benediction with apostles and saints, the Virgin and Child between two attendants. Within, above the arch on the left of the altar, are S. Agnese, S. Praxedis, S. Pudentiana, while beneath is the Lamb of the Apocalypse on the rock of the Church guarded by the four beasts. Beneath are busts of the Blessed Virgin, S. Prassede, S. Pudentiana and Theodora, the mother of the Pope. Above the arch, to the right of the altar, are S. James, S. Andrew and S. John ; while over the altar itself are the Madonna and Child between S. Prassede and S. Pudentiana. Above are Christ and the Apostles. Opposite the altar are the Apostles Peter and Paul guarding an empty throne. One lifts one's eyes from these mysterious splendours so full of a lovely vague music to the roof where Christ reigns surrounded by four angels.

It is not here, however, for all their mystery and glancing gold and strange, beautiful colours, we shall recognise the work of Rome. A real feebleness of expression seems to have fallen on the Eternal City, altogether absorbed, perhaps, in that age, in the tremendous politics which recreated Europe. What her wonderful gift of statesmanship which had just crowned Charlemagne and re-established the western Empire was to lead to in art, we may see, however, in the thirteenth-century altar in the Confession and in the tomb, also by the Cosmati, close by in the chapel of the Crucifix. There, with a nobility and beauty not to be surpassed, she seems to have given back to us all the beauty of antiquity with a new simplicity, a new tenderness and hope.

XVII

SAN GIOVANNI IN LATERANO

LEGEND, eagerly busy for so long with the story of the conversion of the first Christian Emperor, Constantine the Apostate, has not hesitated to accord him also the honour of founding S. Giovanni in Laterano, the mother of all churches, both of the City and of the world. In the bitter pages of Zosimus we see him in 326, loaded with crime, steeped in the blood of his eldest son, his wife, his father-in-law, returning to Rome as it were in an agony of remorse, seeking, well, reconciliation, most of all with his own heart, perhaps, and with the gods, but met always with the same answer, " We have no means whereby a man may purge himself of parricide " ; till at last, weary for peace, he met that strange Egyptian, a Christian from Spain—was it Asio, Bishop of Cordova ?—who assured him that by Baptism all our sins are cancelled out. So Constantine forsook the gods, and ever after followed Jesus our Saviour. And as penance in expiation of those crimes he filled Rome with churches ; with his own hands helping to dig the foundations of the two most famous among them—S. Giovanni in Laterano, and S. Pietro in Vaticano.

Full of inconsistencies, of impossible rumours, as that legend certainly is, it seems to have grown in the manner of legends out of a seed of truth ; though the seed is small indeed. For, in fact, the triumph of Christianity had been assured for nearly thirteen years when Constantine returned to Rome in 326, and the Lateran itself, the palace there, and the church assuredly had been in Christian hands, at any rate since the year 313, the year in which the Edict of Milan established the Peace of the Church, when in October Pope Miltiades held the first Council there against the Donatists. The palace, it seems, had belonged for some centuries to the Laterani, of whom Juvenal speaks ; it had been confiscated in Nero's time, why we do not know, but restored by Septimius Severus. What interests us, however, in thinking of that story of Zosimus is the fact that it had become the property of Fausta, Constantine's wife, was indeed her dower-house, and that, whether as a gift from her or from the Emperor, in the earliest years of the fourth century it had become the palace of the Bishop of Rome.

Of the church, which, as we may suppose, stood within the house, we know nothing, save that it became the citadel of Roman Christianity, an honour it has never forfeited, for even to-day the Lateran takes precedence of all other churches of Christendom : *Omnium ecclesiarum Urbis et Orbis Mater et Caput.* Rumour, however, speaks of its marvellous treasures, among which were the Ark of the Covenant, the Tables of the Law, the Golden Candlestick and the vestments of Aaron, which Genseric stole ; for the Vandals, unlike the Goths, had but little scruple where loot was concerned. Alaric, as we know, entering Rome by the Porta Salaria, amid the horror of his sack was careful of the treasures of the Church. When his barbarians, roaming through the City, came at last upon that " splendid hoard of massy plate, of the richest materials curiously worked," the great king bade them take it up—all of it. Then he marched them " in order of battle through the principal streets, protected with glittering arms the long train of their companions, who bore aloft on their heads the sacred vessels of gold and silver . . ." and laid the treasure reverently in the sanctuary of the Vatican. That was in 410. In 455 Genseric entered Rome at the head of his Vandals by the Porta Ostia, and after a pillage of fourteen days left it, and, taking " all that remained of public and private wealth, of sacred and profane treasure " to his galleys, set sail for Carthage. With him went the treasures of the Lateran, the spoil of the Temple of Jerusalem. When Belisarius took Carthage in 533 he found them all and carried them to Constantinople, where they remained, Procopius tells us, till Justinian sent them to Jerusalem to adorn the Church of the Holy Sepulchre ; but they were lost in the sea.

Before those disastrous days of the fifth century the Lateran had been dedicated to Christ, *Christo Salvatori*, but after the spoliation of the Vandals Leo the Great was compelled to restore it, and it seems that then new titles were given to it, though it has indeed always remained under the dedication of Christ, *Christo Salvatori et in honorem S. Joannis Baptistae et S. Joannis Evangelistae*. It suffered, doubtless, in the awful sack of Totila and the bitter years which followed, and we find Adrian restoring it in the eighth century after Pepin had given him his protection, and it was Leo III, " a priest of the Lateran," who crowned Charlemagne in S. Peter's on Christmas Day in the year 800. Ninety-six years later the Lateran was entirely destroyed by an earthquake—*ab altare usque ad portas cecidit*. Pope Sergius III (904–911) rebuilt it on the old foundations and in the old dimensions. This building stood for four hundred years, till in 1308, on the night of May 3rd, it was totally destroyed by fire. Clement V immediately began to rebuild it, the new church being finished by his successor, John XXII (1316–34), who employed Giotto in its decoration. But misfortune still followed, for in 1360 this building too was burned. Rebuilt by Urban V (1362–70), there seems to have been, by that time, after two fires, but very little of the Sergian Basilica left. Urban's work remained almost unspoiled, though restored by Martin V and Eugenius IV in the fifteenth century, and in the sixteenth century Fontana built the Loggia della Benedizione, the northern façade, for Sixtus V and then in 1650 Innocent X entirely rebuilt most of it, Borromini being the architect. It is this seventeenth-century church we now see ; the great main façade, however, was erected under Clement XII in the first part of the eighteenth century, and is the work of Alessandro Galilei.

Of the church of Urban V very little remains to us, a part of the pavement, which may well be earlier, the tabernacle of the high altar, the cloisters and the mosaics : they but serve to show us what we have lost. Then a great atrium stood before the church surrounded by colonnades, in the midst of which a fountain played in accordance with ancient use. There were set the tombs of the Popes, John X, John XII, John XIV, Alexander II and later, Martin V. The façade of that time, decorated with mosaics of Our Lord and the Four Evangelists, must have been, one may think, something like that of S. Maria in Trastevere ; while on either side the great door stood the statues of S. Peter and S. Paul. Within, the church was divided into five naves by four lines of ancient columns, and the walls were covered with frescoes and mosaics. As to-day, one ascended a few steps into the transept, in the midst of which stood the high altar, the very table at which S. Peter was said to have celebrated Mass, and above rose the exquisite canopy of Giovanni di Stefano, which, though restored, we still possess.

Standing to-day before that immense façade of the eighteenth century, which, splendid though it be as an isolated work of art, has no relation at all to the church, is indeed a mere screen or frontispiece to it, we realise what we have lost. Even the world there does not remain the same. One used to turn away from the church to watch the shadows of the great clouds passing slowly over the Campagna, where in the immense silence the ruined aqueducts still stumble towards the City. To-day all that is gone. It was with the remembrance of that vast solitude that one used to come into the vestibule of S. Giovanni in Laterano before the five doors of the nave, and, passing the statue of Constantine, enter the basilica. And indeed the test was too hard. One's first impression, in spite of a certain largeness, space, and majesty in the church, cannot but be one of disappointment. One cannot deny the spaciousness of those five naves broken by a wide transept, beyond which rises the great tribune splendid with mosaics, nor the beauty and richness of the soffitto roof, all of purple and gold ; but its ancient dignity and repose are spoiled by the pretentious baroque statues, the reliefs on the enormous piers and pilasters which have hidden the ancient columns from our sight. In his own place Borromini is magnificent, but not in a church of so noble an antiquity as this.

All those faults of taste, of modesty, might seem to be expressed to the utmost in the chapels of the nave, of which perhaps the Cappella dei Corsini in the north aisle, built by Galilei in 1704 for Pope Clement XI in honour of his ancestor S. Andrea Corsini, is the best example. There, too, the outlines, as it were the construction, are excellent and strong, the chapel being built in the form of a Greek cross in the manner of Bramante, but all that simple and noble beauty is spoiled by the decoration of it, that is entirely out of place here.

So, little by little one's visit resolves itself into a search for certain treasures that still remain there from one or other of the older basilicas : the fragment of fresco by Giotto on the first pilaster of the right aisle for instance, and the beautiful thirteenth-century monument to Cardinal Guissano close by, and those old sepulchres of the Popes established thereabout. And indeed there is a plenty of beautiful and ancient things there.

And then the high altar guards the wooden table altar used by S. Peter in the house of Pudens and above the heads of SS. Peter and Paul. So we are told.

Passing up the few steps into the splendid transept beside the exquisite Gothic canopy over the high altar, one comes, at the southern end of the cross, upon four columns of gilded bronze which once upheld the Temple of Jupiter Capitolinus, but now adorn the Chapel of the Blessed Sacrament, in which is the supposed table of the Last Supper. Close by one enters the sacristy by two beautiful doors of the twelfth century, and there, too, are some really surprising things—water-pipes of lead from the Palace of the Laterani, stamped with their name, an ancient bas-relief of the old basilica, a crucifix of the thirteenth century, and the two great statues of S. Peter and S. Paul which used to stand on either side of the portal of the church.

The mosaic of the tribune is so much restored that it no longer remains an authentic work of the fourth or of Torriti in the thirteenth century. It was for Nicholas IV that Torriti restored the mosaics here in S. Giovanni, and so they remained till Leo XIII in 1878 enlarged the choir, moving back the tribune.

It was from a window under the portico of Leo IV that Boniface VIII proclaimed the jubilee of 1300. It is probable that both Dante and Giotto were present on the occasion as guests of the Pope, who desired the latter to paint the sides of the portico in memory of that fateful rejoicing. Five years later Clement V fled to Avignon, and the Babylonian Captivity of the Church began. In the confusion and riot which followed, the portico of S. Giovanni was twice burnt and damaged, and it is thus that, of all Giotto's work there, there remains to us but a single fragment, that on the first pilaster of the right aisle. Dimmed by age, cracked, and certainly retouched, this fragment yet remains one of the loveliest things of the church. The Pope shows himself to the people, followed by three clerks, one of whom carried the Bull of Indulgence. When Giotto thus painted his portrait Boniface was in the height of his power, the Papacy seemed indeed the greatest thing in Europe, and there was no other palace in Christendom that might compare with the Lateran.

> *quando Laterano*
> *Alle cose mortali andò di sopra.*[1]

The Papacy had killed the Empire : there followed the tragedy of Anagni, the long exile, and the shame of Avignon.

One passes into the beautiful Cloister which Vassallettus built in the thirteenth century ; but the monastery had been built in the sixth when in 589 the Lombards seized Monte Cassino, and the Benedictines of the mother house fled to Rome. They remained in possession till the end of the eighth century when the monastery was given to the Canons Regular of the Basilica. It was Leo I who in 440 had caused the clergy of the Lateran to live in common under the rule of S. Augustine. They were reformed in 1061, and again in 1294 were expelled by Boniface VIII to make room for secular clergy. After the long exile Eugenius IV restored the monastery to them in 1442, naming them " of the most Holy Saviour." Calixtus III, however, drove them out, and though they returned under Paul II, they were exiled again in 1471, and have never returned.

The Lateran cloister with its wonderful double columns, many decorated with mosaic, the beautiful mosaic work of the architraves and the sculptured heads of the cornice is the masterpiece of the *marmorari romani* of Vassallettus of the Cosmati school of the twelfth and thirteenth centuries.

---

[1] *Paradiso,* xxxi, 34.

The Baptistery, S. Giovanni in Fonte, the Baptistery of
Rome, as rightly understood, its old name, S. Giovanni ad
Vestes, of the neophytes, seems to suggest, was of old approached through the ambulatory of the basilica and the atrium
which Anastasius IV enclosed in 1153. In those days, as for
nearly fourteen hundred years after, the façade faced the
atrium, enclosing the vestibule of S. Venanzio with its two
superb columns of the time of the Flavian Emperors, stolen from
some Pagan building. To-day, however, owing to the enlargement of the apse of the basilica it is necessary to leave
the church and to enter the Baptistery by the door in the
Piazza.

An octagonal building, S. Giovanni in Fonte is upheld
by eight great porphyry columns on which rests the architrave
that supports eight smaller columns on which rests the lantern.
These columns were, as it is said, the gift of Constantine himself who, as the legends tells us, untruthfully it seems, was
cured of a leprosy by Pope Sylvester, who washed him in the
great vase of green basalt that is now the font. Whether that
was a leprosy of soul or body, we may not know, for others tell,
and with no greater truthfulness, that the Emperor here became a Christian, the Pope baptizing him in this very place.

But in truth, when Constantine left Rome for the last time
in 327, it was still as a catechumen, having contrived always
to postpone his christening with the excuse that he wished to be
baptized in Jordan, till he knew himself to be dying, ten years
later, in Nicomedia. It was really on his deathbed that
the Emperor became a member of Christ's Church. Any
doubt that might entertain us concerning matters so weighty is
dismissed by the fact that S. Giovanni in Fonte was only built
in 435 by Pope Sixtus III. It was round this building that
Pope Hilary (461–468) built three oratories, in thanksgiving for
his escape out of the hands of Dioscoros and his followers at
the Council of Ephesus. That on the east, dedicated to S.
John Baptist, is closed to women on account of the sin of
Salome. The Pope brought the bronze doors, it is said,
from the Baths of Caracalla. That on the west is dedicated to
S. John Evangelist. The doors date from the end of the
twelfth century ; the mosaics, the Lamb in the midst of a

beautiful decoration of birds and flowers on a gold ground, are of the fifth century.   The third oratory of Hilary, dedicated to the Holy Cross, has been altogether destroyed.

The Oratorio di S. Venanzio beside that of S. John Evangelist was dedicated and perhaps built by Pope John IV (640–642) when he brought the saint's relics to Rome from Dalmatia.   Its chief interest for us to-day lies in the mosaics of the fifth century within and about the tribune.   There in the midst under the arch we see the Blessed Virgin, a weary, spare figure in the ancient attitude of prayer, attended by S. Peter, S. Paul, S. John Baptist, S. Venanzio, S. Domnione of Salona and Pope John IV, who offers her a model of the oratory.   Above in the arch is a huge bust of Christ between two angels, and on either side are the emblems of the evangelists, and two cities, the heavenly and the earthly Jerusalem perhaps.   Beneath each of these are the figures of four saints —S. Anastasius, S. Asterius, S. Telius, S. Paulinianus on the right, S. Maurus, S. Settimius, S. Antiochianus and S. Cajanus on the left.   The bust of the Saviour, the angels, and indeed all the figures within the apsis seem to be Roman and of an earlier period than those works on the front of the arch which surrounds them.   The very names of these saints seem to protest their alien origin ; while our eyes assure us that that careful delicate work so harmonious in colour and decoration never really came from the hands of a Roman, but owed everything to Byzantium.

This octagonal Baptistery, containing a circular building into which one descended to the font, came to be the pattern of all such buildings in Italy.   There the Bishop, amid a ritual less simple than might seem necessary, officiated, in person for the most part, during the fifty days between Easter and Pentecost.   In the earliest age the person seeking Baptism, almost always an adult, as we may believe, was first stripped naked in the midst of the assembly and then thrice immersed under the hands of the Bishop in the great bath or piscina prepared for the occasion.   And that rite so touching and so humiliating was in truth just a means of escape.   " What dost thou ask of the Church of Christ ? " the priest demanded.   " Faith," answered the neophyte.   " What shall Faith give thee ? "

MOSAIC OF THE APSE, Ninth century (S. Prassede)

ARCADE OF THE LATERAN CLOISTER by Petrus Vassallettus
(S. Giovanni in Laterano)

" Life everlasting." Then followed the Baptism of the Spirit
—the laying on of hands.

That absolute nudity and humiliation of the neophyte
before the congregation soon passed away, laughed out of
existence, half in anger and half in ridicule, by a
world always suspicious of certain forms of insanity :
and almost as soon as separate buildings were devoted
to the rite, those chapels were built as here in S.
Giovanni in Fonte, one on either side for men and women.
Till the end of the fourth century certainly the Baptism of
infants seems to have found many adversaries, but it had, as
Tertullian tells us, been an universal custom even in the
second century. But then the discretion of parents often suspended the Baptism of children till at least they could understand the efficacy of the rite : and even the catechumens were
seldom impatient " to assume the character of perfect and
initiated Christians." For the sacrament of Baptism gave an
absolute pardon of all sin both original and personal, the soul
instantly recovered her original purity and by the promises of
Christ was entitled to a life eternal. Thus it came to be considered, how shall I say, imprudent, to use and so lose a sacrament so salutary and so irrefutable, one, too, that could by
no means be repeated. People began to delay their Baptism
till they lay on their deathbeds, after the manner of the
Emperor, and, assured of salvation by that rite at the last,
were able to indulge themselves in the meanwhile in all the
base enjoyments of the world. The Fathers thundered against
it, but we find even S. Monica refusing out of her love to
christen the little Augustine who seems to have summed up the
pathetic humanity of this excuse in the immortal prayer, " O
God, make me chaste . . . but not yet."

Some magic certainly in the minds of men hung about the
Baptistery even in the fourteenth century, and not least about
that great vase of green basalt here in S. Giovanni in Fonte in
which, as men said, Constantine himself had been purged of his
sins or at least healed of a foul disease by mere contact with that
water under the hands of Pope Sylvester. Was it that which
sent Cola di Rienzo to bathe there on the eve of his coronation ?

Clothed in a parti-coloured robe of velvet, lined with fur

I

and embroidered with gold, crowned with a globe and cross of gold in which was a fragment of the true Wood, the sceptre " of justice " in his hand, he led the procession on that first day of August 1347, all the way from the Capitol to the Lateran, amid the shouting of the people through the streets strewn with roses. Fifty guards with halberds surrounded him, a troop of horse preceded his march, with their drums and trumpets of silver, while over his head floated the great banner of the Republic on which was the Sun in the midst of a circle of stars, and above floated a dove holding an olive branch in its mouth. A band of Roman ladies attended his wife, and the ecclesiastic, civil and military orders followed him under their various banners. It was already evening when they came to the great church and palace " of Constantine," S. Giovanni in Laterano, where, from the hands of " a venerable knight," he was to receive the Order of the Holy Ghost. The first ceremony was the purification, the bath, and it was here, in S. Giovanni in Fonte, he took it in that venerable font, the vase of green basalt, which, as he said later when accused of sacrilege, having been used by a pagan and that was Constantine, could not be profaned by a pious Christian. No action of his life seems to have been so foolish as this, or to have so surely secured him the censure of that superstitious world. Yet he slept in the Baptistery all night, and on the morrow in the basilica " at the hour of worship showed himself to the returning crowds in a majestic attitude with a robe of purple, his sword, and gilt spurs " and then summoned to his Tribunal Pope Clement who was in Avignon and the Electors of Germany " to inform us on what pretence they have usurped the unalienable right of the Roman people, the ancient and lawful sovereigns of the Empire." There, fifteen days later, he was crowned Tribunus Augustus by the most eminent of the Roman clergy with the six crowns of oak, of ivy, of myrtle, of laurel, of olive, and of silver which, he believed, the ancient Tribunes used, and in his hand he held a globe of crystal, the emblem of the world. That was on August 15, 1347 ; exactly four months later, on December 15, in a burst of weeping, he abdicated the government, and a little later fled away to Naples.

That palace " of Constantine," to which Rienzi made his way on that memorable August evening, stood, as does the great building we now see, on the south side of the Lateran, only of old it included the Scala Santa and the chapel of S. Lorenzo at its head, then the Pope's private chapel, and, as it were, the Sistina of the Lateran.   Built at the same time as the basilica, the great entrance and tower were added by Pope Zacharias in the eighth century, and there the papal benedictions were given after an election.   Thence a great staircase led to the midst of the buildings, a labyrinth of rooms, chapels, and galleries much like the present palace of the Vatican.   The most splendid chamber of all was the Banqueting Hall or Triclinium built for the reception of Charlemagne in the year 800.   It was surrounded by ten apses and closed by a magnificent tribune.   The Lateran was the true home of the Popes, till the exile in Avignon, and five general councils were held there, one in 1512.   Then after the sack of 1527 it became ruinous and was altogether destroyed by Sixtus V who employed Fontana to build the present palace in its place. So that all that is left to us of the old palace is the Scala Santa, that staircase of marble by which, according to tradition, Jesus went to face Pilate in the Pretorium, and the chapel of the Sancta Sanctorum at the top closed by a gilded screen : *Non est in toto sanctior orbe locus*—There is no place more holy in all the world.   That beautiful chapel, graceful and delicate, was probably decorated by Cosmatus, the son of Mellini of the great clan of the Cosmati, and is, indeed, inscribed with his name, *Magister Cosmatus fecit hoc opus*, but it has been restored out of all recognition.   Close by rises the great tribune which Clement XII built in 1730 to receive that mosaic of the ninth century, once one of many in the Triclinium : but it was broken as it was being removed, and what we see to-day is merely a copy of the original work which celebrated the coronation of Charlemagne in S. Peter's Church on Christmas Day in the year 800.   The great King appeared not in " the simple dress of his country " but in the habit of a patrician of Rome. After Mass, Pope Leo "suddenly placed a precious crown on his head, and the Roman people cried once more as of old, Long life and victory to Charles the most pious Augustus crowned

by God, the great and pacific Emperor of the Romans."
This act of the great Pope was a surprise to Charlemagne, who
would have wished, it seems, to become Emperor in some other
way—how, we know not ;[1] but the crowning of the Pope
forestalled him. Consecrated by the royal unction, he swore
to maintain the faith and privileges of the Church and offered
rich presents at the shrine of the Apostle. Thus began the
history of the Middle Age. The memory of antiquity had
imposed itself on men, and, deceived by that strange dream,
Dante is not ashamed to desire the salvation of Italy at the
hands of a German.

> *Vieni a veder la tua Roma che piagne,*
> *Vedova, sola e di e notte chiama :*
> *Cesare mio, perchè non m'accompagne ?*

In the Lateran piazza before the northern façade of the
church stands the Obelisk of the Lateran, the most ancient in
Rome. It is made of red granite, is covered with hieroglyphics
and originally stood before the Temple of the Sun at Heliopolis.
It was brought to Alexandria by Constantine to go to Constantinople, but his son gave it to the Roman Senate and it
stood in the Circus Maximus. Sixtus V erected it here in
1588. It is 150 feet high on its pedestal, 105 feet in itself.
This is the largest Obelisk in existence.

---

[1] Cf. Gibbon, *Decline and Fall* (Ed. Bury, 1898), vol. V, p. 283, note 98 ; and
Bryce, *Holy Roman Empire*, cap. 5.

XVIII

SANTA CROCE IN GERUSALEMME

IT was the Empress Helena, the mother of Constantine the
Great, who built this basilica or at any rate a church here
in the Palatium Sessorianum which Sextus Varius had constructed and Elagabalus his son had used for his pleasure.
The Empress, S. Helena, had discovered, as we know, in Jerusalem the True Cross itself and it was into a shrine for this most
precious relic that she converted the great hall of the Sessoriana
and had it consecrated by Pope Sylvester. The reliquary
itself was a golden coffer studded with jewels and about it she
placed four and fifty silver candlesticks, some of eighty pounds
weight, and all the floor and foundation of the great hall she
filled with earth she had brought from Jerusalem and thus the
church got its name. It was Gregory the Great who made the
church one of the titular churches of Rome, and after a disaster
in the eighth century Pope Constantine gave it its columns but
it retained its form of a great hall. In the tenth century a
Benedictine monastery was attached to it and in the twelfth
century the Cosmati built a façade and portico and furnished
the church with a mosaic pavement, part of which remains
to-day, and no doubt decorated it. So it remained in its
beauty till Benedict XIV, who also only less disastrously
restored S. Maria Maggiore by the hands of Domenico
Gregorini, destroyed it all and gave us the characterless building we see. Without and within nothing visibly remains of the
old twelfth-century basilica but part of the Cosmati pavement.
Even the granite columns have been hidden in piers. Nothing
is left of the Sessoriana. In the tribune there remain the
frescoes by Antoniazzo Romano of the Legend of the Holy
Cross, but even these have been ruined by restoration. And
then in the last decade of the nineteenth century the church was
frescoed by a French painter, one Lehoux. On the right of the

Crypt is the Chapel of St. Helena. It was here she placed the earth from Jerusalem. On the vault are some mosaics remade by Peruzzi in the early sixteenth century.

To-day then the church is chiefly interesting for its relics : a large piece of the Cross of Our Lord, the inscribed entablature of the Cross discovered in a sealed casket hidden in the wall in 1492. There are also here the finger of doubting Thomas, one of Judas's thirty pieces of silver, a phial of the Blood of our Lord and other sacramentals. As these relics can only be seen on special occasions, the Title of the Cross for instance on Good Friday, the church is hardly worth a visit. But in passing to or from it and S. Giovanni in Laterano I am always glad of the sight of the great bronze group which was erected to commemorate the seventh centenary of S. Francis. It represents S. Francis and his companions' first sight of Rome. It is most moving and dramatic and bears the eloquent inscription

" A SAN FRANCESCO : ROMA : ITALIA : IL MONDO."

XIX

SAN PAOLO FUORI LE MURA

ABOUT two miles beyond the Basilica of S. Paolo fuori le Mura one comes upon the somewhat meagre buildings of a Trappist monastery, S. Paolo alle Tre Fontane, where, according to the tradition, S. Paul, by order of Nero, was beheaded on a little hill under a pine tree, his head striking the earth three times as it fell ; and in each place a fountain welled up out of the soil, and was later enclosed in a little chapel. Those chapels, it seems, were all that marked the spot, till in the last years of the sixteenth century Cardinal Aldobrandini commissioned Giacomo della Porta to build a church there which was dedicated to S. Paolo—alle Tre Fontane. It was this church which came into the possession of the French Trappists in the middle of the nineteenth century.

But concerning S. Paul we learn that, being dead, Lucina took his body and buried it in her catacomb in the Via Ostia. In the persecutions which followed under Valerian in 258, fearing to lose the sacred relics, not of S. Paul alone but of S. Peter also, the Christians removed them secretly by night, the one from the cemetery of the Via Ostia, the other from the Vatican, and laid them side by side in the Catacomb *Platonia*, under the basilica of S. Sebastiano on the Appian Way. In that act one seems to see already the supreme triumph of the Church, the reconciliation of the irreconcilable : of Peter and Paul, the new founders of the City.

The bodies of the two Apostles remained thus hidden together in the Catacombs till they were buried once more in their own tombs, the one in the Vatican, the other beside the Via Ostia, and later Constantine himself built a shrine or even a basilica in each place. And concerning this the *Liber Pontificalis* is very precise : *Fecit basilicam S. Paulo Apostolo cuius corpus recondidit in arca et conclusit, sicuti Petri*—He made a basilica for S. Paul the Apostle, whose body he put back again in a chest and closed it, and so he did Peter's also.

It was not Constantine, however, who began the great basilica which for more than fourteen centuries stood over the tomb of S. Paul, but rather the three Emperors, Valentinian, Theodosius, and Arcadius, who began to build in 386, whose work was finished under Honorius and decorated by Galla Placida, daughter of Honorius and wife of Adolphus, King of the Goths. Spared by Alaric with all its treasures, it doubtless suffered in the Vandal sack in 455 when Genseric entered the City by this road, nor may we suppose that Totila forgot it. In that disastrous century it was restored more than once ; but it seems to have suffered at the hands of the Lombards in 730, for we hear of Leo II rebuilding it in the eighth century. These spoliations, if such indeed we may regard them, were as nothing to the destruction which followed at the hands of the Saracens in 846. All the country round Rome was overrun and depopulated in that most dreadful incursion. The City scarcely knew how to contain the swarms of monks and clergy fleeing from those ruthless heathen. " Cities, fortresses, villages have perished with all their inhabitants," Pope John VIII wrote to Charles the Bald, begging his succour. " The Bishops are dispersed ; within the walls of Rome are collected the remains of the population, wholly destitute ; without, all is devastation and desolation, nothing more remains to happen save—may God avert it—the ruin of the City. The whole Campagna is depopulated : nothing is left. . . . The neighbourhood of the City has been so utterly devastated that not a single inhabitant, man, woman, or child, is to be found." In those heartbroken letters we seem to understand really for the first time what such an invasion meant.

But the Pope was by no means cowed. He stood for Europe. His activity was extraordinary ; he built a fleet, he made treaties ; but at last, owing to internal dissensions, ever the curse of Italy, he was compelled to purchase peace at the price of a yearly tribute of 25,000 silver *mancusi*. Then events compelled him to flee to France. He returned in 879, on the eve, as it proved, of victory, the victory of Cape Circe which shattered the forces of Mahomet. One of his first acts after that good news reached him was the building of a great wall round the Basilica of S. Paul, even as Leo IV had built one round S. Peter's : to the Leonine City he added Johannipolis.[1] That rocky hill not far from the basilica afforded an excellent support to his fortification, and was probably the site of his fortress. Everything, however, was destroyed, save the cloister of the church, in the great fire of 1823.

Of old, S. Paolo was bigger than S. Peter's, and in spite of restoration kept its primitive character till it was burned to the ground. Entering the new church that as closely as might be has followed the lines of the old, conscious though we are of a splendour of space, it leaves us cold : it is as though one had carefully rebuilt the Temple of Jupiter Capitolinus, carefully, omitting nothing. It is a monument, not a church, and I for one cannot imagine it ever being anything else. Some few things certainly remain from the older building, the magnificent arch of the nave, for instance, supported by two Ionic columns, which Galla Placida built and decorated with mosaics in the fifth century, the tabernacle, the altar itself, the Paschal candlestick, and the cloisters. Restored though they be, these mosaics remain the most beautiful thing in the church, a masterpiece of the first half of the fifth century. Above in the midst, like some enormous vision, Christ is seen at Benediction in a great nimbus of many colours. In heaven shine the symbols of the Evangelists, and below a vast company of saints and certain angels, beneath which are, on one side S. Peter, on the other S. Paul preaching.

That such a work as that moves us so little we eagerly explain to ourselves as the fault of the restorers. And we are eager to offer the same excuse for the Tabernacle of the high altar, which, graceful and charming though it be, seems in some way unworthy of Arnolfo di Cambio.

But the great Paschal candlestick of Vassallettus and Nicolò de Angelis is intact ; carved and sculptured in bands with the figure and passion of Christ, it is unique in Rome.

---

[1] Muratori, *Dissertazioni* (Milano, 1751), tom. i, p. 421, tells us that Gregory IV rebuilt the Città d'Ostia, and called it Gregoriopolis. He gives the inscription he found, which is our proof that John VIII built Johannipolis (Dissertazione xxvi).

As for the Cloister, it is only second in beauty to that of the Lateran.   Begun by Abbot Peter of Capua (1193–1208), it was completed under Abbot John V (1208–1241) and is signed by Vassallettus :   MAGISTER PETRVS FECIT HOC OPVS.

XX

SANTA MARIA MAGGIORE

THE oldest and most beautiful of Roman basilicas, S. Maria Maggiore, illustrates by its fine qualities, obscured though they be by the vandalism of Benedict XIV, the intention of all Latin architecture, its love of largeness, space, and light. If we examine the buildings of antiquity, the Pantheon, for instance, or the Basilica of Constantine, beside the Italian work of the Middle Age, or the Renaissance in the Duomo of Pisa, S. Croce in Florence, or the church of S. Maria della Consolazione at Todi, we see at once that it is just those qualities of space, and light, an effect of space and largeness, contrived with infinite care and precision, with a sort of gift too for entertaining the sunshine, that all Latin architecture, ancient and modern, has in common. In all ages those have been the objects which the Latin builder has most desired, winning them from time to time by different means, coming nearest to a complete achievement perhaps in the Pantheon or the church of Todi, and only half missing them after all, and then really by bad fortune, in the greatest church in Christendom, S. Pietro in Vaticano.

With its vast congregation, its worship in common, its appeal to the multitude, Christianity understood and certainly encouraged this desire, so spontaneous already in the Latin soul, modelling her churches, as it were, on the ancient basilica as convenient for a large multitude and refusing for centuries, not only from a religious motive, to use the temples, small as they were, and fitted after all for a worship rather individual than catholic. It was the Greeks who in the sixth century first built their churches in the temples of the gods ; but long before that the Romans had begun to use the basilicas, places that might seem to have been designed especially for them : and of those which thus passed into Christian service S. Maria Maggiore is at once the oldest and the most splendid.

A whole literature and legend have grown up round the most beautiful church in Rome, the earliest too in the City to be placed under the protection of Mary Madonna, obscuring its origin as in a veil of flowers. There one hears much of Pope Liberius, who is said to have built it ; much of Sixtus III, who dedicated it to the Blessed Virgin, and, if we may believe the inscription still on the triumphal arch, decorated it with mosaics.[1] And while some speak of a fall of snow in August which, as it is said, following on a dream, caused Pope Liberius to build the church which for long was known as *S. Maria ad Nives*, others, apparently knowing nothing of this, call the place *Basilica Liberiana*. And, indeed, it is only of late that the true history of the building has been discovered, as though that criticism which has robbed us of so much that we thought we possessed was eager for once to assure us that here at any rate we have something more ancient and precious than we had dared to believe.

In the *Liber Pontificalis* under the works of Pope Sixtus III (432–440) it is written : *Hic fecit basilicam Sanctae Mariae, quae ab antiquis Liberii cognominabatur*—" here he made a Basilica for S. Mary, which of old was called of Liberius." That was in the fifth century. Eighty years before, about 359, Pope Liberius, we are told : *Fecit basilicam nominis sui juxta macellum Liviae* : " made the basilica named after him near the market-place of Livia." That word *fecit* used in both places might seem to bear twice over the same significance, relative that is and by no means absolute. We cannot depend on it in the earlier entry any more than in the later ; and just as Sixtus had merely added to or repaired an older building, so Liberius seems to have done. But what older building ? We know that the great secular *Basilica Sicinnii* stood on the Esquiline Hill, and both Pagan and Christian writers of the fourth century sometimes call S. Maria Maggiore *Basilica Sicinnii* just as they call it Basilica Liberiana. They speak of it too as being at about this time consecrated to Christian worship.

[1] Cf. J. P. Richter and A. C. Taylor, *The Golden Age of Classic Christian Art* (Duckworth, 1902).

It might seem probable therefore that Pope Liberius merely added a sanctuary to the old basilica, and this probability is confirmed not only by the tiles discovered in the roof but especially by the brickwork of the nave with its arched windows, easily seen from without, which recalls similar work of the time of Hadrian. Our conclusion is, then, that in S. Maria Maggiore we have a classical basilica which has become a Christian church. Thus those forty-two columns of Hymettan marble which uphold the roof are not, as is generally the case, a mere collection of débris from other buildings, but actually a part of the original basilica, which indeed remained, until the eighteenth century, practically what it had always been ; and that it is now less simple and less beautiful than we might expect is the fault of Pope Benedict XIV (1740–58) who restored it according to the taste of his day.

All this, interesting and consoling as it is, becomes of really great importance when we begin to examine the mosaics of the nave and triumphal arch, which, made, as we have been told, under Sixtus III (432–440), still remain to us. After all, we may well ask, if Sixtus did not build the church, is it quite certain that he decorated it ? It is admitted that he dedicated it to the Madonna : if, then, it is to him we owe the mosaics, why are they in no way concerned with her ? And what are they concerned with ? Do they relate, as all the critics have assured us, just Bible histories—are they really stories from the Old Testament such as the frescoes in the Upper Church at Assisi tell of the life of S. Francis ? In fact they are not. They are not stories at all in the ordinary sense of the word ; they are rather didactic than narrative, mystical than evangelic, and they express not the theology of the fifth century but the mysticism of the second and third, of the age of the Apologists. They have nothing to do with the ideas of S. Augustine and S. Jerome (354–430), but are, indeed, an expression of the thoughts of Justin Martyr, of Clement of Rome, of Clement of Alexandria, of Origen, of the Shepherd of Hermas (91–253).

And, if this is so, we may well ask ourselves what they are doing in a church only dedicated to Christian worship in the middle of the fourth century, for by then much of their teaching had become heretical or was forgotten. And that being so, they would seem stranger still as the work of Sixtus III a century later, when indeed they can have had little meaning for any one.

It would seem, however, that the true explanation may be that these mosaics were designed in the end of the second century to decorate the wall of a Roman Palace belonging to a Christian Patrician, for they deal with Christianity in a way that could offend no Pagan—God, the Gods certainly, being in heaven. In that, at least, Christianity was in agreement with her enemies, avoiding this their most telling charge against her—so unthinkable by us—a charge of atheism.

So these mosaics remain to us, in spite of all restorations, the most beautiful as well as the most mysterious pictures in Rome, substantially works of the end of the second and the beginning of the third century, classical in tradition, in style, in means of expression ; summing up for us very perfectly the ideas of the time, the dreams of the Apologists, the mysticism of Justin Martyr, the realism of the Gospel of James—symbols really, symbols of ideas, truths made visible. They do not tell a story but express, as it were, the mysteries of the Christian Faith. We see there, if nowhere else, that it was perfect in the heart of God, from the beginning, and as witness of this mystery, the subject matter itself is typological or else, as most often, we have scenes in which the chief figure is a prototype of Christ. And at last we become aware that what is passing before us is not only the mystery of the Faith, but its history also, the history of that struggle between Europe and Asia in the heart of Christianity, between the Church of the Gentiles and the Church of the Jews ; the words of Justin Martyr in his Dialogue with Trypho seem to repeat themselves over and over again : " Leah is your people and congregation but Rachel is our Church for these and for the servants in both Christ serves even now."[1]

The mosaics of the nave fall into four groups, each gathered, as it were, about a notable figure of the Old Testament— Abraham, Jacob, Moses, and Joshua, with whom we are concerned, not as historical and sacred figures merely, but as prototypes of Christ. We see Abraham with Melchizedek (Genesis

[1] Justin Martyr, *Dial. with Trypho*, cap. 134.

xiv, 18), and the bread and wine on the table, and Christ Himself, who appears in the sky, reminds us of the Eucharist. We see Abraham again entertaining those three strange visitors (Genesis xviii 1, 2, 9, 13)—are they three or one?—which reminds us of the mystery of the Trinity so obstinately opposed to the monotheism of the Jewish Christian. We see Abraham and Lot part asunder (Genesis xiii, 7), and are reminded of the parting of the Christian and the Judaic world. These pictures tell no story, they repeat the Faith, they have not the order of the Bible narrative and are careless of mere fact. Thus, in the story, the three angels appeared to Abraham after the parting with Lot, which happened before the meeting with Melchizedek ; the order is broken, and Isaac was not born when Lot and Abraham said farewell. But in that marvellous composition, perhaps the finest in the church, we see expressed the whole tragedy of Judaism, which, coming out of the desert, a stranger to the Prince of Life, to the sweet variety of the world, must return to it again.

More particular in its symbolism, the second series deals with Jacob, in whom, as it were, is hidden the Prince of Life who won first Leah and then Rachel the beloved for wife, and in whom later we see expressed, almost with the idyllic beauty of the Song of Songs, the Shepherd Bridegroom who leadeth his flock to a fresh pasture. In those nine double pictures, of which Jacob is the central figure, the whole mystery is hidden and expressed. Only seven of them refer to any scene in the Old Testament, the last two being indeed wholly concerned with an expression of the meaning such a mystic as Justin Martyr had found in that fascinating story, for him, at least, charged with marvels. There we see the Shepherd Bridegroom pasturing his flock, which Rachel, " our Church," leads till Laban welcomes them ; Leah, " your synagogue," is left in apprehension and foreboding. Then that shepherd chooses his work, the cure of souls, and his ward, the Church, and, claiming her, is married to her : yet Leah too has an honourable place, for she was Jacob's wife before Rachel .

Four pictures follow in which he chooses his flock, and then four more concerning Hamor and Shechem, and the sons of Leah (Genesis xxxiv, 6-20). While the third series, consisting

to-day of thirteen pictures, the first being lost to us with seven
others, takes Moses as the prototype, which merges at last into
the equally long series in which Joshua appears as the exemplar
of our Lord. It is as though the Church believed that Christ
was already implicit in the Old Testament, and had proved it
irrefutably.

Those pictures, so full, as we may think, of the various
repetitions of the Psalms, lead, as in the Mass, in a procession
of many windings, to Christ Himself. After the Prototypes
we come to the Original ; but still not without mystery.
Those eight pictures which on either side surround the throne
of God, the keystone of the arch, still seek rather to express a
truth than to tell a story.   The scene of the Annunciation is not
followed by the Nativity ; and the Annunciation itself is full of
difficulty for minds so stained with realism as ours ; so far,
perhaps, from reality.   Is it the Annunciation merely or the
whole mystery of the Virgin Birth that we see to the left of the
keystone on the height of the arch ?   The Madonna, already
a queen, attended by angels, passes her time as queens long
since were used to do—how well we know it, since Homer
has told us the very thing—in spinning, drawing a skein of
scarlet wool carefully from a gilt wicker basket beside the
throne on which she sits.   And suddenly that angel falls from
heaven like a snowflake out of the hands of God, whose Son
presently will be hers also.   Not far away Joseph waits dis-
consolate beside the temple, and to him too an angel comes
with that tremendous explanation.   Opposite on the other
side we see as it were the Presentation in the Temple—the
repudiation of Christ by the Jews, as the Gospel of James
tells us.   And then beneath the picture of the Virgin Birth
we see the Adoration of the Magi, the homage of the East to
the Dayspring from on high ; and under the Repudiation
we come suddenly on that strange, delightful scene in which a
Philosopher, surely Plato himself, leads a young man out of the
city into the country where Jesus is, a child still, who with
Mary and Joseph comes to meet them.   Beneath is the scene
of the Magi before Herod and the Priests, and opposite to it
the Massacre of the Innocents ; and under these, the roots, as
it were, of the whole theory or doctrine of the four series of

PASCHAL CANDELABRUM,
by Nicolaus de Angelo and Petrus Vassallettus (S. Paolo fuori le Mura)

ABRAHAM AND LOT, Fourth century (?) mosaic (S. Maria Maggiore)

mosaics on the arch and in the nave—Jerusalem, the home of Judaism, Bethlehem, the birthplace of Christianity.

In those mosaics one seems to have discovered a new world, in which Christianity appears innocent and still full of charm and a certain wideness and serenity of outlook. A true daughter of light, of sweetness and light, she opposes herself only to the obscurantism of the Hebraic superstition, she accepts not only the art and beauty of the Pagan world, but its tolerance also. How she has changed since then we may learn perhaps from the mosaics of the apse, the work of Jacobus Torriti in 1295—on the other side of the Middle Age. Jesus truly, the Madonna also, are little more than magnificent decoration, vast eikons. Something has died in the heart of man in the years between these two achievements.

Beneath this great mosaic, so strangely lovely in its decoration, Gaddo Gaddi, the Florentine, as it is said, with Filippo Rusuti about 1305 made the mosaics of the Life of the Blessed Virgin on the wall between the ogival windows. There we see not an expression of a truth, but a child's fairy-tale, exquisite, and full of the charm of such things—the story of the foundation of the church on the spot where the snow fell on August 5th, as the Pope's dream had foretold him. This is commemorated every year in the Borghese chapel by a fall of rose petals.

Beneath the high altar is the great relic of the church, part of the manger of Bethlehem.

Not far away, just outside the Baptistery, is the beautiful tomb of Cardinal Gonsalvo, Bishop of Albano. The work of Johannes Cosmatus, the son, perhaps, of Jacopo, it is the most beautiful monument in the church, and in itself a sign of that revival of art in the Eternal City which was due to the Cosmati, and which produced that great artist, Pietro Cavallini. The figure of the Cardinal lies robed as a bishop, while two angels lift the folds of the winding-sheet. Over the tomb hangs a cloth worked in mosaic, and above in a trefoil niche is a mosaic of the Madonna with her little Son between S. Matthew and S. Martin.

Close by is the monument which Sixtus V, by the hands of Sarzana, raised to Nicholas IV. And indeed the work of the

K

Renaissance here is as lovely as that of the Middle Age :
the roof of the nave, for instance, the work of Giuliano and
Antonio da Sangallo, seems not less splendid than the matchless though relaid pavement.   And what are we to say of the
celebrated chapels which hold the tombs of Sixtus V and Paul
V ?   One sees them with astonishment here in this Basilica.
They are the beginning of the baroque style in architecture,
the Sixtine chapel by Domenico Fontana, in 1570 heavily
restored ; the Borghese chapel by Flaminio Ponzio is later and
dated 1611.   The Sixtine chapel contains the tombs of
Sixtus V, the rebuilder of the City and of S. Pius V.   The
Borghese chapel holds the tombs of Paul V and Clement VIII.
It also possesses a famous miracle picture of the Madonna.
Both chapels belong to the Rome of the Counter Reform, the
Catholic Reaction, the architectural achievements of which
we shall consider later.

XXI

SAN LORENZO FUORI LE MURA

THE basilica of S. Lorenzo, without the Walls, once so lonely and picturesque, is to-day almost surrounded by a modern suburb, so that you come to it no longer through the meadows of the Campagna, but between houses all the way, by the Via Tiburtina outside the Porta S. Lorenzo. The largest and most populous burial-ground of modern Rome is here ; from the earliest ages there has been a cemetery in this spot, and it was here they buried the second martyr of the Church, the first among the seven deacons of Rome, S. Lorenzo, whose heroic death had so profound an influence on the nobles of the City, that of him particularly it came to be said, " the blood of the Martyrs is the seed of the Church."

It was here, so tradition assures us, that Constantine in his first enthusiasm, if that which was so politic may pass for enthusiasm, built one of the seven churches he is said to have founded in Rome. It was set literally in the midst of the old cemetery, and seems to have been little more than an enlargement of the church in the house of some early patrician convert. Then, in the fifth century, Sixtus III built another basilica close by, these two buildings being united in the thirteenth century by Honorius III, who threw down their apses and built one nave into the other. So the strange and picturesque church of S. Lorenzo was born, the Basilica of Constantine forming the Sanctuary, the Schola and the Confession of Sixtus III the Nave, with the entrance on the Via Tiburtina.

The church of Sixtus III thus united with that of Constantine, divided into three aisles by twenty-two antique, Ionic columns, was completely restored by Innocent IV in 1245. The nave proper, covered by a magnificent wagon-roof spoiled by restorers, holds two precious and beautiful things of the thirteenth century : the pavement of *opus Alexandrinum* and the two ambones, that on the right the most beautiful work of the kind that has come down to us. Simple and severe, the nave contains nothing else that distracts our attention from its own strength and beauty. It is this which was seriously damaged in the war.

Very different is the older part of the building, the great choir raised on high and reached by a flight of steps on either side, and the crypt, half visible, to which a third flight descends in the midst, and from which twelve great Corinthian columns, that may well be part of the original church of Constantine, rise bearing an architrave composed of antique fragments which sustains the beautiful colonnade that forms the tribune. There, on the Triumphal Arch facing the tribune, shines a mosaic of the sixth century, altogether Byzantine in its strange beauty. Beneath this splendour is the beautiful thirteenth-century throne and choir screens, studded with discs of porphyry and precious interlacing marbles, a work, like the ambones, of the Cosmati, as indeed is the magnificent signed ciborium as well as the lovely portico before the church. A splendid *soffitto* roof, all of purple and gold, a work of the early Renaissance, covers the choir.

Descending to the crypt which contains all that is left to us of the half mythical church of Constantine, we find the tomb of Pio Nono, who sleeps there, a martyr among martyrs, as he wished, close to the poor of the city lying in thousands in the cemetery round about.

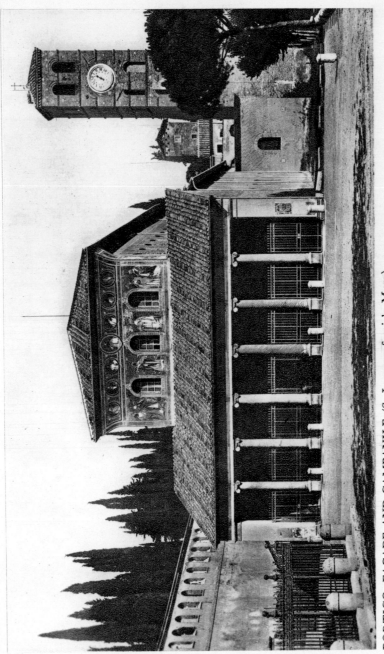

PORTICO, FAÇADE AND CAMPANILE (S. Lorenzo fuori le Mura)

SANTA COSTANZA

XXII

SANT' AGNESE FUORI LE MURA AND SANTA COSTANZA

THE basilica of S. Agnese stands on the Via Nomentana nearly a mile outside Porta Pia. It is said very doubtfully to be a foundation of Constantine but in fact nothing is known of it till the seventh century. It stands over the burial place of the youthful virgin saint below the road ; and in order to enter the church to-day we traverse two courts in one of which, in a modern building, is one of the most grotesque paintings even our epoch has contrived. It represents Pius IX and his cardinals and court falling headlong into the cellar here, which thing befell in 1855 and has been thus commemorated by Tajetti. We descend by a wide flight of steps and come into the beautiful church with its sixteen Corinthian columns of portasanta, pavonazzetto and breccia. Above are galleries enclosed too with marble columns as at San Lorenzo. The church has been restored in the sixteenth and seventeenth centuries. The high altar with its ciborium supported by four columns of rare purple porphyry is of the seventeenth century. Beneath is buried the mortal remains of the little maiden saint.

Agnes was thirteen years of age when as she came from school the son of the Prefect of Rome saw her and loved her and when his father and mother knew it they offered, says Voragine in *The Golden Legend*, to give " much riches with him if he might have her in marriage but she would not." And again and again he came with precious gems and jewels and rich adornments and gifts but Agnes answered him, " I am now loved of another lover and embraced of him of whom the Mother is a Virgin. To him I have given my faith, to him I have commanded my heart." When the young man heard all this he was in despair for he was taken in blind love and he lay down sick on his bed. Then the physicians soon knew his malady and told his father he languished of carnal love to some woman. And the father enquired and knew that it was this woman and did speak to Agnes for his son and she answered that in no wise would she break faith of her first husband. When the prefect demanded who was her first husband, one of her servants said she was a Christian and that she was so enchanted that she said Jesus Christ was her spouse. When the Prefect heard she was a Christian he was glad for the Christian people were in the will of the lord if they would not deny their God. Wherefore the Prefect made Agnes to come to justice and he examined her sweetly and after cruelly by menaces. But Agnes said, " Do what thou wilt, my purpose shalt thou never change." And the Prefect said to her, being all angry : " One of two things thou shalt choose, either to sacrifice to our gods with the virgins of the goddess Vesta, or go to the bordel to be abandoned to all that thither come."

And Agnes answered : " If thou knewest who is my God thou wouldst not say to me such words." Then the Judge made her take off all her clothes and all naked to be led to the bordel, but even as she was, unclothed, God gave her such grace that the hair of her head became so long that it covered all her body to her feet so that her body was not seen. And she made the bordel her oratory. At last came the son of the Prefect with a great company, but they were abashed, and he advanced him for to take the virgin and anon the devil took him by the throat and strangled him that he fell down dead.

"Now when the father heard this he was distraught and they told him she was a Sorceress full of enchantments. Then he would have burnt her alive but the fire would not touch her but the torturers. Then the executioner commanded to put a sword in her body and so she was martyred. And this befell in the time of Constantine the Great which began to reign the year of Our Lord three hundred and nine."

Thus Voragine, and the legend goes on to tell how eight days after her death she appeared, richly apparelled, with a snow white lamb. And so on January 21st every year two lambs wreathed with flowers are placed upon the altar of her church by its titular Cardinal and from their wool nuns make the *pallia* which the Pope sends to all Archbishops and Bishops owing him allegiance.

The only glory of the church, indeed its only interest apart from its architecture, is the mosaic in the apse. In this very Byzantine work of the seventh century St. Agnes appears as in the vision, apparelled like a Byzantine Empress nimbused and crowned with a diadem of pearls which fall too about her head. A large stole of gold, as worn by Byzantine Empresses, with green ornaments, falls from her shoulders to her knees. The hem of her violet robe is a circle of phoenixes, symbol of immortality. Her hands hold a *volumen*, from her left arm falls her virgin's light veil embroidered with flowers. At her feet is the sword, the instrument of her martyrdom, and flames rise on either side of her but do not touch her. To left and right are two pontiffs vested with the chasuble and episcopal pallium. One bears a closed book, the other the model of a basilica. These figures would appear to represent Pope Honorius I (625–638) and Pope Symmachus (498–514). Above the stars which are sown in the firmament appears the hand of God. Below in letters of gold on a blue ground is a long inscription exalting the pontiffs who caused the mosaic to be made.

Perhaps the church of S. Agnese is a little disappointing. Close by, however, just across the Via Nomentana, is the very beautiful mausoleum of Constantina, daughter of Constantine the Great, which is called Santa Costanza. The building itself, in spite of the destruction of the cupola, is of great beauty and the mosaics are of the fourth century and mark the transition from the antique and pagan mosaic to the Christian : the technique is still antique and the mosaic is of marble tesserae on a white background.

The building is a rotunda with an ambulatory with barrel roof. The central rotunda supported a cupola on an arcade borne on twenty-four composite columns in pairs and originally there was a circular colonnade round the outside of the building. The portico remains. It is thus a true mausoleum. Constantina the wicked daughter of Constantine and Constantia her good sister were both buried here in a sarcophagus now in the Vatican. Consecrated as a church in the thirteenth century, in the seventeenth it was "restored" by Cardinal

Veralli and the mosaic of the cupola was destroyed. A
further " restoration " in the early nineteenth century finished
the destruction. An engraving of the seventeenth century
shows us what we have lost. The vault of the cupola was
divided by twelve Caryatidas with monsters at their feet.
Beneath in a broad band round the base of the cupola was the
ocean alive with boats and rafts on which amorini disported.
Above, divided by a vine, the twelve divisions were filled with
biblical scenes. All this has perished.

There remains the ambulatory, the roof of which is covered
with decorative mosaics of the fourth century, the earliest
Christian mosaics we possess ; for amid the decoration of the
vine there are scenes of vintage and again panel after panel
of fruit, of little figures mixed in rounds with birds, of busts
mixed in rounds with flowers and so on. None of this is at
all Christian, but over a doorway is a representation of Our
Lord giving a scroll to an old man, said to be Moses, while He
stretches His right hand to two figures said to be SS. Peter and
Paul. Four lambs are at His feet. There is here much
restoration, as in another mosaic of Our Lord seated. The
date of these two mosaics would appear to be doubtful. No
more interesting Pagan-Christian building is to be found in
Rome, nor I think one more beautiful, half spoilt though it be.

XXIII

SAINT PETER'S

ACCORDING to the tradition which S. Jerome followed, S. Peter came to Rome after his release from prison by the angel in Jerusalem about the year A.D. 42, in the time of the Emperor Claudius, and reigned there as Pope for twenty-five years. However that may be, his presence in Rome was unquestioned until the thirteenth century, when the Waldenses seem to have doubted it, chiefly because they could find no mention of it in the Acts of the Apostles or S. Paul's Epistles. That seems but a lame reason for denying it altogether, and indeed, maintained, as it was, by an unbroken tradition for more than twelve centuries, it is now no longer seriously questioned, though any details of the story of the Prince of the Apostles in the Eternal City must be received with caution. That he died there and the time and place of his martyrdom, which took place after the great persecution by Nero in A.D. 64,[1] must have been well known to every one in the early Church, and the writer of the Gospel of S. John certainly alludes to it in his last chapter.[2] Crucified, as every one believes, on the same day, but perhaps not in the same year, as S. Paul was beheaded, according to the later but more general tradition, he was led, after many months in the Mamertine prison at the foot of the Capitol, with S. Paul along the Via Ostia so far as the little chapel which now marks the place of their farewell outside the Porta San Paolo, when he was led back along the Triumphal Way to martyrdom in the Circus of Nero at the foot of Monte Vaticano.

As one comes to-day from Castel S. Angelo along the new, wide Borgo into the ordered splendour of the Piazza di S. Pietro, and the Vatican City and State, it is only with difficulty

[1] St. Peter himself alludes to this in his " Epistle from Babylon."
[2] John xxi, 18, 19.

one can recall the atrocious drama that was acted there between the years A.D. 64 and 67, when Nero, having, as it was believed, burnt Rome to satisfy his ambition, wreaked the anger of the people on the Christians who, as he said, had caused the fire. Here too, as at the Colosseum, men were thrown to the beasts, women were exposed naked in the arena, children were torn limb from limb, while the frightful spectacles of the Danaides and of Dirce were presented for the amusement of the Emperor's guests to illuminate a nocturnal feast.

Close by the Circus of Nero in the old days was a cemetery, and there the body of S. Peter was laid after his crucifixion. Later, Pope Anacletus, as it is said, built a monument over the grave wherein he too hoped to lie, for the Apostle had ordained him presbyter. Then in A.D. 258, the year of the Valerian persecution, the bodies both of S. Peter and S. Paul were carried secretly into the catacomb beneath the church of S. Sebastian. There they remained till Pope Dionysius (259–268) restored them to their original resting-places. Then after the final peace, Constantine, as it is said, built over their tombs the two basilicas of S. Peter and S. Paul.

To build the church here by the Vatican Hill, the Circus of Nero was destroyed and used indeed as the foundation for the great shrine of the Apostle. Old S. Peter's, founded on Nero's Circus, was a church 380 by 212 feet of pure basilical form, with a wide atrium some two hundred and twelve by two hundred and thirty-five feet, closed by doors and reached by a great flight of thirty-five steps, which the pilgrims, Charlemagne, as one hears, among them, ascended on their knees. In the atrium, booths were set up for the sale of candles, ornaments, and flowers ; even food, figs, and such were sold there for the needs of the pilgrims. There, too, many of the most illustrious princes of the earlier centuries were buried ; among those of our own race who lay there were Conrad of Mercia, Offa of Essex, who took the cowl, and Cadwalla of Wessex, who, as Bede tells us, "forsook all for the love of God." In the midst was a great fountain formed from the pine-cone that crowned once the mausoleum of Hadrian, now Castel S. Angelo.

On the great platform without the atrium the Popes were

used to meet the Emperors, whom they led thence into the sanctuary for their Coronation before the tomb of the Apostle.

Bronze doors flanked by columns divided the platform from the atrium, and five other doors opened thence into the church. The door in the midst was the Porta Argentea, decorated in silver in the sixth century, and inscribed later with the names of the cities Charlemagne bestowed upon S. Peter. To the right were the Porta Romana, which was reserved for women, and the Porta Guidonea for the pilgrims, who, then as now, were led from church to church by a guide. On the left were the Porta Ravennati and the Porta Giudizia for the dead. Beside these was a smaller door, Porta Antica, which owing to its smallness was closed by Sixtus IV, who built the Porta Santa, which, like the Porta Antica, was opened only for the Jubilee.

Old S. Peter's itself consisted of five naves divided by four rows of antique columns. The pavement was of white marble taken from the Circus, which was later gradually replaced by more precious materials. At the end of the great nave was the tribune, covered with mosaics, separated from the nave by a triumphal arch, on which was the great mosaic of S. Peter presenting Constantine to our Lord : in his hand the Emperor held a model of the church. Across the arch lay a huge beam blazoned with the Cross of Christ and the keys of S. Peter, and under hung the great lamp called Pharos, which the Saracens stole in 846 : it had thirteen hundred lights and was lighted only at Christmas, Easter, and the Feast of SS. Peter and Paul.

The Confession before the tribune, reached as to-day by two flights of marble steps, was lighted by silver lamps and was paved with silver, while on a beam of gold stood the silver statues of the twelve Apostles. The shrine, whose panels were painted by some Giottesque master—his work is still preserved in the sacristy—was overwhelmed with the most precious offerings, and was indeed the richest in Europe. And everywhere within, the church was glorious with mosaic. The façade too was covered with mosaics, and the basilica was roofed with gilt bronze tiles taken from the Temple of Venus and Rome.

Beside the atrium stood the Baptistery, built by Pope Damasus and fed with water from Monte Vaticano. It held the Chair of S. Peter, which to-day, exalted, encased in bronze by Bernini, stands over its own altar in the apse of the new church. Not far away stood the bell-tower covered with silver and gold.

To protect these enormous riches, Leo IV surrounded the whole quarter which gradually grew up round the church with a fortified wall, built by slaves, as John VII did for S. Paolo fuori le Mura. This city, in which was the old Borgo—Borgo Saxonum—where our people dwelt and where the Kings of Wessex built a hospice, was known as the Leonine City.

That wall might save old S. Peter's from the invader, but was powerless against the Renaissance Popes who were never guilty of an act more barbarous than the destruction of the most famous church in Christendom, one thousand one hundred and fifty years old at the time Nicholas V began to pull it down in order to build—well, the magnificent and sumptuous church we see.

New S. Peter's was begun by Nicholas V in 1450, and it was consecrated a hundred and seventy-six years later by Urban VIII, some twelve architects having been employed upon it. The first of these was Rossellino, a Florentine, who conceived so huge a church in the form of a Latin Cross that the choir and transepts alone would have enclosed old S. Peter's. In 1455, however, Nicholas V died, and his successor, Calixtus III, was not of the Renaissance. He did little or nothing to the building, while Pius II, who came after him, was too busy in the Romagna and with the Turkish business to be able to devote either time or money to it. When he died the walls were only a few feet high : and Paul II, who succeeded him, was a reactionary. Sixtus IV and Alexander VI were dreaming of quite other things, but Julius II, not less busily ambitious, continued the work Nicholas V had begun, placing it in 1506 in the hands of Bramante ; yet at first he too eyed it with suspicion. Bramante began all over again, making a design in the form of a Greek Cross under a dome. When he died in 1514, so unfortunately for the church, he had done but little towards carrying out his design. Then

ST. PETER'S

PIETÀ, by Michelangelo (St. Peter's)

Raphael was appointed architect. He made a new plan, a Latin cross with a long nave, but dying in 1520, achieved nothing. The work passed into the hands of Baldassare Peruzzi, but when Leo X died not long after, very little had been accomplished. On the death of Peruzzi, Antonio Sangallo was appointed in 1536. He but spoiled Bramante's plan, according to Michelangelo, to whom at his death in 1546 the work passed, Giulio Romano having first been appointed, only to die in the same year.

Michelangelo was already seventy years old when he became capo-maestro. Refusing all payment, he worked, he said, " for the love of God, the Blessed Virgin, and S. Peter." Bound though he was by the plans and achievements of his predecessors, he was able to discard the design of Sangallo, which, besides filling the church with darkness, would have involved the destruction of the Sistine chapel. He took up again the plan of Bramante, a Greek Cross under a dome. " I will throw the Pantheon up there into the sky," he is reported to have said. Every effort was made by the disciples of Sangallo and Giulio Romano to displace him, but the Pope not only confirmed him in his office, but gave him even greater power than before. When he died in 1564 he had finished the drum and made the plans for the dome which Giacomo della Porta erected in 1590. It remains the only perfectly beautiful and satisfactory part of the church.

In 1604 della Porta died and Paul V appointed Carlo Maderna as master of the works. At the order of the Pope he abandoned both Bramante's and Michelangelo's designs, adopting Rossellino's, namely a Latin cross with the long nave at the head of which the altar might gleam and the faithful be edified. The change of those plans over which Michelangelo had laboured for seventeen years turned what might have been one of the most beautiful churches in the world into one of the most imposing.

Maderna finished the façade in 1614. Fifty-three years later Bernini completed the Piazza, his greatest work, with its beautiful colonnades and fountains, and in the end of the eighteenth century Pius VI—whose figure of marble by Canova kneels in the Confessio—built the Sacristy.

Thus was completed the work undertaken by Nicholas V in 1450, but at an expense of more than ten millions sterling and at the cost not only of the destruction of the most venerable church in Christendom, but of a divided Europe ; for it was the sale of indulgences to build the new S. Peter's, a sale pushed too eagerly by Tetzel, that caused the great scandal which gave life and some excuse to the politico-religious movement in central and northern Europe called the Reformation.

Standing in the Piazza di San Pietro to-day we have the beautiful fountains and the colonnades of Bernini on either hand—the colonnades as triumphant a masterpiece in their own way as the dome itself—while in the midst rises the obelisk that once stood in Nero's Circus.

That Obelisk was raised by the genius of Domenico Fontana where it lay, since it was overthrown in the Circus of Nero, behind the Sacristy of the new S. Peter's. Fontana himself in his admirable and illustrated account of the tremendous affair tells us how it was accomplished while all Rome held its breath and Sixtus V threatened with death any who should break the silence. A great religious ceremony marked the raising of the Obelisk. Palestrina himself led his choir— you may see him in procession in Fontana's book—singing perhaps his lovely Offertory *Laudate Dominum quia benignus est*.

All the world knows the story of how at the critical moment as the obelisk rose the ropes began to stretch and to threaten to break when a sailor from Bordighera cried out, *Acqua alle corde*, thus preventing a disaster.

This was the first Obelisk to be set up again in the City, but Sixtus V erected four in all of the ten that Rome now possesses. This in Piazza S. Pietro was erected by Fontana in 1585. It is 82 feet high without the pedestal and has no inscriptions.[1]

---

[1] The largest and oldest of these Egyptian Obelisks, all of them originally brought from Egypt by the Emperors, is that erected by Sixtus before the Loggia di Benedizione of the Lateran in the Piazza there where the equestrian statue of Marcus Aurelius, now on the Capitol, used to stand. This is 105 feet high without the pedestal. It is of red granite and of the 15th century B.C. It was brought to Rome by the Emperor Constantius in A.D. 357. Sixtus erected others before S. Maria Maggiore and in Piazza del Popolo. Six other obelisks are to be found in Rome ; that in Villa Mattei erected in 1582, that in Piazza del Quirinale erected in 1787, that on Monte Citorio erected in 1789, that on the Pincio erected in 1822, that on Bernini's fountain in Piazza Navona erected in 1652 and that upon the elephant before S. Maria Sopra Minerva erected in 1667.

It is ever with new regret one gazes at Maderna's façade over which in huge letters is set the name and title of Pope Paul V, Borghese. The heavy engaged columns, the windows as of a palace, the strange upper storey which has no relation at all to the church, all this obscures altogether the very real beauty and splendour of the church, the great dome of Michelangelo. So one passes up that wide flight of easy steps to the great central door, where are, within the narthex, the gates of bronze which Eugenius IV in the earliest Renaissance caused Filarete to make in envy of the eastern doors of the Baptistery of Florence that Ghiberti had just set up when the Pope presided over the Council of Florence. This central door dates from 1445 and belonged to the old basilica. Side by side with representations of Our Lord, the Blessed Virgin and the Apostles we have scenes of the Council of Florence and the Coronation of the Emperor Sigismund set round a curious series of scenes from pagan mythology, Venus in the arms of Mars, Europa and the Bull, Leda caressing the swan, Jupiter and Ganymede. Moreover, the work has little merit.

One enters the church at last and remains astonished— astonished at its magnificence. Yet perhaps it is not at all what one expected. The largeness seems lost in the general proportion and perhaps in the richness of the material and ornament. It is neither Greek nor Latin but Baroque and its beauty, and it has much, is fundamentally picturesque and romantic. One's eyes are drawn at once to the great baldacchino over the high altar and the innumerable lights about the confessio. Then one's attention wanders, nothing can hold it. The church seems less a church than a city in whose streets one may wander all day long, yet strangely enough the place is always full of silence. . . . But of course everyone's reaction to S. Peter's will be different. For me it remains the most magnificent baroque church in the world.

The centre of the immense and magnificent basilica is the high altar over the tomb of the Apostle ; Michelangelo's dome and Bernini's baldacchino have insured that. The baldacchino is a pictorial rather than an architectural masterpiece. It was erected in 1633 and made from bronze which Urban VIII the Barberini pope took from the roof of the portico of the Pantheon, an act which caused the witty Pasquino to comment, *Quod non fecerunt barbari fecerunt Barberini.*[1] The immense canopy of bronze, supported by four huge twisted columns of bronze covered with golden decoration and the bees of the Barberini, is 95 feet high. And it is a masterpiece. Anything else, anything different would have been insignificant under that dome, which encloses a goodly portion of the heavens and is surrounded by an immortal inscription, the charter of the Catholic Church, in letters nine feet high :

TU ES PETRUS ET SUPER HANC PETRAM
AEDIFICABO ECCLESIAM MEAM ET TIBI DABO CLAVES
REGNI CAELORUM.

The Greeks do not seem to have cared for size, they loved perfection, the Romans, however, were of another opinion, they knew its power.

The four massive piers which uphold the dome are the work of Bramante, but the loggias and their balconies were built by Bernini. They contain and are designed for the display on appropriate occasions of the relics of the Passion : the Spear with which Longinus pierced the side of our Lord, the Veil of S. Veronica which bears the impression of the Divine face, a piece of the True Cross and the head of S. Andrew. The Holy Lance or Spear was venerated in Jerusalem in the sixth century, according to S. Bede, and was taken to Constantinople by the Turks. The Sultan Bajazet sent it to Pierre d' Aubusson, Grand Master of the Knights of Rhodes, who in 1492 presented it to Innocent VIII. The figure of S. Longinus is by Bernini.

Several other works by Bernini are to be found in the basilica, chief among them the famous Chair of S. Peter in the depth of the tribune. This amazing work which clothes in a vast bronze reliquary the reputed Chair of the Prince of the Apostles has been too much disparaged. Like the master's baldacchino it is not so much sculptural or architectural as pictorial, one might almost say a theatrical property. With its wonderful sculptures, and under the window with the dove

---

[1] What the barbarians did not do, the Barberini did.

IACOBO · III
IACOBI · II · MAGNAE · BRIT · REGIS · FILIO
KAROLO · EDVARDO
ET · HENRICO · DECANO · PATRVM · CARDINALIVM
IACOBI · III · FILIIS
REGIAE · STIRPIS · STVARDIAE · POSTREMIS
ANNO · M · DCCC · XIX

BEATI MORTVI
QVI IN DOMINO MORIVNTVR

THE STUART MONUMENT, by Canova (St. Peter's)

CANONISATION CEREMONY,
looking from the High Altar to the Altar of the Chair of St. Peter (St. Peter's)

of the Holy Spirit, it is from a seventeenth-century point of view, and surely now from ours, immensely successful. What else could so fittingly and so dramatically terminate the great church of S. Peter ? If we accept the Chair of the Apostle as a genuine relic it could only be presented incased in a reliquary, and that reliquary considering its contents must be something that could not be disregarded even in the immensity of this the greatest church in the world. Bernini has achieved this and if we examine his work closely we shall easily convince ourselves of the beauty of the details, those angels for instance on either side the throne which is upheld by the four Doctors of the Latin and Greek Churches, S. Ambrose, S. Augustine, S. Athanasius and S. John Chrysostom.

Other works by Bernini here are the tomb of Urban VIII on the right of the Cattedra of S. Peter and the tomb of Alexander VII opposite the pier of S. Veronica. Both are magnificent masterpieces of baroque art.

Opposite Bernini's tomb of Urban VIII is the not less famous tomb of Paul III by Giacomo della Porta. The figures of Wisdom and Justice beneath the enthroned Pope are said to represent the Pope's mother and his sister Giulia, known as Giulia Bella. The Justice was originally nude and this was found offensive, so that Bernini was employed to make a farthingale of tin for the figure.

One or two earlier works in the church are worth all our attention. The famous bronze statue of S. Peter enthroned, under the last pier on the right in the nave dates from the fifth century. It has been venerated and the brazen foot worn with kisses for many generations.

Near the Chapel of the Blessed Sacrament is the unmarked grave of Pierluigi da Palestrina, Principe della Musica :

> Of him whose notes to mortal hearts still bring
> Our Lord enthroned and Seraphs on the wing ;
> Whose winding voices linked in ecstasy
> Draw heaven to earth when earth to heaven would fly. . . .

The Chapel of the Blessed Sacrament has a gilded bronze ciborium by Bernini somewhat similar to the Tempietto at S. Pietro in Montorio, and there is a fresco over the altar

L

by Pietro da Cortona. But its great treasure was the magnificent tomb of Sixtus IV at the foot of the altar by Antonio Pollaiuolo. This has now been removed to the Museo Petriano.

Pollaiuolo also made the monument of Innocent VIII outside the Cappella del Coro. This work of the fifteenth century Florentine, a son of the Renaissance, is not so fine and not so pagan a masterpiece as the tomb of Sixtus IV ; it has, however, the quality of the master.

But it is the works of Bernini here, the marvellous baldacchino with its four glorious angels, the astonishing, but finally convincing bronze of the Chair of S. Peter, the tomb of Urban VIII, the tomb of Alexander VII, to name no others, that lift the monotonous splendour of the church out of its mediocrity, lend it the light of genius and are, save for the Pietà of Michelangelo, perhaps the only things that one remembers here and that glorify the mere immensity of this mighty temple.

Undoubtedly the noblest work of art in the great church is that early work of Michelangelo's. The Madonna della Pietà in the first chapel of the right aisle remains the most beautiful as it is the most perfect of the many works which came from that strong and ruthless hand, so marvellously tender for once. It was carved for the Cardinal di San Dionigi, called the Cardinal Rovano, not long after the Bacchus of the Bargello of Florence. The Madonna is seated on the stone where the Cross was raised, her dead Son in her lap. " He is of so great and so rare a beauty," says Condivi, " that no one beholds Him but is moved to pity. It is a figure truly worthy of the humanity which belonged to the Son of God and to such a Mother ; nevertheless, some there be who complain that the Mother is too young compared to the Son. One day as I was talking to Michelangelo of this objection : ' Do you know,' he said, ' that chaste women retain their fresh looks much longer than those who are not chaste ? How much more, therefore, a virgin in whom not even the least unchaste desire ever arose ? And I tell you, moreover, that such freshness and flower of youth besides being maintained in her by natural causes, may possibly have been ordained by the Divine Power to prove to the world the virginity and perpetual purity of the Mother. It was not necessary in the Son ; but rather the contrary. Wishing to show that the Son of God took upon Himself a true human body, subject to all the ills of man, excepting only sin, He did not allow the divinity in Him to hold back the humanity, but let it run its course and obey its laws, as was proved in His appointed time. Do not wonder then that I have, for all these reasons, made the most Holy Virgin, Mother of God, a great deal younger in comparison with her Son than she is usually represented. To the Son I have allotted His full age.' " Michelangelo was about twenty-four or twenty-five years old when he finished that work. It brought him fame and a great reputation, and there, alone in all his work, on the hem of Mary's robe he has carved his name.

Something of the old humanity stirred now and then certainly in the work of Canova, to be found here not only in the beautiful architectural work of the tomb of Clement XIII, the figure of Pius VI kneeling in the Confession, but especially in that monument which commemorates the last of that unfortunate race which once ruled in merry England. Yes, the most touching and human monument after all in the great church commemorates a tragedy of our race, the passing of the Stuarts, reminding us of the rightful kings of Great Britain, France, and Ireland, James III, Charles Edward, and Henry IX, Cardinal York. Their ashes lie in the crypt, and this monument, where two English boys—*non Angli sed Angeli*—weep beside a tomb, was erected by their royal supplanter George IV, in 1819.

XXIV

THE VATICAN

THE Palace of the Vatican as we see it to-day is not really a palace at all, a building at unity with itself, but rather a group of palaces, chapels, galleries and courts built at different periods, added one by one, since the early part of the thirteenth century, and joined the one to the other by staircases and covered ways. Its prototype is not to be found in any palace in the world but rather in the Imperial buildings on the Palatine Hill which, growing up under successive Emperors little by little, came to form a whole, which, almost shapeless as it was, must have been rather picturesque than beautiful. Nor is this comparison so far fetched as it might seem. The palaces of the Vatican, like the palaces of the Caesars long ago, form the largest and, in many ways, the most splendid building in the world, containing some seven thousand chambers, a multitude of courts and over two hundred staircases.[1]

When the first palace was founded on the Vatican Hill remains a mystery. Tradition asserts that it was in the time of Constantine ; and certainly at the end of the fifth century Pope Symmachus seems to have restored some building beside S. Peter's, and at any rate by the year of Charlemagne's Coronation a palace of some sort was standing on the Vatican, for Pope Leo III escaped thither from his prison in 798, and, as some say, there the great king resided before his Coronation on Christmas Day 800.

When Leo entrenched the Borgo and created the *Città Leonina*, the Vatican became a fortress with S. Peter's as its citadel, till the fire during the siege of Frederick Barbarossa in 1167 : and thirty years later we hear of the restoration, and

---

[1] Cf. Pistolesi, *Il Vaticano descritto ed illustrato*, 8 vols. (Roma, 1829–38) ; Stevenson and Ehrle, *Affreschi del Appartamento Borgia al Vaticano* (Roma, 1897).

new buildings begun by Innocent III and finished by Nicholas
III in 1277 ; but until the Babylonish Captivity the Popes
resided at the Lateran, the Vatican being indeed but a kind of
stronghold.   Its true history, amid much that is vague and uncertain, begins in the last quarter of the fourteenth century
when Gregory XI, led by S. Catherine, having ventured back
from Avignon, chose to live here because of its nearness to
Castel S. Angelo, John XXIII, was his successor, building
the covered way along the wall of Leo from the palace to the
fortress.   In the dreadful years which followed—the years of
the Great Schism—the palace seems to have fallen into utter
decay, and we find Martin V (1417–1431) living in the Colonna
palace near SS. Apostoli, as the Romans tried to force his
successor Eugenius IV (1431–1447) to do ; when he refused,
stoning him down the Tiber so that he was compelled to take
refuge on a pirate's ship and sail for Pisa and Florence.
Eugenius was an exile for the greater part of his pontificate
and seems never to have lived at the Vatican, but his successor, Nicholas V, the humanist, the first of the Renaissance
Popes, rebuilt the palace on a great scale before he began the
work on the new church of S. Peter, which we also owe to him.
It was he who built all that part of the present palace which
stands about the Cortile del Pappagallo, including the so-
called Borgia wings.   His successor, Pius II, was too busy with
the unruly barons of Romagna and with the Turk to concern himself either with the work on S. Peter's or with new plans
at the Vatican.   The next additions were made by Paul II,
who built the Palazzo della Camera, by Sixtus IV, who built
the Sistine Chapel, by Innocent VIII, who built the Palazzo
named after him, and the Belvedere in the gardens which the
buildings of Julius II surrounded, and by Alexander VI,
who added the Torre Borgia, the Sala Regia, and the Sala
Ducale, towards S. Peter's.   All the work of Paul II and the
Palace of Innocent VIII perished to make room for the new
church of S. Peter ;   the rest of the work contrived there in the
fifteenth century remains.

Julius II built those two long wings which brought the
Belvedere of Innocent into the palace itself in the early years
of the sixteenth century.   Then Leo X built the Cortile di

Damaso, so named because the water which supplied the Baptistery, built by Pope Damasus, passed through it, while Sixtus V built the Library and the apartments now used by the Pope, and Alexander VII rebuilt the Scala Regia by the hands of Bernini. The last work of any consequence undertaken at the Vatican we owe to Pius VII (1800–23), who built the magnificent galleries of the Braccio Nuovo, and to Pius XI who built the new Pinacoteca.

Thus the Palace of the Vatican, as we now see it, is the work of some five hundred years. In its first days it was a fortress, in the nineteenth century it became a prison, from which the vicegerent of God never ventured out. It is now again the Palace of an independent Sovereign.

I. THE CHAPEL OF NICHOLAS V

Amid all the living pomp of the Vatican, the Oratory of Nicholas V stands like a little country chapel, as simple as that, and gay as it were with the wildflowers of Tuscany. Of all the sanctuaries of the Eternal City, it alone keeps about it something of the mysticism and charm of the earliest Renaissance—of Beato Fra Angelico. After the material splendours of S. Peter's, the cold magnificence of the great palace of the Popes, it offers you repose. And, indeed, it is a place of perfect happiness, full of sweetness and light. One finds there nothing of Roman pride and solemnity, but, as it were, an intimate silence and joy. And to cross its threshold unexpectedly in the midst of this immense palace, so full of ghosts and unforgettable things, is pure delight.

The work of two Tuscans, Nicholas V and Fra Angelico, as one might expect, perhaps, it still has something of the simplicity and happiness that clings even to-day about every Tuscan church even in Florence ; but it is a more intimate delight we find in this oratory, which seems to express best of all not only the youthful and innocent spirit of the Renaissance which was born in Tuscany, but the very thoughts concerning it of its two most characteristic protagonists—the gracious and beautiful spirit of Nicholas V and the passionate and human genius of the greatest artist of his time, Beato Angelico.

Nicholas V, the first patron of the new learning, of the new spirit, to ascend the pontifical throne, was born in Pisa of poor parents in 1398. Owing to some political misfortune his father, who died when he was about nine years old, left Pisa for Sarzana in the Lunigiana soon after the birth of his second son Filippo, later Cardinal of Bologna. There his childhood was spent in some poverty with his mother, Andreola, who, however, gave him a good education and warned, as Vespasiano da Bisticci tells us, in a dream of his future eminence, not only urged him to pursue his studies, but sent him when he was sixteen to the university of Bologna where he became " learned in all the seven liberal arts." He spent two years at Bologna and then, lacking money, he returned home, but his mother by then had married again, and finding that neither she nor her husband was very rich he went to Florence determined to pursue his studies by means of teaching. There he met Messer Rinaldo degli Albizzi, who engaged him to instruct his sons, and when Rinaldo was exiled he entered the service of Messer Palla Strozzi, so that at the end of two years he had gained enough to return to Bologna. Thus his life began. In Florence he met all those patrons and artists in whose hands lay the future of Europe. He helped Cosimo to form his library, and became the friend and secretary of Niccolò degli Albergati, Bishop of Bologna, who, when Martin V made him Cardinal, took him with him to Rome. Thence he went with his patron, whom he loved as a second father, into France and England on political business. He remained with Albergati for twenty years, and on his death in 1443 entered the service of Cardinal Landriani, who died, however, in the same year. Famous throughout Italy for his learning, the friend of scholars, and a collector of manuscripts, he was presently made Bishop of Bologna by Eugenius IV and sent as Papal Legate into Germany. He got so little, however, out of his bishopric, for Bologna was at war with the Holy See, that he was compelled to borrow money from the Medici, Cosimo giving him a general letter of credit to all his correspondents. His embassy was so successful that in 1446 Eugenius gave him the hat, and a few months afterwards he found himself Pope, taking out of gratitude to his early patron, Niccolò degli Albergati, the title

of Nicholas V. Pacific, without political ambition, his reign
was remarkable for his protection of the new learning, his
splendid patronage of scholarship and the arts, his destruction
of old S. Peter's, his plans for the great church of Rossellino,
and his work at the Vatican. He was not maybe without
pedantry, but he was the first Pope who preferred scholars
and artists to monks and friars. He secured for the Renaissance the allegiance of the Church. It was the irony of cir-
cumstance that he should die in a moment of misfortune just
after the fall of Constantinople.

Great as were his services rather to humanity than to the
Church, the work of such a man is easy to forget, and indeed
in all Rome there is only this little chapel in the Vatican
which vividly reminds us of him.

It was in 1445 that Pope Eugenius had invited Fra Giovanni
da Fiesole to Rome, where he remained till, Eugenius dying
in 1447, Nicholas V besought him to decorate the new chapel
he was building at the Vatican. Illustrious throughout Italy,
Angelico appeared to the Pope, Vasari tells us, " a person of
most holy life, as he really was, gentle and modest, so that when
the Archbishopric of Florence became vacant he offered him
the preferment, but Angelico entreated his Holiness to provide
himself with some other person since he did not feel capable of
ruling men." It was on his recommendation that Frate
Antonino was appointed. A Dominican, one of the first to
enter that order at S. Domenico at Fiesole, Angelico was the
greatest painter of his day in Italy. Early a traveller, during
the dispute as to the proprietary rights in the convent, he visited
Foligno and Cortona, returning to Fiesole in 1418. But all
central Italy was known to him later ; with his pupil, Benozzo,
he painted in Cortona, Perugia and Orvieto, and seems to
have wandered all over Umbria. He was sixty-two years old
when Nicholas invited him to paint in his study at the Vatican,
which was later transformed into the chapel we know.

There on the walls Angelico has painted the life and death
of SS. Stephen and Laurence. In the lunette to the right as
one faces the window, we see the Ordination of S. Stephen.
He kneels, his head newly shaven, before the altar, while S.
Peter presents to him the cup and platter of the Communion,

and behind, the " multitude of the disciples," called together for the occasion, watch while the new deacon is ordained.   S. Stephen had been appointed to minister to the widows of the Grecian Jews, and in the second fresco we see him preaching to them while they sit on the ground even as the women do to-day in southern Italy and Spain, enthralled by the sweetness of his eloquence, their emotions touched, as women's are, by the beauty of words.   In the background the men are assembled ; less moved than the women, they seem to argue, as men will, concerning the matter of the sermon.   In the lunette on the left are the two scenes of the saint's martyrdom. In the first he is seized at the city gate by certain Jews, Paul among them.   In the second he kneels on the hillside, caught, as it were, in the arms of God, heedless of the stones that fall so thick about him.   But one among the murderers—is it Paul again ?—holds his stone listlessly, as it were in doubt, clutching his robe in his left hand, as though, moved by that rapt figure, he found some undreamt-of misgiving suddenly in his heart.

Beneath these wonderful paintings, Angelico has told in fresco the story of S. Laurence.   In the first we see the Pope Sixtus, masquerading as Nicholas V, ordaining him, even as S. Peter had ordained Stephen.   In the second, the same Pope gives the treasures of the Church into his keeping, while the soldiers stand ready to arrest him.   In the third, S. Laurence, standing in the portico of some basilica, surrounded by women and children, distributes alms to the poor, the halt, and the blind.   In the fourth we see him before the Emperor Decius, who sits under an arch upheld by pilasters from which a beautiful tapestry is hung.   Without we see the trees and the blue sky ; while the saint in the power of a soldier waits patiently, his hands bound, for the sentence of his judge. Instruments of torture already lie on the ground, and later, as we see, he is led away to die, blessing his gaoler as he goes to that awful death which Angelico painted there on the right, but which is completely spoiled.

As one looks at these living and exquisite pictures, the work of an old man of sixty-three, one is chiefly struck, perhaps, by their freshness, as though the influence of Rome had revealed to a mind, enclosed till then in a country cloister among the wildflowers, the realities of the world, of life, that contemporary life which was about to become so splendid. The gentle friar, who has dreamed his life away among the saints and has walked hand in hand with Jesus, as it were, has become, under the influence of the Eternal City, the most perfect and the most satisfying of naturalists, not copying life but creating it, out of a profound realisation of it. Some joy always secretly in his heart has led him, suddenly so observant of men, to just this realism, as we might say, which is so new and so charming a feature of his work here in the Vatican. Consider then that woman who in the ministration of S. Stephen, lightly, lightly holds her child's hand, oblivious of everything but the emotion which the saint's words have suddenly awakened in her heart : or that blind man, who, when S. Laurence distributes alms, approaches with so uncertain a step, one hand stretched out before him, the other holding firmly to the trusty staff : it is as though we had really seen these people, so surely has Angelico drawn them from the mere details of life, of life in the Eternal City. How well they must have loved one another, those two, the Pope who was the greatest humanist in Italy, an eager archaeologist, a lover of all beautiful things, and the artist who had, long and long ago, mistaken earth for heaven in his joy at its perfection, only to find here at last, it might seem, that it was in some sort the only truth he might really apprehend.

II. THE APPARTAMENTO BORGIA

The Appartamento Borgia, situated as it is under the Stanze of Raphael, looking on the one side into the court of the Belvedere, and on the other into the Cortile del Pappagallo, formed part of the palace which Nicholas V had built in great part, but had died too soon to complete. It was Alexander VI who finished the work begun by Nicholas, adding the tower named after him which became so famous. It was in these rooms, decorated for his delight by Pinturicchio, that Alexander spent the splendid disastrous days of his pontificate. Here in a strange and almost fabulous luxury he lived for eleven years,

half fearful under the eyes of Cesare his son, forgetting everything in the beauty of Giulia Farnese. It was here, too, that
he died at last after that fatal dinner with Cardinal Adriano
of Corneto. Cesare Borgia, the wonder of the world, occupied
the vast apartment on the second floor, which was later
decorated by Raphael, and is known to us as the Stanze di
Raffaele.

After the death of Alexander VI, the Appartamento Borgia
was abandoned to the nephews of Julius II, the Pope dis-
carding it in his hatred of the Borgia House. Then when
Sixtus V built his new palace it was deserted, till in 1527 it
was used as a sort of *caserna* by the rabble of de Bourbon.
Infinite damage was done at that time, but not more than in the
seventeenth century, when two conclaves were held there, the
walls and frescoes being ruthlessly spoiled by the erection of
cells for the Cardinals. Gradually the apartment, a favourite
with no one but its builder, came into the hands of servants.
Later, in the time of Pius VI, these were turned out, the spoiled
frescoes were painted over, and the place was used as a picture
gallery, then as a museum and library. Its present rehabilita-
tion we owe to Leo XIII, who set about restoring it in 1891,
when the library was removed. It was not, however, till
1897 that the whole apartment, consisting of six rooms, the
two last belonging to the tower, was accessible, the frescoes
having been uncovered and carefully restored, and the whole
place set in order.

It was in the first days of his pontificate that Alexander VI
set Pinturicchio to work on the decoration of these rooms, which
he was able to occupy about two years later, in 1495. In the
three years that had then passed since his election in 1492 the
five inner rooms had been painted by Pinturicchio and his
assistants, the outer room, the Sala dei Pontifici, by which we
enter the apartment to-day, being painted later under Leo X
by Perin del Vaga.

Pinturicchio's work, the work which he at least designed,
begins in the Sala della Vita della Madonna, where we see
certain of the joyful mysteries of the rosary of the Blessed
Virgin : the Annunciation, the Nativity, the Adoration of the
Magi, the Resurrection, the Ascension, the Descent of the Holy

Spirit, and the Assumption. Above on the ceiling are the Evangelists and Fathers. The second room, Sala dei Santi, is decorated with scenes from the lives of SS. Susanna, Sebastian, Barbara, Antony Abbot, and Paul the Hermit; an exquisite Madonna and Child, and S. Catherine disputing with the Philosophers. In the third room, Sala delle Arti, are allegorical figures of Geometry, Arithmetic, Music, Rhetoric, and Grammar, while over the door is a tondo of the Madonna and Child. In the fourth room are the Prophets, and in the fifth the Sibyls. Side by side with these Christian scenes and figures are set incidents from old religions, such as the stories of Isis and Osiris, of Juno and Io. While scattered everywhere are flowers and fruit, birds, sphinxes, and hydras, interwoven with the bull of the Borgia.

But what is most interesting to us perhaps in all this gay and decorative work is the fact that it is full of portraits. In the fresco of the Resurrection, for instance, Alexander himself kneels before the newly risen Christ, while we may see all the pontifical court of the day in the dispute of S. Catherine. It is Cesare Borgia who appears as the Emperor Maximus, and Lucrezia herself, the sweetest and most tranquil of women, then about fifteen years old and on the eve of her marriage with Giovanni Sforza, the young man in a red cloak in the right-hand corner of the picture, appears as S. Catherine. Among the many Oriental personages in the same picture we may identify two certainly; for the prince who stands close to the throne and is dressed in a purple cloak is Andrea Paleologus, Lord of Morea, who had just lost by the death of his uncle, Constantine XIII, the crown of Byzantium; while the other wearing a splendid turban, standing on the Emperor's left, is Djem, the brother of the Sultan Bajazet, and the inseparable companion of Cesare.

According to Vasari, " Over the door of one of the rooms Pinturicchio portrayed the Signora Giulia Farnese in the face of a Madonna; and in the same picture is a figure in adoration of the Virgin, the head being a portrait of Pope Alexander." Vasari, however, seems to have confused these frescoes with the picture now in Valencia, where a donor, perhaps Alexander VI, kneels before the Madonna. In these rooms, as we have seen, the Pope kneels, the triple tiara on the ground beside him, before the risen Christ ; while the only Madonna here which seems to be a portrait is the tondo over the door of the Sala dei Santi, where she holds her little Son in her arms as He reads from a book of hours.   May we see in that pale and exquisite face as true and realistic a portrait of Giulia Farnese " Sponsa di Cristo " as we have of Alexander in the kneeling figure of the " Resurrection " ?   That delicate, voluptuous mouth was made, one might think, rather for kisses than for prayers, that golden hair, a veritable fleece of gold, which she would unbind and let fall so that it covered her even to her feet, and as the Florentine ambassador said, made her in truth a sun—*Parava da farla un sole*—scarcely hides itself under the half transparent veil.   It may well be that this is the divine Giulia Bella whom the Pope so loved, that even in the company of Lucrezia she might not leave Rome for a single night without his express permission.   If it be, we have in these rooms portraits of the chief personages of that reign, Cesare himself, that tongue of fire, as we have seen, masquerading as the Emperor.   A contemporary medal in the British Museum, if need be, confirms the portrait as his.

III. THE SISTINE CHAPEL

To pass from the chapel of Nicholas V, from the Apparta-mento Borgia even, into the Sistine Chapel, is to realise what in Rome at any rate the Renaissance had become little by little in the first half of the sixteenth century.   Built for Sixtus IV by the Florentine Baccio Pintelli about the year 1473, the Sistine Chapel is a great oblong building with a vaulted ceiling, a hundred and forty-seven feet long by fifty wide, the pavement being of fine mosaic work in the manner of the Cosmati. Divided into two parts by a beautiful screen of marble, the work of Mino da Fiesole and Giovanni Dalmata, it is sur-rounded by a marble bench set against the wall while within the screen is a tribune for singers, a *cantastoria*, a grave and noble work which, spoiled as it has been by gilding, remains for the most part of the fifteenth century.

This plain and simple building, round the lowest course of

which Raphael's tapestries were to have hung, where now we see a painted curtain, is lighted by twelve narrow windows set high in the walls under round arches. Beneath these windows, like a frieze, are set the famous frescoes by painters of the fifteenth century, those on the right being scenes from the life of Christ, those on the left scenes from the life of Moses ; the prophecy, as it were, and the fulfilment facing each other in that narrow room, but without any real significance. No, the problem that we see triumphantly solved in the Sistine Chapel and yet with a sort of failure after all, had nothing to do with the doctrine or faith of the Church. It was rather a question of aesthetics than of theology which presented itself to that master, whoever he may have been, who directed the famous company of artists Sixtus IV had brought together to decorate his private chapel. Who that master was we do not know, but many facts in that scheme of decoration seem to suggest the name of Perugino.[1] An Umbrian whose immense reputation was greater at that time than that of any other artist who has worked here, he was certainly accompanied by an assistant whose work appears there, while he himself began the series somewhat as Giotto had done perhaps in the upper church at Assisi. Those three frescoes by Perugino which Michelangelo destroyed at the bidding of Pope Clement VII to make room for his great painting of the Last Judgment may well have set the pattern, as it were, of the frieze that was to pass quite round the church, and as though to remove all doubt Pinturicchio, his assistant, painted the second panel, now the first, of each series on either side the high altar, the Journey of Moses and the Baptism of Christ. Beside these two Umbrians worked the greatest masters of Italy in the last

---

[1] Vasari affirms that the general direction was in the hands of Botticelli. However that may be, a contract dated the 27th October 1481 gives us the names of the artists employed here. There were three Florentines, Cosimo Rosselli, Botticelli, Ghirlandajo, and one Umbrian, Perugino. Each of the masters doubtless brought with him several pupils ; among them, however, we only know Piero di Cosimo, the pupil of Cosimo Rosselli, and Pinturicchio, the pupil of Perugino. The work had probably already been begun in the spring of 1481, the artists promising to complete it by the 15th March 1482. A document of January 1482 tells us that of the ten frescoes spoken of in the contract only four were finished ; two hundred and fifty ducats being paid for each. To hasten the completion of the work a new artist was engaged, Luca Signorelli. The work was actually finished on 15th August, 1483, when Sixtus IV consecrated the chapel. Cf. Crowe and Cavalcaselle, *History of Painting in Italy*, under " Signorelli."

quarter of the fifteenth century : Luca Signorelli, half Umbrian, half Tuscan, the true master in painting of Michelangelo Buonarotti ; Sandro Botticelli, who alone was thought worthy to be named in Leonardo's treatise on painting ; Domenico Ghirlandajo, whom one had wished to cover the walls of Florence with portraits of her citizens ; Cosimo Rosselli, and his pupil Piero di Cosimo.

Those three frescoes over the high altar, with which Perugino began the two series that together surround the whole chapel, were the Assumption, in which was a portrait of Sixtus IV, and on one side the Nativity of our Lord, and on the other the Finding of Moses. These paintings, so unhappily lost to us by the ruthless vandalism of Clement VII, who bade Michelangelo paint in their place his tremendous fresco of the Last Judgment, were confirmed in the example they set for the decoration of the chapel by the work of Pinturicchio, who beside them, in the first spaces of the long walls north and south of the altar, painted the second scenes in the life of Christ and of Moses—the Baptism of our Lord and the Journey of Moses. Pinturicchio was twenty-eight years old at the time of his first coming to Rome, and these two frescoes were his first great commission, won for him, doubtless, by the influence of Perugino. A second-rate painter at best, superficial and full of excuses for the gaiety and even childishness of his work, in these two early paintings we see him not merely at his best, but really a greater painter than he was ever to be again. Still under the strong and really imaginative influence of Perugino, these works, we find, have infinite details copied from him, but in both pictures the composition as a whole is not at all like the almost clairvoyant work of Pietro Vannucci. The groups are a little confused and crowded, the pictures seem eager to tell a story, the beautiful fairy landscape, strange with toppling rocks, and fair, fantastic trees, has nothing of the actual truth of Perugino's world ; it has come to us, yes, out of the pictures of Fiorenzo di Lorenzo and out of the heart of a child, Pinturicchio himself, with his mind full of such fairy business. Here and there we are surprised by the energy or sheer beauty of a figure or a face, and immediately ask ourselves whether here we may not find the hand of Perugino, such work being indeed almost out of place among so much that is merely pretty and charming : that woman so seriously busy with a religious rite, for instance, or that company of young Florentines in the background there, who seem with her to be the only real people in a world of ghosts, a child's dream of a world, that passes like an untroubled yet intricate music into forgetfulness.

It is the same with the picture of the Baptism of our Lord. How confused it is, without any simplicity ; how crowded with figures that one might think had but little concern with the true subject of the picture ; and among them Christ and S. John—copies almost from Perugino's predella now in Rouen—seen like a vision. Are they aware, then, of that cloud of witnesses, real people, concerned after all with their own business, who have somehow failed to understand that it is Jesus who stands there in Jordan—or Tiber, is it ?—and that God Himself will presently speak from heaven ?

Besides these two light and lovely works, so restless and un-real, Botticelli has painted two pictures, which have been called the Youth of Moses, his sojourn in the desert, and the Temptation of our Lord.

The Temptation of our Lord ! That confused and enig-matic picture was the first work Botticelli painted here, and one is doubtful after all what the subject may be ; for the scenes of the Temptation are in the background, three little vignettes almost overwhelmed by the landscape and that great Temple about which surges a restless crowd. Far away to the left, under a grove of trees, Jesus faces Satan, dressed as a monk, who would persuade Him to change the stones into bread. In the midst of the picture, on the topmost pinnacle of the Temple, He faces the devil again, who would have Him tempt God ; while to the right all the glory of the world passes before Him, its price infidelity, the worship of a lie : but already the tempter flees away, unmasked at last by the words, " Get thee behind me, Satan," while angels come swiftly to minister to the Son of God, who presently returns out of the silent desert to our world. There He finds—so Botticelli seems to suggest—the consequences of the success of the first Temptation which ended so differently from that

THE TEMPTATION, by Michelangelo (Sistine Chapel)

THE MADONNA OF FOLIGNO, by Raphael (Pinacoteca Vaticana)

just over, in the Fall of Man. On the right a leper healed, the type of sinner, saved now by the victory of Christ, approaches the altar, aided by two of his friends, while on the left his wife advances, carrying on her head a covered basket in which are the two doves. In the midst the high-priest receives from a young Levite an earthen platter in which is the blood of the bird sacrificed, with which, according to the prescribed rite, he sprinkles him who was sick and is healed, cleansing him from the moral stain of his sickness. Who can have invented this curious and mystical theology? Can it have been the work of Botticelli, or was the subject in all its intricacies given him by the Pope? Certainly the whole picture tends to flatter Sixtus IV, for the façade of the temple is an exact reproduction of the front of the hospital of Santo Spirito which he had built, and then, Franciscan as he was, with a peculiar devotion, as he said, for St. Francis, he would appreciate the healing of the leper, since their care had been among the first commands of Il Poverello. Nor does the symbolism, or allusion rather, end here, for in the background to the left of the Temple one sees the church of S. Francesco at Assisi, and there, too, the oak, the badge of the della Rovere family, to which Sixtus belonged. Opposite this fresco, meant so cunningly to flatter the Pope, stood the Episcopal throne, so that his eyes always rested upon it.

This composition, which, in its main details at any rate, one may believe to have been forced on Botticelli, confined him, too, in the work opposite to it, the Youth of Moses, for he was compelled, in order to keep to the sequence, to include seven episodes of Moses' life, from the murder of the Egyptian to the exodus, within a single picture. But, left more to himself, perhaps, than in the fresco of the Temptation, he was far happier in his achievement. Unexpectedly, charmingly, he has chosen for his central motive not one of the more famous scenes of the life of Moses, often so full of tragedy and dramatic force, but a scene altogether simple and idyllic, his meeting at the fountain with Jethro's daughters. Full of sweetness and grace, Moses is here, from the theological point of view doubtless, a prototype of the Good Shepherd, but it is perhaps the last thing we remember as we look on that fair scene, where

M

a young man, gentle now and full of a certain shy kindness, is glad in the service of beautiful women, bowing before them, a shepherd, not like Christ, but like Paris on Mount Ida. Just there we forget the terrible and majestic figure of the Old Testament, to find it again in the scenes round about, so different from the quiet episode of the foreground, the murder of the Egyptian, the chastisement of the two Hebrews who fought together, the escape from Egypt, the vision in the fields among the flocks of Jethro, the exodus at the head of his people.

Two scenes follow this in the story of Moses, the Destruction of Pharaoh and his Host in the Red Sea, by Piero di Cosimo, and Moses on Mount Sinai, by Cosimo Rosselli, the work of a master and his pupil, the first of which was painted to flatter Pope Sixtus, who had in August 1482 overwhelmed the Neapolitans by the hand of Roberto Malatesta.

Opposite these paintings are the Calling of Peter and Andrew, by Domenico Ghirlandajo, and the Sermon on the Mount, another work by Cosimo Rosselli. In the first, a quiet scene in strong contrast to the Destruction of Pharaoh's Host which faces it, we find the innumerable portraits that Ghirlandajo always introduced into his work.

The fifth scene in the story of Moses, the Destruction of Korah, Dathan, and Abiram by fire, the work of Botticelli, faces the fifth scene in the story of our Lord, Christ giving the keys to Peter, the work of Perugino.

The fresco of Botticelli, the third picture from his hand in this chapel, is less beautiful certainly than the youth of Moses, but different in sentiment as it is, not less remarkable.

In the centre, Moses, with a marvellous gesture full of confidence and force, calls down punishment from heaven on the false Levites who have questioned his authority, while Aaron, the true priest, gravely celebrates the appointed sacrifice. To the right a few faithful are about to stone one of the rebels ; to the left the earth opens to swallow Dathan and Abiram, while Eldad and Medad prophesy in the camp according to the Scripture.[1] The moral, as one might say, of this extraordinarily violent and yet splendid composition is graven on the triumphal arch there, to wit that none should aspire to the

[1] Numbers xi, 26.

honour of the sacrifice save only he whom God has chosen even as He chose Aaron.

Perugino's work opposite, perhaps the most beautiful composition in the chapel, confirms and bears out these words, as we might expect. The Delivery of the Keys to S. Peter he called the fresco, but he has built there behind the mere subject of the picture a beautiful church in the new manner of the Renaissance, delicate and lovely, with round arched porticoes at the sides leading into an octagonal temple that reminds one of the Duomo of Florence as seen from the corner of the Via del Proconsolo ; and on either side far away in the spacious Piazza are set two triumphal arches, again in the new manner, that after all was but the old Roman style come back again with a novel sort of freshness upon it—a real new birth into a world that had never been able to satisfy itself with that gloomy, fantastic, not quite sane, Gothic work, and was already impatiently awaiting this new birth of old classical things. Far away behind the beautiful buildings the whole world is filled with evening, and you gaze past the delicate fantastic trees to the near valley, wide and full of peace, and the mountains that the sun has kissed when night falls. That hurrying crowd of people, those delightful gesticulating figures, and even this company of disciples round Christ who is founding His Church—something as lovely and as new as that Temple before which they linger—how little they mean to us ! It is not from them that we receive the emotion this fresco never fails to give ; an emotion aesthetic, if you will, but really religious too, something that we shall find in scarcely a picture that has been painted before this time, comes from the sky full of the quiet evening light, from the delicate clouds that seem to be sleeping, that are shaped like wings, and from the landscape itself that is full of the breadth and coolness of evening, the holiness of the hour after the sunset. It is as though these people, just saints and apostles after all, as we discern, with our Lord in the midst, were a vision that in the quietness of the evening had surprised our hearts, busied for the moment with a thought of that invisible Church which so beautiful and fair a Temple had brought to us. The whole world seems to be blessed. And it is just that very perfect suggestion of evening, in Umbria at least, that gives us this emotion, that has made Perugino's work so beloved. Alberti has told us that when he saw the meadows and the hills covered with flowers in springtime he wept, he knew not why ; and it might seem that something of this pantheism, that strange stirring of the spirit at the thought of the earth from which we are sprung, has been understood by Perugino, for it is the one thing he never ceases to express. His figures, always a little aloof from life, more or less dream people, often beautiful but always a little fantastic, a little sentimental, as we might say, became less real, less actual, as he grew older ; he seems continually to have repeated himself, to have been content to care little about them ; but his landscapes are always full of eagerness and peace, which he found in that world of valley and mountain and lake which surrounds his home and birth-place. There he seems to have found everything that might satisfy him, and he returns to it again and again, as though, as indeed it was, it were something divine, something that in a world that was continually passing away remained always, in its profound and living beauty, the one thing that could never fail him, in which he would always find, as both before and after him so many poets and children have done, the very garments, as it were, of God, whose voice as of old we may still hear at evening " walking in the garden."

Two other works remain to complete the series on either wall, Cosimo Rosselli's fresco of the Last Supper, a mediocre work enough, and the Death of Moses, by Luca Signorelli, or as some think, Bartolommeo della Gatta, which would leave Signorelli unrepresented here. Lacking in a certain dignity and passion, it is but a disappointment whoever may have been the painter.

The decoration of the walls of the chapel is completed by the twenty-eight full-length figures of the Popes, subscribed with the name of each and the years of his reign, painted by many artists, among them Ghirlandajo, Botticelli, and Fra Diamante, between the windows.[1]

---

[1] Ghirlandajo is responsible for Hyginus and Zephyrinus to the left of the altar, and Anacletus, Pius I, Victor I, and Felix to the right, while over the entrance he painted Damasus. To Botticelli are assigned, on the left, Evaristus, Cornelius, and Stephen, and on the right Soter and Sixtus II.

Above these, supported by marvellous and gigantic figures of sibyls, of prophets, of slaves, and athletes, stretches the roof of Michelangelo, that new heaven which is the old earth, beautiful with the life of man, his love which brought disaster and all joy, the wild story of the world, which ends on that vast wall above the altar where he has painted the Last Judgment, or is it the Resurrection ?

This ceiling, so heavy with life that it always seems to crush us under the weight of its tremendous story, was painted for Pope Julius II, between the years 1508 and 1512. Condivi tells us that it was Bramante and other rivals of Michelangelo who suggested to Julius that the great Florentine should paint the vault of the chapel of Sixtus IV in order to distract the Pope from works of sculpture, and because they thought he would either refuse the commission and so anger the Pope, or accepting it, do far less well than Raphael had done in the Stanze.

" Michelangelo," Condivi goes on, " who as yet had never used colours, and knew the painting of the vault to be a very difficult undertaking, tried with all his power to get out of it, proposing Raphael and excusing himself, in that it was not his art and that he would not succeed, refusing so many times that the Pope was almost in a passion. But, seeing his obstinacy, Michelangelo set himself to do the work, which to-day is . . . the admiration and wonder of the world ; it brought him so much fame that it lifted him above all envy. . . . The shape of the ceiling is what is commonly called a barrel vaulting, resting on lunettes, six to the length and two to the width of the building, so that the whole formed two squares and a half. In this space Michelangelo has depicted firstly the Creation of the world, and then almost the whole of the Old Testament. He has divided the work after this fashion : beginning at the brackets, where the horns of the lunettes rest, up to almost a third of the arch of the vault, the walls appear to continue flat, running up to that height with certain pilasters and plinths imitating marble, which project into the open like a balustrade over an additional story, with corbels below, and with other little pilasters above the same story, where sit the prophets and sibyls. The first pilasters grow from the arches of the lunettes, placing the pedestals in the middle, leaving, however, the greater part of the arch of the lunette—that is to say, the space they contain between them. Above the said plinths are painted some little naked children in various poses, who, in guise of terminals, support a cornice, which binds the whole work together, leaving in the middle of the vault, from end to end as it were, the open sky. This opening is divided into nine spaces ; for from the cornices, over the pilasters, spring certain arches with cornices which traverse the highest part of the vault and join the cornice on the opposite side of the chapel, leaving from arch to arch nine openings large and small. In the smaller spaces are two fillets, painted like marble, that cross the opening in such a way that in the middle rest the two parts and one of the bands where medallions are placed, as shall be told in due course ; and this has been done to avoid monotony, which is born of sameness. Now at the head of the chapel, in the first opening which is one of the smaller ones, is seen how the omnipotent God in the heavens, by the movement of His arm, divides light from darkness. In the second space is how He created the two great lights. The Creator is seen with arms extended : with the right He lights the sun, and with the left the moon. With Him are child-angels ; one on the left hides his face against the bosom of his Creator, as though shielding himself from the harmful light of the moon. In the same space on the left God is seen turning to create the trees and plants of the earth, painted with such art that wherever you turn He appears to turn away also, showing the whole of the back down to the soles of His feet—a thing most beautiful, which shows what may be done by foreshortening. In the third space the great God appears in the heavens again with a company of angels, looking upon the waters and commanding them to bring forth all those forms of life nourished in that element, just as in the second He commands the earth. In the fourth is the Creation of Man. God is seen with arm and hand stretched forth as if giving His commandments to Adam, what to do, and what not to do ; with His other arm He draws His angels about Him.[1] In the fifth is how He drew woman from the side of Adam. She comes forth with her hands joined, raising them in prayer towards God, bending with gracious mien and offering thanks as He blesses her. In the sixth is how the

[1] Woman perhaps and her progeny in the fold of His garment. Adam seems reluctant to accept life. How languidly he lifts his finger to touch the hand of the Creator ! Woman, however, in the next picture is all joyful.

devil tempted man. From the middle upwards the wicked
one is of human form, and the rest of him like unto a serpent,
his legs transformed into tails winding around a tree . . .
on the other side of the space the two, Adam and Eve, are
seen driven forth by the angel, terrified and weeping,
flying from the face of God. In the seventh is the sacrifice
of Abel and Cain. . . . In the eighth is the Deluge, when
the ark of Noah is seen in the distance in the midst of the
waters ; some men attempt to cling to it for safety. Nearer
in the same abyss of waters is a boat laden with many people,
which, both by the excessive weight she has to carry and
by the many and tumultuous lashings of the waves, loses her
sail, and, deprived of every aid and human control, she is
already filling with water and going to the bottom. It is
an admirable thing this picture of the human race so
wretchedly perishing in the waves. Likewise, nearer to
the eye, there still appears above the waters the summit of a
mountain, like unto an island, on which, fleeing from the
rising waters, collect a multitude of men and women who
exhibit different expressions, but all wretched and all
terrified, dragging themselves beneath a curtain stretched
over a tree to shelter them from the unusual rains ; and
above them is represented with great art the anger of God,
which overwhelms them with water, with lightnings, and
with thunderbolts. There is also another mountain-top
. . . much nearer the eye, and a multitude labouring under
the same disasters, of which it would be long to write all
the details ; it shall suffice me to say that they are all very
natural and tremendous, just as one would imagine them
in such a convulsion. In the ninth, which is the last, is
the story of Noah when he was drunken with wine, lying
on the ground, his shame derided by his son Ham and
covered by Shem and Japhet.

" Under the before-mentioned cornices which finished
the walls, and above the brackets where the lunettes rest
between pilaster and pilaster, sit twelve great figures—
prophets and sibyls—all truly wonderful as much for
their grace as for the decoration and design of their draperies.
But admirable above all the rest is the prophet Jonah,
placed at the head of the vault, because contrary to the
form of this part of the ceiling by force of light and shade,
the torso, which is foreshortened so that it goes back away
into the roof, is on the part of the arch nearest the eye, and
the feet and legs which, as it were, project within the walls,
are on the part more distant. A stupendous performance,

which shows what marvellous power was in this man of turning lines in foreshortening and perspective.

" Now in the spaces that are below the lunettes, as well as in those above which have a triangular shape, are painted all the genealogy, or should I say all the ancestors, of the Saviour, except in the triangles at the corners which come together, so two make up one of double area. In one then above the wall of the Last Judgment is seen how Aman, by command of King Ahasuerus, was hung upon a cross ; and this was because in his pride and arrogance he wished to hang Mordecai, the uncle of Queen Esther, for not honouring him with a reverence as he passed by. In another corner is the story of the brazen serpent, lifted by Moses on a staff, in which the children of Israel, wounded and ill-treated by lively little serpents, are healed by looking-up. Here Michelangelo has shown admirable force in those figures that are struggling to free themselves from the coils of the serpents. In the third corner, at the lower end of the chapel, is the vengeance wreaked upon Holofernes by Judith, and in the fourth that of David over Goliath.

" These are briefly all the histories. But not less mar-vellous is that part which relates to certain nudes which sit upon plinths above the before-mentioned cornice, one on either side, holding up the medallions which, as has been said, appear to be of metal ; on which in the style of reverses, are designed several stories, all, however, appropriate to their principal histories. . . . But to tell the particulars of these things would be an infinite labour, a book for them alone would not be enough ; therefore I pass them over briefly, wishing rather to give a little light upon the whole than to detail the parts. . . . He finished all this work in twenty months without assistance, not even for the grinding of his colours. It is true that I have heard him say that the work is not finished as he would have wished, as he was prevented by the hurry of the Pope, who demanded of him one day when he would finish the chapel. Michelangelo answered : ' When I can.' The Pope, angered, replied : ' Do you want me to have you thrown off this scaffolding ? ' Michelangelo hearing this said to himself, ' Nay, you shall not have me thrown down,' and as soon as the Pope was gone he had the scaffolding taken down, and uncovered his work upon All Saints' Day. It was seen with great satis-faction by the Pope (who that very day visited the chapel), and all Rome crowded to admire it. It lacked the retouches *a secco* of ultramarine and gold in certain places, which

would have made it appear more rich. Julius, his fervour
having abated, wished that Michelangelo should supply
them ; but he, considering the business it would be to re-
erect the scaffolding, replied that there was nothing important wanting. 'It should be touched with gold,'
replied the Pope. Michelangelo said to him familiarly,
as he had a way of doing with his Holiness : 'I do not see
that men wear gold.' The Pope said again : 'It will seem
poor.' 'Those who are painted here were poor,' Michelangelo replied.

" Michelangelo received for this work and all his ex-
penses three thousand ducats, of which I have heard him
say he spent in colours about twenty or twenty-five."

So far Condivi. But this profound and wonderful vision
of life by no means decorates the chapel of the Popes : it
dwarfs it. The air is so full of shapes that we can see nothing.
In this place, where for centuries the vicegerents of God
have been chosen, Michelangelo has created a multitude of
sublime figures : Adam who so languidly, so reluctantly
touches the outstretched hand of the Creator ; pitiful humanity
and our beautiful world drowned in the bitter unforgivable
flood ; the mighty sibyls bowed under thoughts they dare only
express in mysteries ; the tortured prophets, the sacrificed
messengers of God, the athletes and the slaves. And above all,
overwhelming everything, stands the huge fresco of the Last
Judgment.

> O thou who from Carrara's marble breast
> Hewed those dread forms of slavery and unrest,
> Dark Day, dire Night, and with a brush of fire
> Judgment proclaimed on man and man's desire. . . .

IV. THE STANZE OF RAPHAEL

When, after the brief reign of the successor of Alexander
VI, Julius II mounted the throne of S. Peter, such was his
hatred of the Borgia that he refused to occupy the apartments
that recalled their " unspeakable memory," preferring the
suite of rooms on the first floor of the palace, which Nicholas V,
who built them, had himself used. These rooms had already
in greater part been decorated by Perugino, Sodoma, and

Peruzzi, but Julius, caring nothing for the work of his predecessors, ordered these frescoes to be destroyed, so that they might be painted according to his own wishes by Raphael Sanzio, just then come from Florence, in his twenty-sixth year. It was in 1508 that Raphael began the work, which was not finished till 1517. In these four rooms, in spite of the destruction and vandalism of the sack of 1527, we still have perhaps the most wonderful series of decorations in existence. They were not, however, painted in the order in which we now see them, the Stanza della Segnatura being the first to be completed, then the Stanza d'Eliodoro, third the Stanza dell' Incendio, and fourth the Sala di Constantino.

In the Stanza della Segnatura, begun in 1508 and finished in 1511, the arabesques on the ceiling are all that remain of Sodoma's work here ; the design is still his, but the figures in those four circular frames on a gold ground of mosaic— Theology, Philosophy, Justice, and Poetry, and the four square panels, Adam and Eve in the garden, a figure representing Astronomy, the Judgment of Solomon, and Apollo and Marsyas—are from the hand of Raphael. Under the medallions on each of the four walls is a scene, as it were, illustrating it. Thus the crowned fair figure of Theology points with her right hand to the famous " Disputa," which is painted on the wall beneath.

This picture, one of the most subtle and beautiful pieces of decoration in the world, has been called the " Disputa," the discussion or debate. It is an allegory, as it were, of Theology, even as the so-called " School of Athens " opposite is an allegory of Philosophy.

" There," Vasari tells us, " the master has depicted heaven, with Christ and the Blessed Virgin, S. Giovanni Battista, the Apostles, the Evangelists and the Martyrs, all enthroned amid the clouds ; and above them is the figure of God the Father, who sends forth His Holy Spirit over them all, but more particularly on a vast company of Saints who are celebrating Mass below, and some of whom are discoursing concerning the Host which is on the altar.[1] Among these are the four Doctors of the Church

[1] The Host, as the symbol and summit of the Catholic Faith, is naturally the centre to which every line leads, to which every thought tends.

(to wit, SS. Jerome, Augustine, Ambrose, and Gregory the Great), who are surrounded by numerous Saints, S. Domenico, namely, with S. Francesco, S. Thomas Aquinas, S. Bonaventura, Duns Scotus, and Nicolaus of Lyra. Dante, Savonarola,[1] and all the Christian theologians are also depicted, with a vast number of portraits from life. In the air above are four children who are holding open the Four Gospels ; these are figures which it would not be possible for any painter to surpass, such is their grace and perfection."

Yes, Raphael has shown us there every form of belief, the most ecstatic with the most cold, the most spontaneous love and faith beside the most long-sought-out ; S. Francis sits there with S. Thomas ; S. Augustine with Duns Scotus. But who are these two fair young men who stand on either side in the foreground, but indeed without the assembly? They look like philosophers : can it be then that, eager to give everything its due, Raphael has thought to express in those two delightful figures the fascinating doubt of his age ? Who can say ? Certainly one could wish to follow them a little way from the logic of the doctors to speak with them of the life of man and the beauty of the world.

It might seem to be just that which is being discussed by the two great philosophers, of whom one was a poet, in the " School of Athens." There we see Plato and Aristotle engaged as it were in argument, in discussion certainly, amid a crowd of attentive listeners. Close by, Socrates passes with his own group of disciples. One can see he is still asking those favourite questions of his, so exasperating and bewildering, as he counts off his premises on his fingers, true wisdom perhaps lying on the steps in great content all the time, close beside that little eager company, in the person of Diogenes, " who had no needs." An older man writing busily, with a tablet before him on which is inscribed the musical scale, may well be Pythagoras ; while not far away we see the astronomers Ptolemy and Zoroaster, and Euclid the measurer.

But, after all, what strikes us most in this picture dealing

[1] Dante is there for that he was a theologian, almost as much as he was a poet ; but Savonarola appears because he was the enemy of the man Julius hated, Alexander VI.

so easily and surely with the greatest matters, is its value as just a picture, its decorative value, that is, its marvellously lovely expression, not of any profound or subtle thought but of its own element, a certain spaciousness, confined, as we perceive at last, within very narrow material limits, but that seems infinite. It is the very triumph of decorative art, come at last to perfection in one who had been the pupil of Pietro Perugino. The difficulty of such an achievement, greater here by far than in the " Disputa," for there all heaven lay open to our eyes, is scarcely felt till, in an effort to understand what is really consummate in the art of Raphael—and no man has been praised so much for the wrong things—we perceive here his real triumph. That palace or temple, all of earth, full of the measured beauty of the work of man, is not less infinite in its spaciousness after all than the whole circuit of the world, the limitless kingdom, light on light, of the sky. And this is the real triumph of Raphael, not that he has summed up the ancient and the mediaeval world and expressed them in the terms of the Renaissance, but that into that narrow, cramped room he has brought an infinite beauty. How awkward were those spaces he had to fill we realise best of all, perhaps, in the " Parnassus," where the astonishment of his victory recalls the difficulty he had to overcome. That window which so inopportunely, as one might think, breaks into the symmetry of the semicircle he had to fill became in his hands the opportunity of his triumph. Above it he drew a hill, yes, Parnassus itself, obtaining thus two small foregrounds below and a somewhat wider plane above. There in the height, under the laurels, Apollo is seated among the Muses, Homer too, and Virgil with Dante, whom he led not alone through the mazes of Hell and Purgatory. Apollo, caught in the ecstasy of his own music, is playing on a violin, looking upward in rapture, and his music inspires Homer to sing as he too gazes, but with sightless eyes, into the heaven whence comes this mystery. Beneath are the mortals, Sappho, Pindar, Virgil and Horace, Dante and Petrarch, and the rest.

If the " Parnassus " shows less beauty of space than the " Disputa " or the " School of Athens," it is not surprising,

the miracle being that it is what it is. The figures, however, are less splendid than the composition : the Muses, for
instance, being but mere lifeless imitations of antiques, the
" Ariadne " of the Vatican, the " Suppliant Woman," and
such. In looking on these figures one thinks regretfully of
Botticelli's beautiful group in the " Primavera." As for the
Sappho, it is as though here Raphael had thought to compete
with Michelangelo, and had only contrived to prove his in-
feriority to that master, in the creation of life certainly ; this
unfortunate figure is a sort of caricature of the sibyls of the
Sistine Chapel. The decoration of the room was completed by the symbolical figures of Fortitude, Prudence, and
Temperance on the opposite wall, which fail to rouse our
enthusiasm, and by the two scenes from the history of
Jurisprudence there, the delivery of the secular and ecclesiastical codes, with which his work in this room came to an
end.

In the Camera d'Eliodoro, Peruzzi worked on Raphael's
designs. Far less decoratively lovely than the work in the
Sala della Segnatura, the paintings here are more imposing,
more plastic in effect, more realistic in their illusion. Their
subject resolves itself into the Triumph of the Church. Under
certain scenes from the Old Testament, " God's Warning to
Noah," the " Sacrifice of Isaac," " Jacob's Vision," " Moses
before the Burning Bush," the work of Peruzzi, Raphael has
painted four frescoes, the " Expulsion of Heliodorus from the
Temple," the " Mass of Bolsena," " Attila repulsed from Rome
by Leo the Great," and the " Liberation of S. Peter," in allusion to the triumphs of Julius II over his enemies. The
Expulsion of Heliodorus from the temple is told in the second
book of the Machabees. For it seems that Seleucus, King of
Asia, hearing from one Simon, of the tribe of Benjamin, who
had fallen out with the high-priest about disorder in the city,
whispered to the friends of Seleucus how that the treasury in
Jerusalem was full of infinite sums of money, and that it was
possible to bring all to the king's hand. And the king chose
out Heliodorus his treasurer, and sent him to bring the money.
So Heliodorus came to Jerusalem, and, courteously received by
the high-priest, told him why he had come and the whole

truth. And the high-priest answered that there was such money laid up for the relief of widows and fatherless children. But Heliodorus answered again that it must be brought into the king's treasury. And the high-priest, white with fear, prayed before the altar, and the whole city was consumed with terror. Nevertheless Heliodorus executed that which was decreed. " Now as he there presented himself with his guard about the treasury, the Lord of Spirits and the Prince of all power caused a great apparition, so that all that presumed to come in with him were astonished at the power of God and fainted and were sore afraid. For there appeared unto them an horse with a terrible rider upon him, adorned with a very fair covering, and he ran fiercely and smote Heliodorus with his forefeet, and it seemed that he that sat upon the horse had complete harness of gold. Moreover, two other young men appeared before him, notable in strength, excellent in beauty, and comely in apparel, who stood by him on either side and scourged him continually, and gave him many sore stripes. And Heliodorus fell suddenly unto the ground, and was compassed with great darkness. . . ."

Such is the story. And Raphael, with that extraordinary talent of his for gathering a multitude of various things into unity, into himself chiefly, has combined here the different incidents of that story into a single picture, not as the old painters might have done, by a series of scenes only held together by the frame, but in a real and essential unity that violates neither time nor place. He shows us Heliodorus leaving the Temple laden with spoil, we see there the women and children—that fine touch in the story, " the women, girt with sackcloth under their breasts, abounded in the streets, and the virgins that were kept in, ran some to the gates, some to the walls, and others looked out of the windows ; and all holding their hands toward heaven, made supplication "—rushing through the streets, witnesses of the divine interposition, the sudden advent of that glorious rider, terrible and beautiful as the lightning, the prostrate Heliodorus, smitten in an instant, calm though fallen, unhurt as yet, about to be trampled underfoot, the youths rushing forward to strike him with their rods.

In the "Miracle of Bolsena,"[1] where a doubting priest celebrating Mass finds the Host stained with blood, we have a composition not less original certainly than the "Expulsion of Heliodorus." The effective drama that in the hands, perhaps, of an earlier, and certainly of a later painter would have expressed itself in the astonishment of the incredulous priest, is found here in the gesture of the crowd. The central figure is motionless, turned to stone, as it were, really afraid with amazement. But in the crowd we see a marvellous crescendo of astonishment, of ecstasy. It passes over the nearer group of choristers like a wind over a field of tulips, their bodies sway in an almost involuntary adoration. On the steps of the altar people are pressing and crushing one another in a terrible excitement which reaches its climax in that figure in the foregound, the woman who, suddenly aware, has leapt up, and with a marvellous gesture of adoration strains forward in an ecstasy of worship, herself an absolute expression of passionate faith. The priest so breathlessly kneeling there is seen in perfect profile, and opposite, on the other side of the altar, as it were, facing him, in profile too, kneels the Pope, Julius II, as he had ordered, cold and unastonished at the sudden revelation of a truth he had known from the beginning. It is a marvellous portrait, and only less splendid is that group of Cardinals in the background.

Opposite the "Miracle of Bolsena" Raphael and his pupils painted the frescoes of the "Deliverance of S. Peter." In the midst we see the Apostle roused by the angel between his sleeping guards in prison ; on the one side, still as it were in a dream, he is led by the angel back into the world ; on the other the watch is roused when his escape is known. This fresco, like that beside it, "Attila repulsed from Rome by Leo the Great," which is in part from Raphael's hand, celebrates the retreat of the French from Italy after the battle of Ravenna in 1512.

The last work in these rooms was the "Burning of the Borgo," in the room which bears its name, Sala dell' Incendio. It seems to lack a certain unity, and indeed is mostly the work of Giulio Romano.

[1] Dates 1511-14 ; by Raphael himself.

We return again and again only to the Stanza della Segnatura, which with his portraits, and a few wonderful easel pictures offer us the explanation why Raphael's name has for so long been the most famous and the most beloved in modern art.   There at least he has achieved the calm perfection which we attribute to the classical age, of which, indeed, he is the somewhat fragile representative—a god born out of due time, who could never grow up or grow old.   For even as his work has something of the perfection of the antique, its correctness and ideality, so in his own body he was beautiful and delicate.   Without the great nervous strength of so profound, so subtle a personality as Leonardo, or the immense physical virtue of Michelangelo, he died at thirty-seven years of age.   And he seems to have absorbed in so short a time, all, or almost all, that was best in his contemporaries, and to have added to it something of the serenity, the quiet delight in beautiful things for their own sake, that were so conspicuously his own.   It is as a scholar among masters we see him, content even to the end of his life to learn and to absorb everything that was fair, with which he came in contact ;   not the art of painting alone, but the scholarship, the philosophy, the history, the poetry of his day, its interpretation of the classics also, transforming them into his own terms, and finding in them the serenity and beauty of his own nature.   The giant energy, the tragic rebellion of Michelangelo were impossible for him.

Of all that imperious, lawless, and splendid age, Raphael is the saviour.   The presence of his nature is like a fair soft light over everything, or like a perfect flower in the midst of a battlefield.   Rather than any saint, or soldier, or philosopher, or man of genius, he serves as the type of the Renaissance at its highest ;   and his acquiescence—if we may so call it—is nothing more than the failure of all art to express, to do more than shadow forth that perfect state which Plato has seen lying in the heavens, which S. Paul has assured us is there eternal.

V. THE PINACOTECA

We come upon Raphael's work again in the small gallery of pictures, the nucleus of which the British Government presented to Pius VII, after the defeat of Napoleon and the occupation

of Paris in 1815. By the efforts of the Duke of Welling-
ton and Lord Castlereagh, the French were forced to return
the loot of the Italian campaigns, but time pressing, Canova
was given only ten days to collect it in Paris. The consequence was that of all the pictures stolen in the wars and
distributed among the French cities, since the Louvre could
not contain them, Canova found only some seventy-seven in
the short time at his disposal ; these, however, were among
the most precious works in existence. They were dispatched
across the Alps to Rome at the expense of the British Government,[1] and should have been redistributed to their owners.
Pius VII, however, deprived Perugia not only of the picture
that was in Lyons, which Canova could not obtain and which
the Pope presently gave the people of that city leave to keep,
but of the two pictures by Perugino which were returned and
which are now in this gallery. Cesarei, the patriotic *gon-
faloniere* of Perugia, wrote time after time to Rome to deliver
the works which England had returned not to the Pope, but
to Italy. For a time he got no answer. Then at last in
October 1817 Cardinal Consalvi wrote to say that " the allied
powers " had presented all the pictures " to the Sovereign
Pontiff as Head of the Pontifical States from which they had
been stolen." In consequence of this, and for the benefit
of students, the Pope proposed to keep the pictures. Thus
Pius VII set a precedent which the kingdom of Italy has
followed, to the enormous loss of the Holy See.

Though all the Italian schools of painting are represented
in the Pinacoteca of the Vatican thus so strangely founded, it
takes its rank among the great collections of the world rather
by reason of its quality than its extent. Of the chief Tuscan
school, the school of Florence, it possesses a considerable number of works of the fourteenth century including some very
beautiful predella panels by Daddi. Of the fifteenth century
it boasts works by Fra Angelico, Lorenzo Monaco, and Fra
Filippo Lippi—a Coronation of the Blessed Virgin, the Angels
being from the hand of Fra Diamante.

The Madonna and Child, by Fra Angelico, is a small picture

[1] The British Government spent some £30,000 in the affair ; the rest of the
allies contributing nothing.

on a gold ground, in which the Virgin, with our Lord in her
lap, sits enthroned between S. Catherine and S. Dominic.
In her hand she holds a white rose set with thorns, and about
her is a company of angels, flowers of Paradise, one may think,
gathered about the Rosa Mystica.

The two *predelle* originally formed part of the altarpiece
now in the Perugia gallery which Fra Angelico painted for
the chapel of S. Niccolò dei Guidalotti in the church of S.
Domenico there.   In the first panel we see the birth of S.
Niccolò, who, on the day he was born, stood up as they washed
him and praised God.   Later we see him listening to a sermon
in a meadow sprinkled with flowers ; and again he secretly
drops three bags of gold into the house of the poor nobleman
whose three fair daughters could not marry because they were
portionless.   In the second panel we see the saint during a
great famine bidding certain sailors unload the corn with which
their ships were laden for the relief of the starving city, promising that on their arrival in Byzantium, whither they were
bound, they should have suffered no loss.   In these lovely
works of the early fifteenth century we seem to have returned
how far on our way to the simplicity and beauty that too soon
were to pass into the self-conscious loveliness of the high
Renaissance.

The most subtle master, the most rare Leonardo himself, is
represented here by an unfinished picture of S. Jerome.   It
was bought by Pius IX from Cardinal Fesch, who had the good
fortune to find part of it in a heap of rubbish.   Not much later
the same Cardinal, by a sort of miracle, found the other part
in a cobbler's shop, where it served as a covering for the bench.
Looking on this S. Jerome to-day we see, what Leonardo above
all so well understood, how the soul may wear out the body,
as a sword will wear out its scabbard.   Alone in the desert, in
the shadow of those fantastic rocks, the saint has literally
lost himself in God, and is already become a part of the universal, from which for a moment the body had sought to
isolate him.   The shadow will creep away at noon and the
sun will pour down upon him, midday will pass into the
languor of afternoon, into evening, into the coldness and
silence of night, but dawn when it comes in all its tragic

beauty will find him still as it were in the arms of the Eternal, for God only fills his eyes, and for him there is no other pleasure or loveliness. In that terrible embrace his body has become, as it were, a mere shadow, an appearance confronted at last by reality.

The Umbrian School is very well represented here in the work of Niccolò da Foligno, of Melozzo da Forlì, Gentile da Fabriano, of Perugino, Pinturicchio, Lo Spagna, and Raphael.

The great altarpiece of the " Coronation of the Virgin " by Niccolò da Foligno, in which some sixty-three saints take part in the great ceremony amid a host of angels, is one of the most splendid of his strange and melancholy works. In the midst is the Virgin, like a lily bent before the dawn, crowned by the Day-Spring heralded by a galaxy of angels. Above we see a vision of Christ crucified reigning on that cruel throne we gave Him. In the pinnacles are certain bishops, and below cherubim and half figures of saints. On the left is the Blessed Virgin, then S. Catherine of Alexandria and S. Agata. On the right are S. John the divine, S. Mary Magdalen, and S. Reparata of Florence. Below are two rows of saints, among them S. George, S. Ambrose, and S. Augustine, S. John Baptist, S. Paul, and S. Sebastian. Then in the lower part of the picture we see the twelve Apostles, and beside them the first two martyrs, S. Stephen and S. Laurence ; while a host of virgins seems to wait on the Madonna.

Besides this magnificent work Niccolò has here a triptych of the Crucifixion, with S. Mary Magdalen at the foot of the Cross, and in the side panels certain saints, while in the medallions above we see David and Isaiah.

Perugino's work, after that of Niccolò da Foligno, seems altogether joyful. He was about fifty years old when he painted the " Enthroned Madonna " of the Vatican. His life had been a continual wandering. Famous throughout Italy he had painted in the Sistine Chapel as well as in Florence and Northern Italy. Alien though he was from the tradition of Florence as from the material glory and splendour of Rome, and assuredly with but little in common with the painting of Venice just then about to dawn on the world, he had yet entranced these divers cities by the beauty of such dreams as this—those mystical and quiet visions that came to him down the valleys of Umbria. Painted for the Cappella dei Priori of Perugia, it was finished about 1496. There seems to have been some trouble about the decoration of this chapel owing to the vanity of the magistrates, who, during their term of office, had employed a certain Pietro di Maestro Galeotto to paint a picture of the Madonna and Child, with their portraits as donors. This the artist failed to accomplish, and the Priori turned to Perugino, in November 1483, making an agreement with him to paint the picture in about four months for a hundred florins. But Perugino was called to Rome in December of that year, and therefore failed to carry out his commission. Coming to Perugia again in 1495, he found the chapel still without its picture, and he then entered into another agreement with the Priori to paint the altarpiece, but for a higher sum. This is one of the pictures which Pius VII did not return to the Perugians. Under a great baldacchino the Madonna sits enthroned, the Jesus Parvulus standing on her knees ; beneath, round about the throne in the manner that Raphael was to use later for the Ansidei Madonna, now in the National Gallery, four saints stand intent on some service of adoration. Perugino has signed the picture : *Hoc Petrus de Chastro Plebis Pinxit.*

The panel in which we see three saints—SS. Placida, Flavia, and Benedict—is part of a picture of the Ascension which Napoleon stole from the church of S. Pietro dei Cassinesi, in Perugia, and which is now in Lyons. This also the Perugians claimed, in vain, as we see. But mark how Time brings about his revenges ; in 1860 the church of S. Pietro in Cassinese in Perugia was alone permitted to retain its works of art because it had befriended the army of Victor Emmanuel.

The last work given here to Perugino is the "Resurrection," which originally came from the church of S. Francesco in Perugia. Vasari gives it to Pietro, but Crowe and Cavalcaselle think it to be an early work by Raphael, while Morelli gives it wholly to Lo Spagna : Mr. Berenson, however, agrees with Vasari, adding that it is a late work of the master. In a lovely and wide landscape such as Perugino knew and loved so well stands the tomb, a work of the Renaissance, three soldiers sleeping about it while one is awake. Over the tomb in a mandorla of light the risen Christ hovers, while an angel bows in adoration on either side. If this indeed be the work of Perugino, it must have been painted in his last years, when he had lost grip on his art. It is certainly not the youthful work of Raphael.

Pinturicchio, whose work is at its best in Rome, is represented here by a fine picture of the " Coronation of the Blessed Virgin." Above in heaven our Lord, between two seraphs playing musical instruments, crowns Madonna the Queen of Angels, while below in the world kneels S. Francis of Assisi, a cross of gold in his hand, amid the twelve Apostles, gazing upwards at the wonder in the sky ; S. Louis of Toulouse and S. Anthony of Padua kneel on the right, while to the left are S. Bonaventura and S. Bernardino of Siena. Originally painted for the nuns of La Fratta at Umbertide, only the upper part seems indeed to be from the hand of Pinturicchio, the rest being the work of pupils.

Another Umbrian, Melozzo da Forlì, is represented here by one of the most splendid portrait groups of the Renaissance. For long assigned to his master, Piero della Francesca, this fresco, for it is a fresco transferred to canvas, was painted to celebrate the restoration of the Vatican library by Sixtus IV ; Platina having been appointed as librarian of the great collections Nicholas V and Sixtus IV had formed there. It is apparent that Sixtus, Platina, two attendant Cardinals, and a couple of inferior persons are portrayed from life in the library itself, whose square pillars and panelled ceilings with their ornament, are drawn with a precision of perspective the which Melozzo learnt in the school of the great painter of Borgo San Sepolcro. The Pope sits on the right in a great chair, his hands clasping the terminal balls of its arms. To the left stand the two Cardinals, Pietro Riario, his profligate son, created Cardinal in his twenty-sixth year, and Giuliano della Rovere, later Pope Julius II. Platina, the librarian, the historian of the Popes, kneels before Sixtus, and behind him stand two attendants.

From this marvellous and realistic work one passes to the pictures of Raphael, those three great pieces with the two little

predelle which have made the fame of the gallery. The
" Coronation of the Blessed Virgin " dates from 1503 as do
the *predelle* of the Annunciation, Adoration of the Magi
and Presentation in the Temple, which belong to it. The
monochrome " Faith, Hope and Charity " is of 1507. The
" Madonna di Foligno " with Sigismondo Conti as donor was
painted in 1511–12 and the famous " Transfiguration " is of
1519–20, the lower part being from the hand of Giulio Romano.
What can one say of these pictures save that they are Raphael's?

The Sienese are very numerously represented here. Though
there is nothing by Duccio, there is a panel of Christ Blessing
by Simone Martini, the most exquisite Sienese master of the
fourteenth century, and a Crucifixion with six saints below by
his follower Barna. A beautiful small panel of " Christ before
Pilate " is from the hand of that great master Pietro Lorenzetti.
By Taddeo di Bartolo we find two panels of the Dormition and
Assumption of the Blessed Virgin.

Of the fifteenth century Sienese we find here a panel by
Sassetta of S. Thomas Aquinas praying before a Crucifix,
a predella panel from his first altarpiece (1423–6).

There are also here many predella panels by Sano di
Pietro, who is always at his best in these small works ; and a
panel by Vecchietta of the miracles of some Saint.

Of the other schools of Italy represented in the Vatican
gallery the most important is the Venetian. Carlo Crivelli
has at least one picture here a " Pietà " full of an almost
gorgeous distress, while the S. Bernardino which is attributed
to him is a curious and even fascinating work of his school.
The " Portrait of a Doge," is said to be a copy by Titian of a
work by Bellini, but Titian is represented by a signed canvas
of the Madonna in glory with six saints, an altarpiece painted for
the Cappella di S. Niccolò in the cloister of the Frari Church
in Venice. Painted about 1523, in the eighteenth century
it was in the Quirinal Palace, and Northcote tells us that the
picture was then cut into two parts. Even now something is
missing, for the topmost part with the dove is gone.

The other Venetian paintings here consist of a " S. George
and the Dragon " by Paris Bordone, a " Madonna and Saints "
by Bonifazio Veneziano, " S. Helena," ascribed to Veronese,

but more probably the work of a pupil, and a " Pietà " which seems to be from the hand of Bartolommeo Montagna.

Among the other pictures here is the only example in Rome of the work of Moretto, a " Madonna and Child," so injured that it can scarcely be reckoned among his works, while the naturalistic school is well represented by the famous masterpiece of Domenichino, the " Communion of S. Jerome," and by Caravaggio in the wonderful but not pleasing " Deposition," one of the most important and profound works of that school.

Among the few foreign pictures here, some Murillos, a Poussin, some Dutchmen, the brilliant full length portrait of King George IV by Lawrence is an unexpected and a delightful codicil to this recently brought together and newly housed collection.

XXV

CASTEL SANT' ANGELO

THE mausoleum of Hadrian, the fortress and prison of the Popes, is the chief stronghold too of modern Rome.
Built by Hadrian about 135 for his own tomb, it served as the Imperial sepulchre till the time of Septimius Severus, and enormous as is the present castle, two hundred and twenty feet in diameter, and more than seventy feet high, it is little more than the stump of the Mausoleum, which stood on a great square platform of stone, each side a hundred yards long, covered from base to summit in Parian marble, surrounded on the four sides by pilasters which upheld two galleries one above the other, supported by two rings of columns, between which were set an immense number of statues, while the whole was crowned by a pyramid capped by a huge fir-cone of bronze or marble. Such was the sepulchre which Hadrian built, perhaps in envy of hushed Egypt, and certainly to the despite of " great Augustus."

It was Aurelian who, in the end of the third century, first turned that lonely tomb into a fortress, using it as a bastion for the bridge in his great defence of the City. Thus, what had been the wonder of the world for something less than a hundred years in some sort became the citadel, the prize at which every besieger was to aim, the key, as it were, of the City.

In 410 it was pillaged by Alaric, who seems to have done little damage after all, for about a hundred years later Procopius gives us a description of it, in which we see that certainly till 530 it must have been much as it always had been. " The tomb of the Roman Emperor," he said, " is outside the Porta Aurelia, distant from the wall about a bow-shot, a memorable sight. For it is made of Parian marble, and the stones fit closely one into another without fastening. It has four equal sides, each about a stone's-throw in length, and in height overtopping the walls of the City. Above these are placed statues of men and horses made out of the same stone, marvellous to behold." That was written before the gallant defence of Belisarius against Vitiges, the Goth, in 530. That siege, as we know, came to an end before the great fortress, when, thinking to take it by surprise, the Goths crept up under cover of the colonnade that then joined S. Peter's to the Castle. Their catapults, that tremendous artillery, were, it seems, useless, and the enormous size of the fortress made it difficult for them to know what was happening either within or behind it. Swiftly and silently they gathered under the walls and rushed to the assault, when in despair the defenders, without other ammunition and at the point of starvation, suddenly thought of the statues, and immediately tearing them down hurled them on the Goths, hundreds of whom were crushed under their weight. There, mingled with the dying, the most precious works of art were hacked to pieces by the kicking horses, the maddening soldiery, and the stones which followed them. So by a stratagem which, as has been said, Polyphemus might have used against Ulysses, the Mausoleum of Hadrian was destroyed.

The ruin got its name of Sant' Angelo, which it has borne ever since, in the time of S. Gregory, who, with Rome on his hands half destroyed by pestilence, used to assemble the people at dawn and lead them to S. Peter's singing *Kyrie Eleison*. " Now because the mortality ceased not," says Voragine in *The Golden Legend*, " S. Gregory ordained a procession in which he did bear an image of Our Lady, which, as is said, S. Luke the Evangelist made which was a good painter ; he carved it and painted it after the likeness of the most glorious Virgin Mary. And anon the mortality ceased, and the air became pure and clear, and about the image was heard a voice of angels that sang this anthem, *Regina Coeli Laetare*. And at the same time S. Gregory saw an angel upon a castle which made clean a sword all bloody and put it into the sheath, and thereby S. Gregory understood that the pestilence of this mortality was passed, and after it was called the Castle Angel."

Three hundred years go by, and Castel Sant' Angelo had become a prison, and then like a sign in heaven, coming no man knows whence, the new Messalina appeared in the awful years that began the tenth century, Theodora, in all but name Queen of Rome. She made the castle her palace, and reigned there with her daughter for nearly forty years. Beautiful, ambitious, and relentless, Theodora had married one of the noblest personages in Rome, Theophylactus the Senator and Consul. The mistress of the Marquis of Tuscany, with the help of her lover and her husband the City passed into her hands. Caught by the beauty of a young priest at Ravenna, she made him Pope John X, so that he might be near her, and, as Liutprand says, " that she might enjoy him more easily." Already she had given Marozia her daughter as a virgin to Pope Sergius III, who had wished to exhume the body of Formosus that he might submit the cadaver to the censure of a synod. By this monster Marozia conceived a son whom she was to make Pope. Thrice married, each time more advantageously, to the Duke of Spoleto, the Duke of Tuscany, the King of Italy, she dreamed of the Empire. In 928 her husband, Guy of Tuscany, at her bidding strangled Pope John X, her mother's creature, in Sant' Angelo, and in his place she set up Leo VI, whom she deposed presently because she feared him. Stephen VIII replaced him, but he died of poison after a reign of a year and eight months. At the election which followed she seemed to have the world in her grasp, for she elected her own bastard by Sergius III, Pope John XI. In the event, however, she was deceived. John XI and his younger brother Alberic conspired together, and deserted by all, she was imprisoned in a convent, where she died.

That family, only evil continually, as Liutprand assures us, has been compared both with the Atreides and with the Borgia, but Sant' Angelo can show other crimes as great as theirs, though not so famous. In those dungeons Stefano Porcari died, and Oddo Colonna, the victim of that assassin, Sixtus IV, whose most inveterate foes were of that house of which he said, " he cared not whom the Colonna served." They took him at his word.

An " ungovernable liking for discord " seems to have been the chief characteristic of Sixtus IV, who sought to kill Lorenzo and Giuliano de' Medici at the altar in the moment of the elevation. When he was forced to make peace with Naples, he still kept Ferrante's allies, Cardinals Colonna and Savelli, in prison, and it was not till the end of the year that he released them. The Colonna knew him, and when Orsini was made Cardinal on the same day that they got justice, they but waited for the return of the protonotary Oddo to act. He entered Rome on April 28, 1484, and the Orsini flew to arms. Then the magistrates appealed to the Pope to save them from civil war. Sixtus sent for Oddo, who, knowing the Pope, sent his excuses in return. Again the Pope summoned him, and he was about to obey, was, indeed, already mounted, when his friends prevented him, dragging him by force back to his palace. Then Sixtus declared him guilty of treason and ordered him to be taken. The Orsini stormed the Colonna palace and sacked it ; then Oddo, to prevent further slaughter, surrendered to Virginio Orsini, who carried him to the Pope, but scarcely, for Count Girolamo Riario tried thrice to stab him on the way : but Orsini had passed his word.

Sixtus imprisoned him in Sant' Angelo. There they tortured him, slowly dragging him to pieces, calling in now and then a Jewish doctor to keep him alive that they might torture him again. Then, lest indeed he should die, they prepared to kill him. " On the last day of June," says Infessura, who loved him, " about an hour and a half after sunrise, the Holiness of our Sovereign Lord caused the protonotary Colonna to be beheaded in Sant' Angelo. . . . Now when he was brought forth out of prison early to the cage above the castle, he turned to the soldiers about him and said that he had been grievously tortured, and for that cause he had said things untrue. . . . He would not let them bind his hands, but he knelt down quietly at the block, and forgave the executioner, who asked his pardon. He called thrice on Christ, and at the third time that word and his head were severed together from his body. Then they put the body in an open coffin and carried it to S. Maria Transpontina. And presently, though none beside dare come to take it away, his mother came, and she took her son's head from the coffin and held it up to the people, saying, ' Behold the justice of Sixtus.' . . . So they took him away at

length to SS. Apostoli and buried him in the Chapel of the
Colonna there.   But all saw first the torments which he had
suffered, in his feet which were bound with rags, in his fingers,
which were turned quite about, and his head, where the scalp
had been raised as with a great knife.   And they had dressed
him up like a zany to insult him withal.   I, Stephen, saw it
with my eyes, and I, with Prosper Cicigliano, who had been
his vassal, buried him. . . ."

As for the Borgia, they seem to haunt Castel Sant' Angelo
even yet.   One meets them everywhere.   Alexander VI
restored the place by the hands of Antonio Sangallo.   It was
their great fortress, and of all those he held for good or evil
Cesare held this longest.   It was not before their need that they
restored the place and built the subterranean way into it
from the Vatican.   Charles VIII was on the Via Francigena,
and presently in Rome.   Then on January 7, 1495, Alexander
VI fled by the secret way into the fortress.   Meanwhile
Charles was besieged by the enemies of the Borgia, who
begged him to depose the Pope, but he seemed, and rightly, to
doubt his fitness to denounce any one at all.   Mad, a profligate
and a fool, Charles was, though he knew it not, at the mercy
of the irrefutable Pope.   " Alexander has his detractors,"
replied that great incorrigible man by the mouth of Cesare
Carojal and Riario, " yes, he has his detractors, but he knows
that Jesus too was accused as a winebibber and a friend of
publicans and sinners.   And then at least he is not a hypocrite.
. . ."   Which last was but the truth.   Charles, had he been
capable of judging any one, should have remembered he was a
man of action.   To use against the Pope the irregularities of his
private life was, the Italians thought, " a low trick."   Alexander's personal morality had nothing to do with politics.   So
they spoke of politics.   There in Sant' Angelo they had
been wise enough to think of little else.   Twice the French
artillery was trained on the castle, where a piece of the wall had
fallen on the day Charles had entered Rome ; twice it was
withdrawn, and then at last, on January 11, terms of peace
were arranged, Charles withdrew his demand for Sant'
Angelo, and was permitted to conquer Naples, where he and
his host were overwhelmed by an immortal pestilence.

Alexander VI kept Sant' Angelo, it might seem, that there he might hide himself both from God and man. It was on the morrow of the murder of the Duke of Gandia that he took refuge there, perhaps most of all from himself.

The Duke, Alexander's elder son, was murdered, it seems, near the house of Antonio della Mirandola, who had a daughter famous for her beauty. He had been to sup with his mother, Vanozza, at whose palace a large party had assembled, among whom were Cesare and Giovanni Borgia. It was dark when the Duke of Gandia and Cesare mounted and left with a small company of servants. At the Palazzo Cesarini, where Cardinal Sforza lived, the Duke bade his brother farewell, pleading private business. Dismissing all his servants save one, he followed a mask who had frequently visited him at the Vatican and who had already spoken with him that night at supper. He went towards Piazza Giudea, and there bade his servant await him. Then taking the masked figure up behind him on his mule he rode away. He was seen alive no more. The servant was suddenly attacked by armed men, and hardly escaped with his life. The rest is the story of the Slavonian woodseller who traded on the Ripetta near the Ospedale degli Schiavoni. He said that to protect his cargo which he had just unladen he was sleeping in his boat moored to the bank when he was awakened. He saw two men—it was about one o'clock—approach cautiously from the street on the left of the Ospedale. They went away and returned with two others : who presently signed to a rider on a white horse, who bore behind him, slung across the horse, a corpse, held in place by two others on foot. They went to the place where refuse was thrown into the Tiber, and there the two men seized the corpse and flung it into the water. When the rider asked if it had sunk, they answered, " Si, signore " ; but he, looking again, saw the mantle floating there, and one of the men pelted it with stones till it sank. Then all went away.

Two days later the Duke of Gandia's body was discovered with the throat cut and eight other wounds. He was dressed as usual, and in his pocket was his purse, in which were thirty ducats. The body, which was found below the city, was placed on a barge and taken to Sant' Angelo.

From a window there the Pope watched the procession at midnight, which, under the torches, bore the body of his elder son to S. Maria del Popolo for burial. According to custom, the cadaver was exposed without coffin, the face visible to all. As the torch-light fell on the face—the procession being about to cross the bridge—the Pope came face to face with his son. It seemed to him that he saw the scene of the murder ; he knew the culprit : " I know who did it," he exclaimed in his anguish, weeping for the first time, and veiling his head he gave himself up to his agony in silence.

Was Cesare the murderer ? *In ogni modo si crede sia stato gran maestro.* The charge was not brought against him till nearly nine months later, and it rests rather upon the fear his name came to inspire, on the suspicions of the suspected Orsini, Ascanio Sforza, and Mirandola, as well as of him who was afterwards Julius II. Guicciardini and Machiavelli, however, assert that it was Cesare's deed ; and his victims here in Sant' Angelo might seem to bear witness against him, Astorre Manfredi, the beautiful and glorious hero of Faenza, whom he cast into the Tiber bound hand and foot, Cardinal Orsini, who was so swiftly driven mad by poison and murdered : but in fact there is no answer possible to-day.

As for Pope Alexander VI, Borgia, was he the monster tradition will have it he was ?

Rodrigo Borgia was over sixty when he became Pope Alexander VI. Yet he is accused, though of late years more and more *sotto voce*, of the most exhausting, as well as the most perverse vices, of poisoning his cardinals for gain, of debauching his own bastards, and finally of dying by the poison he and Cesare had prepared for another. But, not one of these crimes, accepted without question for centuries, can be proved, and it is even a matter of grave doubt whether the children attributed to him were really his.

We know Rodrigo Borgia to have been a man of much charm, a hard worker, very abstemious in food and drink, and, according to Pius II, " a model of earnestness and modesty ". Pope Calixtus, his uncle, made him Cardinal in 1456, and in the following year, at the age of twenty-five, Vice-Chancellor ; that is, head of the Papal internal organization and second in dignity only to the Pope himself ; and he held this office through the reigns of four succeeding Popes till he himself became Supreme Pontiff by unanimous election (which might seem, by the way, to dispose of the charge of simony), in 1492. No charge of any kind seems to have been made against him till he became Pope.

As Pope he showed himself to be not only by far the best statesman in Italy, but one of the best in Europe. When Charles VIII was invited and admitted into Italy by Ludovico Il Moro of Milan, for the conquest of Naples, though the Pope could not prevent the invasion he brought it to futility and defeat. He made the marriage and the reign of the Catholic Kings in Spain possible, and promulgated the most far-sighted and complete public law for Rome in the whole history of the Papal City ; and he it was who in 1493, in the famous Bull, *Inter Cetera Divina*, drew the line dividing the Americas. Had he lived a little longer, the whole history of Italy might have been different, and her confederation might have antedated her unity by some 400 years.

There were, of course, two rulers in Alexander. He was Pope, and it might seem impossible to find fault with his exercise of the Papal function. But besides being Pope he was the ruler of an Italian State, and posterity has confused these rôles and has insisted on regarding him as Pope in all his activities.

Personally, he was inevitably a man of his time. Pastor, the historian of the Papacy, will have none of him because he had children. But he did not have children while he was Pope, and if he had it was no new thing. Pius II, Sixtus IV, Innocent VIII, his predecessors, had children, and his malignant successor, the root, we may suspect, of the Borgia myth, had three daughters. But then Alexander VI was a Spaniard and a foreigner. As a Prince, Alexander was of the standard of his times, more lavish, more brilliant, more successful than his contemporaries. He was not alone in having children : it was in their beauty, intelligence and energy that he was alone. The loveliness of Lucrezia, the ruthless ability of Cesare, were enough to draw all men's eyes, and envy and malice were not slow to use the scandal. And when Cesare began to carry out

his own—or were they Alexander's ?—ideas for the organization of the States of the Church and the defence of Italy at the
expense of innumerable illegitimate vested interests, the destined victims were quick to use against him the traditional
Italian weapon, Calumny—Calumny, the subject of Botticelli's strange picture. Perhaps the Borgia myth is their
revenge.

None of those sacks which Rome had suffered at the hands of
Alaric, Genseric, Guiscard, or Charles VIII can compare for
horror with that which befell her in 1527, in the time of
Clement VII, just twenty years after the death of Cesare.
That army of brigands, German, Italian, Spanish, that, with
the Constable de Bourbon at its head, really forced him step
by step across the Apennines, through Val d'Arno and Siena,
by the Via Francigena and Viterbo to the siege of the Eternal
City, literally beggars description. Again and again de
Bourbon wrote to the Pope for money to appease his host,
but with little chance of staying a march that was more terrible
than a thunderstorm between the mountains and the sea.
On May 3 they swept through Viterbo, and by sunset of May
4 they were at Isola Farnese, six miles from the City. Then
in the misty dawn of May 6 they advanced to the last attack,
as ever, on Sant' Angelo. In that dense fog the fire of the
defenders was ineffectual. De Bourbon, it seems, had led his
men, and when he reached the walls had seized a ladder and
called them to follow. He had scarcely put his foot on the
first rung when a ball struck him in the groin. A little later he
died, murmuring in his agony, " To Rome, to Rome." That
morning Cellini, whose adventures in Sant' Angelo then and
later are too well known to be repeated here, had gone with his
friend Alessandro, the son of Piero del Bene, and two others to
reconnoitre about the walls of the Campo Santo. There on
the ramparts they took up their station. At last, after
watching the battle, Cellini proposed that they should go home,
seeing that their own men were already in flight. " Would
God we had never come here," said Alessandro. Angered at
this Cellini answered, " Yet since you have brought me here I
must perform one action worthy of a man." Then directing
his arquebus where he saw the thickest of the fight, he aimed

VIEW OF CASTEL SANT' ANGELO AND ST. PETER'S as it used to be

PULPIT, by the school of the Cosmati (S. Cesareo)

exactly, as he says, at one whom he "remarked to be higher than the rest." In the fog he could not see whether he was on foot or on horseback. "I discovered afterwards," he tells us, "that one of my shots had killed the Constable de Bourbon, and from what I subsequently heard he was the man whom I had first noticed above the heads of the rest." However that may be, the death of de Bourbon was by no means fortunate for Rome. No one but he could even pretend to command the mixed host of villains and barbarians who presently had the City in their hands. The Borgo was taken on the day he died to the cry of *España, España*, and Clement fled along the subterranean way into the Castle, where he presently surrendered the City. Then followed a scene of appalling horror. "Forty thousand ruffians, free from all restraint, gratified their elemental lusts and passions at the expense of the most cultivated population in the world. They were worse than barbarians. . . . Rome was at the mercy of a host of demons inspired only with avarice, cruelty, and lust. . . . The Germans were the most ferocious at first; and the Lutherans amongst them set an example which was quickly followed of disregard of holy places. The Spaniards excelled in deliberate cruelty. The Italians were the most inventive, and hounded on their comrades to new fields of discovery. Those who had taken refuge in the churches were dragged out by the Lutherans; vestments, ornaments, and relics were seized by greedy hands. Monasteries were stormed and sacked; nuns were violated in the streets. . . . The streets were filled with the dying and the dead, amidst whom the soldiers staggered to and fro laden with heavy bundles of spoil. The groans of the dying were only interrupted by the blasphemies of the soldiers and the shrieks of agonising women who were being violated or hurled out of the windows."

This frightful spectacle lasted for three days. On the fourth the barbarians began to quarrel among themselves about the division of the booty. But they were told by their leaders to enjoy what they possessed. "The Germans were ready to obey, and turned to drunkenness and buffoonery. Clad in magnificent vestments and decked with jewels, accompanied by their concubines, who were bedizened with like

o

ornaments, they rode on mules through the streets, and imitated with drunken gravity the procession of the Papal Court. The Spaniards were not so easily contented. They had no pleasure in anti-papal demonstrations. . . . There still remained the discovery of secret hoards of wealth and the possibility of extracting ransoms from those who had possessions or friends elsewhere. For this purpose they had recourse to every refinement of cruelty. They hung up their prisoners by the arms ; they thrust hot irons into their flesh or pointed sticks beneath their finger nails ; they pulled out their teeth one by one, and invented divers means of ingenious mutilation."

Meantime, Clement, trusting in the strength of Sant' Angelo, was bent on gaining time, hoping against hope that the traitor Duke of Urbino would arrive to relieve the City. But in vain. On June 5, 1527, the Pope signed the capitulation, and on the 7th the garrison of Sant' Angelo marched out, and was replaced by Germans and Spaniards. Clement was a prisoner in the hands of the Emperor.

The state of the City may be more easily imagined than described ; Rome was starving. The flight of the Pope to Orvieto on December 6 may be said to mark the end of the Renaissance. It was a new and far less human régime that returned to the Vatican.

XXVI

SANTA MARIA AND SANTA CECILIA IN TRASTEVERE — THE WORK OF PIETRO CAVALLINI

TRASTEVERE, that region apart, which for centuries was the last of the thirteen Rioni that divided the City, lies on the right bank of the Tiber about Janiculum, between the river and the wall of Urban VIII, between Porta S. Spirito and Porta Portese. Always the abode of the people, Trastevere remains even to-day the most Roman quarter of Rome, the poorest part still, where one may see, not always without admiration, the indestructible simplicity of the Latin race, its shamelessness, its unaffected acceptance of the promiscuities of life, its frankness and gravity. There of old, not far from the Port, lived the Syrian porters, who bore the litters all day long through the gay streets of the marvellous capital of the world, the Jewish money lenders, the sailors and bargemen of the Tiber, the dock labourers who unloaded on the quays the corn from Sicily and Africa, the precious wine from Chios, the merchandise from the East, the marble from Paros and Luna.

Not far from the Port, in the midst of this region full of the poor, a Taberna Meritoria, a sort of Hospice for the destitute, had been established in the earlier days of the Empire, and, presently abandoned, is said to have been given by the Emperor Alexander Severus to Pope Calixtus I, who built there as early as 222 a place of assembly, a church, in the very place where, on the first Christmas night, a river of oil had burst forth from the soil, that Fons Olei, which afterwards named the building. That the Christians should have met together thus in the poorest part of the city as early as the third century, might seem likely enough, but that Calixtus I built a church here is difficult to believe, though tradition asserts that he was martyred hereabout and buried close by on the Via Aurelia, so that already in the time of Constantine the place was known as Area Callisti. It is then the true history of S. Maria in Trastevere begins, in the fourth century, when Pope Julius I built a church here which was named after himself, and another on the Via Aurelia over the tomb of Pope Calixtus. This basilica, built between 337 and 352, was restored in the ninth century by John VIII, who had the walls painted in fresco : but already fifty years before, in 828, Gregory IV had added two aisles to the nave, building a *Schola cantorum* in the midst, and, raising the tribune, had laid the bodies of Calixtus and S. Calepodius to rest there. The church, however, which John VIII had restored in the ninth century, was entirely rebuilt by Innocent II in 1130, and it is for the most part his church we see to-day when we pass into S. Maria in Trastevere. It was he probably who dedicated it to the Madonna : and it is certainly to him we owe the mosaic of the façade so gay in colour and ornament, representing the Virgin and Child between the wise and foolish virgins, ten figures, eight crowned, their lamps lighted in their hands, two uncrowned, with their lamps unlit : while on one side kneels Pope Innocent himself, on the other Eugenius III, who completed the work.

The same qualities of colour and decorative beauty, the same defects too are seen in the mosaic of the apsis where the Madonna, wearing a marvellous crown and draperies of gold, sits beside our Lord on the same throne, between S. Calixtus, S. Lawrence, and Pope Innocent II, S. Peter, and the Popes Cornelius and Julius, with S. Calepodius. Beneath the throne are the two sacred cities—as it were, Jerusalem and Bethlehem, above the four rivers, beside which the twelve sheep of the Apocalypse stand on either side the Lamb of God.

The same luxury of ornament without any real beauty of form is found again on the arch of the tribune, where we see, under a decoration of angels and flowers, Isaiah and Jeremiah and on either side a tree and the symbols of the Evangelists, and over all the Cross above the seven candlesticks. Lovely as these mosaics are, and seen certainly to the best advantage in a church so beautifully proportioned and so fine still, with its rich, Ionic columns, in spite of the frightful restorations of Pius IX, it is for the sake of Pietro Cavallini, master of Giotto, that we are come to S. Maria in Trastevere.

That *dottissimo e nobilissimo maestro* of whom Ghiberti writes with so much enthusiasm, seems almost to have escaped our notice till the discovery of his frescoes at S. Cecilia in Trastevere. Vasari, who has so much to say of every Tuscan master, tells us nothing of Cavallini's birth, but speaks of his labours in many parts of Italy ; labours unconfirmed to us save in Naples, where we know he was employed in 1308 by King Robert. All his work in Southern Italy, however, seems to have perished, and though much of what may well be his painting is still to be seen in Latium, it is really as the mosaicist of S. Maria and the painter of S. Cecilia in Trastevere, and perhaps in the Upper Church of S. Francesco at Assisi that we know him to-day, " Dottissimo fra gl' altri maestri," as Ghiberti says, and almost certainly in some sort the master of Giotto.

There in S. Maria in Trastevere he has covered the lower part of the tribune and the arch of the tribune with mosaics. On the sides of the arch are the Birth and Death of the Virgin ; in the Tribune itself the Annunciation, the Nativity of our Lord, the Adoration of the Magi, the Presentation in the Temple. In this truly marvellous work, Byzantinism has altogether disappeared ; and instead he contrives a sort of realism that has the energy and gesture of life, with something certainly of its strength, its pathos too, and fleeting beauty. Looking on his work one begins to understand the strength and achievement of that Roman renaissance of the twelfth and thirteenth centuries which we know best in the work of the Cosmati.

It is the influence of the antique, its influence on behalf of life, that we find so expressive in the wonderful frescoes in the Coro delle Monache at S. Cecilia in Trastevere. Finished in the last decade of the thirteenth century, in those frescoes the future of European art is already decided. They cover three sides of the coro, and spoiled as most of them are, the most

important among them, The Last Judgment, is happily the
best preserved ; the upper part in which we see Christ, the
Blessed Virgin, and the Apostles, being on the whole in fairly
good condition.   Looking on those figures we seem once more
to be in the presence of Roman work, not merely of work done
in Rome, but of work which for the first time for many centuries stands in a true relation to the antique.   There is no
trace at all of Byzantine influence.   The heads are full of a
natural beauty and force, the drapery falls in ample folds with
a certain freedom and dignity.   Christ seems to wait for some
interval in an angel's song, the Madonna seems about to
speak again the words of the *Magnificat*, the angels gather
round our Lord with a new eagerness, one can almost hear the
whisper of those restless wings.   It is the dawn, as it were, of
a new Easter, and we seem to hear again, with a new meaning,
the old beautiful words of the Canticle, for the Prince of Life
being raised from the dead dieth no more : death hath no more
dominion over Him.

What that death was we may see at once and understand if,
leaving the convent, we enter the church of S. Cecilia in
Trastevere through the beautiful atrium under the portico,
with its antique Ionic columns, above which are some rude
mosaics of the ninth century.   Other work of the same period
still decorates the raised tribune, the Redeemer between S.
Paul, S. Agata and Pope Paschal, to whom we owe the work,
on the one side, and S. Peter, S. Cecilia and Valerian, her
husband, on the other, above the lamb and twelve sheep.
To such a matter of rule, precept upon precept, line upon
line had the beautiful art of Byzantium come, four hundred
years before Pietro Cavallini banished it from the West for
ever.

One wanders away through the lovely spoiled church before
the altar of Arnolfo down to the tomb of S. Cecilia, and the
touching fallen figure of " Hevenes Lilie," by Stefano Maderna.
It was so they found her in the catacomb in the sixteenth
century, seemingly sleeping.   She was not the least of those who
in the earliest days of the Church lost their lives for Christ's
sake.   Rich and sweetly nurtured, well beloved, not least by
Valerian, her husband :

This mayden bright Cecilie, as hir lyf seith,
Was comen of Romayns, and of noble kinde,
And from hir cradel up fostred in the feith
Of Crist, and bar his gospel in hir minde ;
.   .   .   .
And when this mayden sholde unto a man
Y-wedded be, that was ful young of age,
Which that y-cleped was Valerian,
And day was comen of hir mariage,
She ful devout and humble in hir corage,
Under hir robe of gold, that sat ful fayre,
Had next hir flesh y-clad hir in an heyre.

And whyl the organs maden melodye,
To God alone in herte thus sang she ;
" O lord, my soule and eek my body gye
Unwemmed, lest that I confounded be. . . ."

So she told Valerian, her husband, that she had an angel
who guarded her.

" I have an angel which that loveth me,
That with greet love, wher-so I wake or slepe,
Is redy ay my body for to kepe. . . ."

And he, anxious to see this wonder, desired her to show
him that angel which had cost him her love. But Cecilia
answered that he could not see him unless he were baptized,
and he, moved by anxiety and curiosity, consented. So she
sent him to " the gode Urban the olde " in the catacombs of
the Via Appia, who baptized him.

" Valerian goth hoom and fint Cecilie
With-inne his chambre with an angel stonde ;
This angel hadde of roses and of lilie
Corones two, the which he bar in honde ;
And first to Cecile, as I understonde,
He yaf that oon, and after gan he take
That other to Valerian, hir make."

So he called his brother whom he loved, Tiburtius, and he
too was taught by S. Cecilia, and being baptized, saw too the
angel, and Cecilia claimed him as her brother. Not long after
they were martyred by the Prefect Almachius. Valerian and
Tiburtius were quickly dead, but Cecilia who had given their

wealth to the poor and so disappointed Almachius, was ordered
to be burned in the heating-room of the great bath in her house.
There she remained for a night and a day unharmed, when an
executioner was sent to kill her, but he left her but half dead,
for she lived for three days after.   Then they buried her privily
with many tears.

> Seint Urban with his deknes, prively
> The body fette, and buried it by nighte
> Among his othere seintes honestly.
> Hir hous, the chirche of seint Cecile highte ;
> Seint Urban halwed it, as wel he mighte ;
> In which unto this day, in noble wyse,
> Men doon to Crist and to his seint servyse.

XXVII

SANTA MARIA SOPRA MINERVA

THE church of S. Maria sopra Minerva, the only "Gothic" church in Rome, stands on the ruins of a Temple of Minerva, built by Pompey in return for his victories in Asia. A church has stood within the precincts of the temple since the middle of the eighth century at any rate, when the Greek nuns of Campo Marzio had their convent there, *S. Maria in Minervium*, which, however, they presently abandoned. More than five hundred years later, in 1280, Pope Nicholas III, pulling down the ruins of the old church, began to build in its place the church we see, S. Maria sopra Minerva, after the designs of the Dominicans Frati Sisto and Ristoro, who had already built S. Maria Novella in Florence : but the new building does not seem to have passed into the hands of the Dominican Order till 1370.

S. Maria sopra Minerva can never have been able to bear comparison for beauty or charm with her Florentine sister, and to-day certainly, after suffering the most miserable restorations, she is less than ever the peer of the "sweet bride" of Michelangelo, but at least she has this in common with her rival that she is a museum of Tuscan art. Yet there, too, she comes short, for though she possesses work of Filippino Lippi, of Mino da Fiesole, of Michel Marini, of Baccio Bandinelli, of Raffaele da Montelupo, of Baccio Bigio, and even Michelangelo, she has nothing, or almost nothing, to put beside the Rucellai Madonna, the work of Orcagna, of the painters of the Cappella degli Spagnuoli, of Masaccio, or of Ghirlandajo.

The decoration of the Strozzi chapel in S. Maria Novella at Florence was entrusted to Filippino Lippi on the 21st April, 1487 ; but in a letter written from Rome on 2nd May, 1489, while acknowledging the debt of kindness and of gratitude

which he owed to that noble Florentine house, he excuses himself for neglecting his commission, saying that he is already
busy in the service of Cardinal Caraffa, " as good a patron as
any man can desire," and describing, not without enthusiasm,
the splendour of the paintings with which he was then decorating his chapel in S. Maria sopra Minerva. These frescoes
represent the Blessed Virgin and the Triumph of S. Thomas
Aquinas, while in another part of the chapel we see the
Annunciation with the figures of the donor and his patron,
S. Thomas Aquinas, and the Assumption of the Blessed Virgin.
In the Triumph, S. Thomas kneels, as it were in ecstasy, before
the crucifix and hears the words spoken to him by our Lord :
Bene scripsisti de Me, Thoma.   In the background the world goes
on its way, the quiet world that surrounded the saint.   A
friend who would visit him is prevented by his servant, who
evidently speaks in a whisper.   In the silence a dog suddenly
barks, and a child drops his crust, startled by the noise : and
as though to emphasise the enthralling stillness that has fallen
on the world, two women stand listening to the whispers of
the servant, a little disturbed even by the careful footsteps of
him who is coming down that flight of steps yonder under the
arches.

Beneath this fresco we see another of S. Thomas enthroned
between Philosophy and Theology and two other figures
trampling on a fallen heretic, enjoying the spectacle of Arius,
Sabellius and Averroes prostrate in the foreground.   It is the
very spirit of the Domincan Order.

As for Filippino's work, it is full of splendour and force, a
little excessive perhaps, a little too eager in its movement,
but possessing nevertheless the true secret of great composition
in a certain rhythm and boldness admirably used and expressed.

Of all the works of art, sculptures, and paintings in the
church, but one, and that the earliest, is by a master of the
Roman school, the rest are from the hands of strangers.   The
solitary example of Roman art is the tomb close to the Caraffa
Chapel of the Bishop Guglielmus Durandus, the masterpiece of
Johannes Cosmatus.   The Bishop is represented at full length
on the slab of the tomb, which is covered with an embroidered
cloth, while two angels lift the curtains.   In the recess formed

by an arch borne on inlaid pillars sits the Virgin enthroned, holding Bambino Gesù in her arms, and on either side stand S. Dominic and another saint. The tomb, restored in 1817, as an inscription tells us, is perhaps still the loveliest, as it is certainly the simplest thing in the church.

It was the exile in Avignon which killed the Roman schools of sculpture and of painting, art generally being lost without a patron, so that when Eugenius IV returned from that second exile in Tuscany he was compelled to look thither for his artists, as did Nicholas V after him, till it seems to have become the custom always to employ strangers in all artistic matters. In S. Maria sopra Minerva we see their work by no means at its best. In 1454 Mino da Fiesole came to Rome, and, among his innumerable works, left in S. Maria sopra Minerva the tomb of Francesco Tornabuoni, his compatriot. The less lovely work of Maini, a statue of S. Sebastian, is in a chapel close by, while Michelangelo, a little feeble for once, has left there a statue of Christ which fails to move us at all, and might well be the work of a mediocrity. And as though one could not have too much of such work, Baccio Bandinelli and Raffaele da Montelupo have been at work here too, building the tombs of Leo X and Clement VII, the Medici popes. Nor is this all, for if it is a Lombard hand we see at work in the magnificent monument of Cardinal Tebaldi, the hand of Andrea Bregno, in the passage from the chapel on the left of the choir, we come upon the tomb of Fra Giovanni Beato Angelico, who died in the convent here in 1455 : HIC JACET VENERABILIS PICTOR FRATER JOANNES DE FLORENTIA ORDINIS PRAEDICATORUM MCCCCLV.

Yes, in S. Maria sopra Minerva one seems to have entered a Florentine church that has come into the hands of strangers, and if not Florentine certainly Tuscan, for the body of S. Catherine of Siena, the Dominican tertiary, is under the high altar, the chief relic of the church.

XXVIII

THE AVENTINE AND ITS CHURCHES

OF all the hills of Rome the Aventine, now built over, alone, precipitous and almost uninhabited as it was till lately, used to impress one with its own beauty and serenity. It was as though the ancient curse of the Patricians were still heavy upon it. Something certainly of those far-off days seemed to linger about its shadowy, deserted ways, among the gardens there, where the almond trees were so strangely lovely and in summer the *cicala* wearied one with its song ; where many an ancient church still counted the Ave Mary through the centuries, half-forgotten in a world of silence and of flowers. That seclusion, as of a hill without the city, now gone, seems to have belonged to it even in antiquity ; thither the Plebs assembled to oppose the Patricians, and there the Bacchic orgies were held by that secret society whose discovery so startled the Republic—a host of frenzied men and women naked in the woods sacrificing by night to the Maenads such children as they might entice into their mysteries. Later there were temples there, too, for the shadowy Aventine had always been, as was supposed, the abode of some deity :

> *Lucus Aventino suberat niger ilicis umbra*
> *Quo posses viso dicere, Numen inest.*

"Divinity is there," said the Roman world, awed by the silence of the woods, and so the hill was crowned with temples, the most renowned and splendid being that of Diana, which stood on its very summit in the midst of a grove where that pale goddess seems to have been worshipped from the time of Servius Tullius to the time of Alaric the Goth.

As we pass to-day from S. Maria in Cosmedin, where the shadow of the Aventine mixes with that of the Palatine hill, turning into the Via della Greca and so almost at once into the Via di S. Sabina, we come presently to the very place sacred once to Diana, but now to another virgin, S. Sabina, whose church stands in the ruins of the ancient temple.

Built by Peter, an Illyrian priest, in the fifth century, the church of S. Sabina was almost entirely restored and spoilt about 1587 by Sixtus V. But this spot was already sacred to Christianity long before the foundation of the church ; for there, as we read, the noble lady Marcella had her palace, and, after she became a widow, was converted to Christ about the year 400. Retiring almost completely from the world she sold all her possessions save her house, giving all to the poor, receiving there on the Aventine only those who came to speak with her concerning the love of Jesus. Thus she gathered about her a small company which heard S. Jerome expound the Gospel, meantime devoting themselves to charity. They do not seem to have lived in common, and certainly they had no rule, but we may discern there the very spirit of monasticism in the beautiful gravity of their hearts.

Then, in August 410, Alaric and his Goths surprised the City. Drunk with lust and wine, those rude soldiers, who had broken into Italy as into a new world, were soon sacking and burning Rome. And although they respected the churches, when they came to the Aventine they did not scruple to loot the palace of Marcella. To their demand for money and treasure, she could only reply that she had nothing, since Christian like themselves, though they were Arian, she had long sold all, as Christ had said, and given to the poor. Thinking she lied, and nothing might seem more likely, they took what they could, violating both her and her companions and setting fire to the house. Naked and wounded, towards evening those poor women made their way to S. Paolo, where on the morrow Marcella died.

It was some fifteen years later that Pope Celestine I began to build in that very place, beside the Temple of Diana, among the ruins there, the church of S. Sabina, which Sixtus V destroyed, so that very little remains to us to-day even of its primitive form ; while the mosaics which once adorned it have perished altogether save for the fragment over the door in the nave, where, on a blue ground, we may see an inscription recording the foundation of the church, and on either side the figure of a woman holding an open book, representing, as it is written, the *Ecclesia ex Circumcisione* and the *Ecclesia ex Gentibus*, the Church of the Jews and the Church of the Gentiles ; while above are the emblems of the four Evangelists.

The church has been completely restored and with its columns of Hymettan marble has the appearance of an early Christian basilica, but what remains to us of ancient beauty belongs to the doors of cypress wood, which are not only the most beautiful things in the church, but among the most precious remnants of primitive Christian art. Carved in the fifth century, they are divided into twenty-six panels representing scenes from the Old and New Testaments, and though these are no longer in their proper order, for they were re-arranged, as we now see them, by Innocent III about 1198, when he added to them some work of his own time, the scene of the Crucifixion for instance, they remain representative work of the fifth century, the time of the foundation of the church. There we see Elijah borne to heaven in the fiery chariot accompanied by an angel, like a Roman Victory. Then Pharaoh crosses the Red Sea, which recalls the great horsemen, the glory of Monte Cavallo ; Christ is adored by the wise kings in Phrygian dress ; S. Peter denies his Lord to a damsel like a Roman Empress.

The beautiful door-jambs of marble are of the time of Honorius III, who, in the thirteenth century, greatly enlarged the church, fortifying it with walls and towers. He spent, indeed, much of his time there, dying there at last not before he had placed S. Sabina in the care of the Dominicans.

Tradition assures us that S. Dominic himself often came to the place, and points to an orange tree still growing in the garden as of his planting. But amid so many diverse memories we are like to forget S. Sabina altogether. And truly we know little about her. Converted, as it is said, by her Greek slave, Serapia, she was one of Hadrian's martyrs. She lies now with Serapia in the Confession before the high altar, the two bodies having been brought hither from the catacombs. It seems doubtful, however, whether S. Sabina ever existed.

The new Giardino di S. Sabina offers one a wonderful view of the City.

Close beside S. Sabina stands another half-deserted church,
that of S. Alessio—S. Alessio, the pilgrim who left home on his
wedding morning, and after seventeen years returned to the
City to beg, unknown, at his parents' door, here on the site of
his church.   This happened, as it is said, in the fourth century.
But of old, as it seems, the church bore another name : and it
was not till the first years of the thirteenth century that
Honorius III reconsecrated the church to receive the relics of
S. Alessio.

Approached through a charming courtyard of the sixteenth
century the building itself has little enough of antiquity ; yet
a church hereabout was given by Benedict VII in 975 to a
fugitive in Rome from Arabian persecution, the Greek Metro-
politan, Sergius, who founded beside it a great monastery of
Basilian monks.   In the twelfth century this monastery was
divided and renamed ; one part, called S. Bonifacio, being
given to the Benedictines, who held it till 1231 ; the other,
S. Maria in Aventino, coming into the possession of the Knights
of Malta.   To this period belongs the beautiful campanile,
which with two columns from an iconostasis of fine workmanship of the thirteenth century—Cosmati work, adorned with
mosaic—is in fact all there is left, for the church was spoiled
in the eighteenth century.

So on a Sunday morning in the marvellous Roman summer
one may pass from church to church on the way to hear Mass
sung at S. Anselmo, close by.

The great Benedictine College of S. Anselmo stands in the
midst of its gardens and *poderi* just opposite S. Alessio.   Begun
in 1892 and finished in 1896, S. Anselmo was built by Leo
XIII, as a college for black Benedictines of all nations.   And,
here, truly better than anywhere else in Rome, one may hear
the very song of the early Church, that long drawn-out, sweet
melody, that might seem to have been born with the mystery
of the Mass, but is really more universal and more ancient, the
very tones, indeed, instinctive with beauty and humility in
which man has always spoken with the gods.   For the plainsong is by no means an exclusively Christian music, it seems
to have been used by all peoples and all religions, it is indeed
an universal hymn of praise, of assurance, plaintive, too, and

full of the repetitions of love, the expressions of an universal joy, an universal weariness.

Returning a little on the way from S. Anselmo past S. Sabina, we come to the Via di S. Prisca, and following it come presently to her church, where in the house of Priscilla, to whom S. Paul sent greeting, was the *Ecclesia Domestica*, in which S. Peter lived when he was in Rome. The house fell into ruin, but before the end of the fifth century a basilica was built amid its ruins and this Pope Adrian I restored in 721, as Calixtus III did in 1455. Their work was, however, altogether destroyed by Cardinal Giustiniani in the early part of the seventeenth century, so that to-day there is almost nothing there worth the trouble of seeing. Yet one cannot altogether pass it by, for this was perhaps the first place in the City where two or three were gathered together to worship Jesus.

It is another monastery of Basilian monks we come to when passing down the Via di S. Prisca, and crossing the Viale Aventino we enter the church of S. Saba with its memories of the seventh century and the Byzantine dominion. Divided now into three naves by ancient columns, it is but a fragment of the old Greek church with its five naves and great mosaics. Nothing seems to be left from those far-off times, and indeed from all the centuries it has kept nothing save the fine double portico, the restored work of Jacobus Cosmatus, the mosaic pavement, the ambones, the Bishop's throne and the screens signed by Vassallettus, the twelfth-century Roman artist who built the Lateran cloister.

Across the vague waste to the south, still within the walls, we may see the tower of S. Balbina by the Baths of Caracalla, but to reach it we must return to the Viale Aventino. Taking thence the Via Aventina and then the Via di S. Balbina we come to the small and ancient basilica, built, as it is said, by Gregory the Great in the end of the sixth century. To it was attached a small monastery whose walls still remain, as does its tower, so beautiful from far away. Some importance belonged to it in the fifteenth century when the Prior had the privilege of reading the Gospel of Easter in Greek in the Papal chapel. It is now just an orphanage in the care of certain Poor

PORTICO AND FAÇADE, by Pietro da Cortona (S. Maria della Pace)

CAMPANILE, by Borromini (S. Andrea delle Fratte)

Clares. Some beautiful relics of its former glory still remain
to it. The great tomb of Stefano de Surdis decorated with
the mosaic of the Cosmati ; an episcopal throne of the same
exquisite workmanship. An altar decorated with bas-reliefs,
among them the Crucifixion, by Mino da Fiesole, built in the
fifteenth century by Pope Paul II in old S. Peter's, stands on
the south. The great open roof and the three round windows
are all that remain to us of any antiquity in the building
itself, which has been more than once restored within the last
hundred years.

Following the Via di S. Balbina down into Via Porta di
S. Sebastiano, and turning there to the right, we come to the
Basilica of SS. Nereo ed Achilleo beside the Baths of Caracalla.
Built, as it is said, by Leo III at the beginning of the ninth
century, but older than that, it might seem, by nearly four
hundred years, SS. Nereo ed Achilleo guards the bodies of
those two martyrs brought here from the catacomb on the
Ardeatina in the sixth century. Its great days, however,
were in the twelfth century, when it was one of the most important churches in Rome. Falling into ruin, it was restored
by Sixtus IV in 1471, and later, too, by Cardinal Baronius,
who, loving the place, besought those who should come after
him, " for the glory of God and the merits of those martyrs "
to spoil nothing but to keep it always as it had been of old.

> *Presbyter Card. successor quisquis fueris*
> *Rogo te per gloriam Dei*
> *Et per merita horum martyrum*
> *Nihil demito nihil minuito nec mutato*
> *Restitutam antiquitatem pie servato.*
> *Sic te Deus martyrum suorum*
> *Precibus semper adjuvet.*

So it is by his intervention that, unlike S. Saba and S.
Balbina, SS. Nereo ed Achilleo keeps still about it something
of its austere and mystic beauty. Consisting, as it does, of a
nave and two aisles divided by octagonal pillars, its ancient
cosmatesque pavement remains at least in the presbytery,
while the choir is still enclosed within its marble balustrade,
with the two ambones on either side the altar, the ciborium,
the Bishop's throne, the Paschal candlestick, all works of the

P

Cosmati school. The mosaics of the apse have unhappily
perished, but those of the arch remain from the earliest part
of the ninth century, the time of Leo III. There we see in
the midst the Transfiguration, and on one side the Madonna
enthroned, on the other the Annunciation. And then the
beautiful Episcopal throne, from which Gregory the Great
read his twenty-eighth Homily on the Gospels, still remains.

Close by is the very similar church of S. Cesareo also known
to Gregory the Great. It is a basilica of a single nave much
restored in the sixteenth century and now again in the restorer's
hands. But nevertheless it still contains some precious works
of the Cosmati. The lovely ambone or pulpit on the left, for
instance, with its wonderful overlay of porphyry and mosaic
is a most typical Roman work of the twelfth or thirteenth
century. The other ambone is inferior, but still a genuine
thing. The choir screens, the Bishop's throne, the altar,
but not its modern canopy, are all fine works of the Cosmati
brotherhood, and help us to ignore the mosaics of the tribune
by the Cavaliere d'Arpino.

At the southern foot of the Aventine, by the Porta S. Paolo,
are the Pyramid of Cestius, the Protestant Cemetery and the
ancient Porta Ostiensis. The Pyramid is the sepulchral
monument of a certain Caius Cestius Epulo, who died *ca.*
12 B.C. Like similar pyramidal monuments in Rome, now
destroyed, it was built of brick covered with marble.

The Protestant Cemetery Shelley describes as " the romantic
and lovely cemetery of the Protestants under the pyramid
which is the tomb of Cestius and the mossy walls and towers,
now mouldering and desolate, which formed the circuit of
ancient Rome. The cemetery is an open space among the
ruins, covered in winter with violets and daisies. It might
make one in love with death, to think that one should be buried
in so sweet a place."

Shelley was writing, I think, of the old cemetery, now closed,
where he lies who said his " name was writ in water "—John
Keats. Those are strange words and one wonders what
suggested them, though the fact of his dying so tragically,
so young and without any general recognition of his genius
may explain their bitterness. As for the words themselves,

perhaps so eager a lover of Spenser may have recalled in his
last hours those lines in the *Amoretti* :

> One day I wrote her name upon the strand
> But came the waves and washed it away ;
> Again I wrote it with a second hand,
> But came the tide and made my pains his prey.
> Vain man, said she, that dost in vain essay
> A mortal thing so to immortalise,
> For I myself shall like to this decay
> And eek my name be wiped out likewise . . .
> My verse your virtues rare shall eternise
> And in the heavens write your glorious name.

Close beside Keats' grave is that of his friend, Joseph Severn,
who nursed him dying and to whom we owe the last portrait
of the poet.

Shelley, or rather the heart of Shelley—*Cor Cordium*—is
buried in the newer cemetery adjoining the old. Here lie
many other Englishmen, among them Edward Trelawney,
who snatched Shelley's heart from the pyre on the sea-shore
near Viareggio where the body of the poet was burned.
John Addington Symonds lies here too, and many Germans,
among them the son of Goethe.

> The One remains, the many change and pass ;
> Heaven's light forever shines, Earth's shadows fly ;
> Life, like a dome of many-coloured glass,
> Stains the white radiance of Eternity,
> Until Death tramples it to fragments.—Die,
> If thou wouldst be with that which thou dost seek !
> Follow where all is fled !—Rome's azure sky,
> Flowers, ruins, statues, music, words are weak
> The glory they transfuse with fitting truth to speak.

XXIX

THE COELIAN HILL AND ITS CHURCHES

THE Coelian Hill was, with the Aventine, among the most deserted and silent quarters of Rome, but it too has now been much built over. Its memories belong almost wholly to the Middle Age, scarcely anything to be found there dating from pagan times. Indeed this *Mons Querquetulanus* seems to have had but little part in the life of the ancient city; its name even coming to it from a stranger, Coelius Vibenna, an Etruscan who helped Romulus in his war with Tatius after the Rape of the Sabine women. But if it lacks Pagan memories, its medieval possessions are of some importance. Certainly to the English pilgrim—and Catholic or Protestant, who is not a pilgrim in Rome?—the Coelian, with its memories of S. Gregory, will be among the most interesting quarters of the Eternal City.

In the first centuries of Christianity there was not in all Rome a region more populous, inhabited as it was by the better classes and splendid with beautiful dwellings. The temples which stood there, mere names to us now, included those of Jupiter, of Minerva Capita, of Diana, of Isis, and of the Emperor Claudius, built to his memory by Agrippina, and everywhere among the gardens rose baths and stadia and the houses of the patricians, the palace of Verus for instance, of the Laterani, the villa of Tetricus, while S. Clement lived there in the first century, the Valerii in the fourth. It is then amid the memory at least of an ancient splendour and civilisation that we find Gregory, the future pope, living at the foot of the hill in the middle of the sixth century.

One comes to the church of S. Gregorio Magno from SS. Nereo ed Achilleo along the Via di Porta S. Sebastiano, or from the arch of Constantine along the Via di S. Gregorio, now Via dei Trionfi, that shady and quiet road, verily a triumphal way between the Palatine and the Coelian hills. The great church stands close to the Porta Capena above a sloping piazza full of trees, from which a great flight of steps leads up to the doors of the atrium, which, grass-grown and silent now, still stands before the sanctuary. Thus, though the church is in fact a construction of the seventeenth and eighteenth centuries, in some ways, I know not how, it evokes in its desertion and its silence that heroic figure who, in the midst of an age full of tragedy, sent us the religion of the Prince of Life. For it was hereabout that Gregory had his home, which in 575 he turned into a monastery that he might live there under the rule of S. Benedict. Fifteen years later the Roman people dragged him from his cloister and, to our eternal gain, forced him to take the throne of Peter, the first monk who sat there, and one of the greatest of those who, out of the religion of Jesus, have forged a weapon to subdue the world. It is fitting that England should have stood first in the mind of such an one. All the world knows the story of that meeting in the Forum with the English boys who were so fair that they seemed to Gregory not Angles but Angels too lovely for hell. So the great Pope sent Augustine, parting from him here on the green sward before the church ere he set out for England.

The church and monastery which Gregory is said to have built on the site of his own home, fell into ruin, in the disastrous years that followed his death ; it was not till a hundred years later, in the time of Gregory II (715-731), that they were rebuilt and placed not only as at first, under the protection of S. Andrew, but also under that of Gregory then declared a saint. Through the next seven hundred years we know but little concerning the place save that it was still used and inhabited in the fourteenth century. In the latter part of the sixteenth century Gregory XIII gave the monastery to the Camaldolese Order, who in some sort still hold it. Then in 1633 Cardinal Borghese restored, and in great part rebuilt, the eighth-century church of Gregory II, the façade and atrium being built by Soria. As architecture, the interior of the church fails to interest us, as it was completely rebuilt in 1725. Certain tombs, however, in the cloistered court, several memorials of English Catholic exiles remain ; among them that of Sir Edward Carne, the last ambassador of England to be accredited to the Holy See. He was appointed by Henry VIII, and recalled by Elizabeth.

Within the church those rebuildings and restorations have left but little that may interest us. The chapel of S. Gregory in the south aisle, and the tiny chamber hard by, are all that is left, it is said, of the house of Gregory. Leaving the church by a door in the north aisle, we come into the garden with its three little chapels of S. Andrea, S. Sylvia, and S. Barbara, built by Cardinal Baronius under a single colonnade. The first commemorates the first church built by Gregory and destroyed by Robert Guiscard in 1084, and holds two famous frescoes, the work of Guido Reni and Domenichino. The second marks the spot where S. Sylvia, Gregory's mother, was buried ; while the third holds still the ancient marble table where the saint sat each day with twelve poor men he had brought in from the highway to feed and serve.

S. Gregorio possesses another tomb, that of the courtesan Imperia, the mistress of Agostino Chigi. She was so beautiful that she was the wonder of Rome. Raphael painted her as the Phrygian Sibyl in S. Maria della Pace. She lies, however, here in S. Gregorio and this is her epitaph :—

IMPERIA   CORTISANA   ROMANA
QVAE   DIGNA   TANTO   NOMINE
RARAE   INTER   HOMINES   FORMAE
SPECIMEN   DEDIT
VIXIT   ANNOS   XXVI   DIE   XII
OBIIT   MDXI   DIE   XV   AVG.

Leaving S. Gregorio and crossing the shady piazza we turn to the right into the Via di SS. Giovanni e Paolo, coming between the old garden walls to the great church of that name in the hands of the Passionists, spoiled within by restoration, but still with its noble bell-tower and portico for the most part as they always have been. But then we have come here not for the sake of the church but rather to see that Roman house so lately excavated beneath it. It was the dwelling of Giovanni and Paolo.

Tradition tells us, and here certainly we have nothing more

to depend on, that in the time of Julian the Emperor, two officers of his court, Giovanni and Paolo—we know only their Christian names—were executed by his order in their own dwelling for the crime of " Christianism," which, it may be, was not merely a belief in the religion of Jesus. We hear, too, that their dwelling and their sepulchre were later transformed into a church by the Senators Byzantius and Pammachius, and that this church named after them was just the Basilica of SS. Giovanni e Paolo, on the Coelian Hill. And truly nothing might seem better established than the fame of these two martyrs whose names appear still among the few that are written in the Canon of the Mass. Nevertheless it seems doubtful whether Julian, the restorer of Hellenism, would have cared to put to death or even to persecute those who failed to understand him. However that may be, the tradition which shows him as a successor of Decius and Diocletian is in part at least confirmed by the discovery of Padre Germano, who found a house and church under the present basilica of SS. Giovanni e Paolo. But it matters very little whether Julian were guilty or no. What chiefly interests us is the fact that here at last, in the Eternal City, we have an ancient Roman house, the property of a private citizen. Even so it is the only one of its kind in Rome, and its rarity does not end there. Happily, almost perfect as it is with its reception rooms, its baths, its store-houses and cellars, and indeed all the surroundings of the *vita antica*, it is yet a Christian dwelling, and as such the only example indeed left to us in Europe.

The history of the discovery is interesting. Padre Germano, the Passionist, was one of those born archaeologists who need but a hint to be sure of the way, and without instruction almost achieve more by instinct than a *savant* may do with all his learning. Before he began to excavate he had understood that much of the masonry of the present church was of the third century, the walls of the perimeter for instance, and that to the south along the Via di SS. Giovanni e Paolo, which is still in its primitive state with its six ancient arcades and two orders of windows corresponding to the two upper floors of the house. Seeing these things he was convinced that the present church was not so much built on the ruins of a building of the third

century as constructed out of it : that in fact very little had
been destroyed, and that what was before him was merely a
transformation. His " heart full of sweet thoughts," as he
said, with exactly twenty francs in his pocket, the present of a
friend, he began his excavation, which has resulted in giving to
us the only Roman house, that is not an official residence, in
the Eternal City. It is of his romantic work we think to-day,
as, led by a Passionist father, we descend into that strange
Christian palace.

For the house under that great basilica is just that. One
of the largest and most beautiful of the innumerable dwellings
of the Coelian Hill, it occupied an area of some seven thousand
square feet. Nearly fifty feet high, consisting of a ground-
floor and two stories, it offered to its inhabitants one of the finest
views within the City. From its windows and terraces one
might see the Palatine and the Palaces of the Caesars, the
Temples of the Forum, the Capitol, the Colosseum, the Baths
of Trajan and of Titus. On the east it reached almost to the
Temple of Claudius. On the south it looked over the palaces
and tenements that lay between it and the Aurelian wall to
the Campagna and the great roads lined with tombs that led
southward to the hills.

There were in Rome two kinds of houses, the *insulae*, or,
as we might say, mansions or flats inhabited by many families,
each with its own apartment, and the houses proper, where a
single family rich and powerful dwelt alone, even as to-day
in France or England. In Italy such a dwelling is still called a
palazzo, and it is in truth one of these that Padre Germano has
discovered on the Coelian Hill. Built, as they seem to have
been, if one may judge by the discoveries at Pompeii and Hercu-
laneum rather than by any written description, all on one plan
but with an infinite variety of detail, the ancient palaces for
the most part consisted of a *protyrum* which opened on to the
road, a sort of vestibule which led into the great rectangular
atrium, surrounded by columns in the midst of which, under the
open sky, was a fountain. To the right and left of this atrium
were the rooms for domestic business, and beyond, opposite
the *protyrum*, opened the *tablinum*, the principal chamber of the
house, the salon or reception-room. Beyond this opened

another *atrium* called the *cavaedium*, around which were set the most private parts of the house where the master dwelt with his family and where were to be found the bedrooms, dining-rooms, library, and so forth ; this second atrium forming a sort of garden where often statues stood about a green lawn mixed with roses. It is on this plan that this palace on the Coelian Hill was built, but with numerous modifications due to individual taste or the necessities of the site. And in examining this ancient Roman house one is struck once again, as often before, by the darkness that must have filled the rooms. The more private apartments certainly received no light save by the door, and one is compelled to suppose that the Romans lived a more public life than ourselves, passing the day at the baths or in the Forum, and returning to their houses only at evening, when, the lamps being lighted, those dark, cool rooms were pleasant and quiet after the noise and sunshine of the City.

But among the most interesting features of this palace on the Coelian are its upper floors, which, so rarely preserved, assure us of the truth of Petronius's words, when he tells us that the Roman houses " towered into the sky," and indeed, as we know, the buildings grew so high within the city that Augustus and Trajan sought to limit them, the one to seventy feet, the other to sixty. No doubt the mansions in which numerous families dwelt were, even as to-day, the highest, this palace, great as it seems, falling short by more than ten feet even of Trajan's limit. Within we find, as I have said, the usual arrangement of a Roman house. We see the great Bath chamber, in the midst of which is a huge earthenware basin, where after the massage and the vapour baths, the bather refreshed and cleansed himself. This great room was in the midst of the house, and underground and about it were set the apartments for the slaves, the store-houses and cellars, full still of the great vases of wine and oil, some of which are marked with the monogram of Christ, and were doubtless set apart for use at Mass, others with various signs denoting foreign or home-grown wines. These rooms were, of course, bare, but the more splendid apartments were decorated with marble, sculptures, paintings, and mosaics, almost nothing of which remains, save the pavements and certain wall-paintings which have happily escaped destruction.

The *triclinium*, which opens out of the *cavaedium* on the right, is partly lined with white marble to a height of some two yards, and above are painted around the room two life-size, draped Genii, one of whom is winged. They are caught in a great garland of flowers that, from one to the other, winds round the chamber, while birds wander among the flowers at their feet, and others fly, as it were, in the sky above them, which once doubtless covered the ceiling, now perished. All this seems to be pagan work ; but in a room close by, where the earlier paintings have been destroyed, we come upon what seem to be the symbols of Christianity, figures of fish and doves, the most ancient emblems of our Lord and the Holy Spirit. But it is in the *tablinum* we find this Christian work at its best, fourth-century painting of a real beauty and character covering all the walls and those parts of the roof which remain. There, amid painted pilasters, arcades, and the usual Roman decoration, under a rich frieze of flowers and leaves, the acanthus among them, one sees on the roof two sheep and two goats placed alternately on either side a tree, to which they turn, as though on either side of our Lord were set the good and the bad. With these compositions six others altogether different are mixed. Is it the Apostles we see reading or praying, the four evangelists with SS. Giovanni and Paolo ? Who knows ? We call these paintings Christian, but there might seem to be little if anything there that might not be just the decoration of a pagan house. Even the praying youth in the room close by might seem to have as much in common with the statue in Berlin as with anything essentially Christian. But we are told that this figure so calm and expressive is an emblem of the Church. It may be so.

What then we are supposed to have here under our eyes is a Roman palace belonging to some great Roman family in the service of the Emperor. Splendidly decorated in pagan times, when SS. Giovanni e Paolo owned it, it was in part re-decorated with paintings of Christian symbols, vague and almost secret that could in no way offend a world still mainly pagan. Of the two saints we know really nothing, save the rumour of their martyrdom and their early fame in the Church. Tradition tells us that in the fourth century Byzantius, a senator, and his son, Pammachius, the friend of S. Jerome, built a church in the house of the two martyrs, and a chapel there lately excavated still possesses a fourth-century altar *in situ*. Known certainly in the fifth century as *Titulus Bizantis* or *Titulus Pammachii*, the church was restored by Pope Symmachus in 499 and twice in the course of the eighth century. In the thirteenth century the present church and portico were built, the former having, as we see, been restored again and again out of all recognition.

Leaving SS. Giovanni e Paolo and following the road that bears their name one comes presently to the Arco di Dolabella which once carried the Acqua Marcia across an ancient street. Close by is the gate of the old convent of the Trinitarians, S. Tommaso in Formis with its fine Cosmati portal ; the convent stood where now we see the Villa Mattei.

The Order of the Trinitarians, in England called Crutched Friars, an order of Mendicants really, but having little or nothing in common with the Franciscans or the Carmelites, was founded by S. Jean de Martha towards the end of the twelfth century for the redemption of captives. That is why our Lord is represented in the mosaic by the Cosmati above the gate between a white and a black slave whom He came to set free as S. Jean de Martha perceived. The work of the Order was properly the redemption or ransom, from the Saracens and the Arabs, of captives, some nine hundred thousand of whom it is said to have thus set free.

Close by is the very ancient church of S. Maria in Domnica or the Navicella, as some call it, because of the marble boat which stands before it. One of the most ancient churches in Rome, the house, as it is said, of Cyriaca where the Christians met in the time of the great persecutions, it alone in Rome has retained its ancient title of Dominicum. It is chiefly interesting to us to-day, however, on account of its fine mosaic on the tribune arch, a work of the early ninth century, where we see the first extant portrait of a Pope, Paschal I, in alb and stole, kneeling there beside the Madonna enthroned with her little Son between the Angels.   Tradition tells us that Raphael and Bramante restored the place in 1500 to the order of Giovanni de' Medici, afterwards Leo X.

But the finest building still existing on the Coelian Hill is the great round church of Santo Stefano Rotondo, with its fine mosaic and beautiful columns.   Larger of old than it is now, its pillars built into the outer wall forming a second circle surrounded in its turn by a wall, S. Stefano is a Christian building of the fifth century.   In the seventh century Pope Theodore brought there the bodies of the martyrs, Primus and Felicianus, burying them in the porch which was then turned into an apse and decorated with mosaics.   There we see the shining cross under a bust of our Lord with saints on either side.   We seem to have here a shy attempt at representing the Crucifixion which was not permitted till a century later.

The paintings of every sort of atrocious torture here by Pomarancio and Tempesta are too horrible and realistic to look upon.   They are in truth " *le sublime des âmes communes*," as Stendhal very justly said.

XXX

ROMA BAROCCA

THE transformation of Rome from a classical to a medieval city had been brought about by a universal catastrophe, the fall of the Empire in the West ; the transformation of Rome from a medieval and renaissance city to the baroque city which, in spite of modernisation, we still know, was also brought about and accompanied by an immense disaster, the Protestant revolution in which half Europe seemed to have been lost. It was this disaster which changed the form of S. Peter's church, it was this collapse which inspired the activities of the Jesuit Congregation, and produced the Counter-Reform, the Council of Trent, and finally the Catholic Reaction which altogether changed the aspect of the City, the very face of Rome.

Such a transformation had been foreshadowed in the work of so prophetic a master as Michelangelo, in the tragic tomb of Julius II in S. Pietro in Vincoli, for instance, where something overwhelming, something monstrous suggests itself ; not only in the gigantic figure of the Jewish Moses which seems like a caricature of Donatello's noble figure of S. John the Evangelist in Florence.

But it was not Julius II or even Michelangelo who changed the face of Rome ; it was Sixtus V. If one ignores the modern vulgarities imposed on Rome since 1870, it is really Sixtine Rome in which we move and have our being. It was Sixtus who drove the roads over the Quirinal, Viminal and Esquiline Hills, one of which has always borne his name, first as Via Felice and still as Via Sistina. It was Sixtus who erected the four great Obelisks. It was Sixtus who built the Vatican Library and the Sixtine Chapel in S. Maria Maggiore as a reliquary for the major relic of the church and as a resting place for S. Pius V, who loved him, and for his furious, ferocious, talkative self : all this by the hand of his favourite

225

engineer and architect Domenico Fontana, assisted as to the tombs by a handful of sculptors. It was Sixtus who built the Piazza of the Lateran, the Piazza del Popolo, the Acqua Felice, which bears his name,

But it was not Sixtus who built the church of Il Gesù, it was Vignola in the time of S. Pius V and that was in some sort the beginning of the whole transformation. This church, the headquarters of the new Society of Jesus, founded by the Spaniard S. Ignatius of Loyola, might seem to be the first reaction in architecture in Rome to the revolution in the north. As Vignola built and planned it for Cardinal Alessandro Farnese, a gift to the Society, it was not at all what it became later in the hands of Giacomo della Porta, still less what it is to-day. It was, as Vignola had it, a very plain and severe building, as San Giovanni de' Fiorentini still is, a rebuke and denial as it might seem to the luxury and splendour of Renaissance Rome, that had become a legend in the mouth of Luther and his " protestants." Begun in 1568 its great architect died in 1573 and the church was completed by Giacomo della Porta in 1584. It seemed and it was a novelty, though it in some sort recalled, vaguely enough, the basilica with its long nave ; but it had discarded aisles and columns and consisted of a single, rather short rectangular nave the sides of which were chapels, with a shallow transept surmounted at the crossing by a cupola over an octagon drum, the apse beyond being shallow too and semi-circular. In the angles on either side the apse Vignola contrived two circular chapels. The altar stood against the wall in the shallow apse and was thus visible from every part of the church, the focus of all who entered. The light came from the windows above the cornice and in the drum and so the church remained in some obscurity—this again was a novelty conducive, it was thought, to recollection and prayer. The church was thus rather puritanical, as we might say, in its severity and exactly corresponded not merely with the taste and convictions of its architect, but with the mood of the Counter Reform.

The church of Il Gesù established a fashion, for it perfectly expressed the disposition of the time, frightened by the revolt of the north ; and almost all the churches built in Rome

between 1570 and 1630 follow more or less closely the lines of
the Gesù, for instance : S. Maria in Vallicella (the Chiesa
Nuova, S. Philip Neri's church—1575, Martino Longhi) ;
S. Maria ai Monti (1580, Giacomo della Porta,) ; S. Girolamo
degli Schiavoni (1585, Martino Longhi) ; S. Giovanni de'
Fiorentini (1588, Giacomo della Porta, and Carlo Maderna) ;
S. Andrea della Valle (1591, Pietro Olivieri and Carlo
Maderna) ; S. Maria della Vittoria (1605, Carlo Maderna) ;
S. Susanna (1603, Carlo Maderna) ; S. Isidoro (1622, Antonio
Casoni) ; SS. Domenico e Sisto (1622, Vincenzo della Greca) ;
S. Ignazio (1626, Orazio Grassi). Some of these churches, it is
true, the Vallicella for instance and S. Giovanni de' Fiorentini
have divided the broad single nave into aisles and deepened
the transept, but largely these and other churches of
the first period of the Baroque style derive from the
Gesù. This, however, was not quite universal, S. Giacomo
degli Incurabili in the Corso with a façade by Carlo Maderna
was built by Francesco da Volterra and has an eliptical plan
and in S. Maria Maggiore the Sixtine and the Borghese chapels
have the form of a Greek cross under a dome and so has S.
Carlo ai Catinari, a lovely temple rather than a church,
built in 1612 by Rosati in honour of S. Carlo Borromeo. But
in S. Giovanni de' Fiorentini the original design even of Michelangelo was abandoned for the long nave, as it was in S. Peter's
itself.

But presently it began to be clear that all was not lost, that
the disaster which had threatened to destroy Catholic civilisation was not to happen, that the barbarians far from advancing
had been thrown back by a new Leo in the form of Ignatius
Loyola and his sons. The old Europe, Christendom, the
Europe of the Empire was still intact within its old frontiers
of the Rhine and the Danube. What was lost, grievous
though it might be, was only, save for a single province, the
outer barbarian lands that had never known the Empire.
The sky cleared, the severe and even puritanical mood of the
Counter Reform disappeared, giving place to an almost
uncontrollable joy, the enormous enthusiasm and energy of
the Catholic Reaction so perfectly expressed in the full Baroque
of Pietro da Cortona (1596–1669), Giovanni Lorenzo Bernini

(1598–1680), Francesco Borromini (1599–1667), Alessandro Algardi (1602–1654).

Pietro da Cortona began the upper church of SS. Martina e Luca over the old seventh-century building where he is buried and partly at his own cost in 1634. It is his most important work in architecture, a beautiful thing, if overloaded with ornament, full of light—a Greek cross under a dome. About the same time Francesco Borromini began S. Carlo alle Quattro Fontane (S. Carlino), elliptical in shape with eight Corinthian columns on each side, not a straight line anywhere. The much criticised, but most skilful undulating façade was only finished in 1682. These two churches in their turn seem to have set a fashion and were followed by a whole series of churches with central naves, Borromini himself in 1653 building S. Agnese in Piazza Navona, a Greek cross under a dome, Bernini building S. Andrea al Quirinale in 1658, elliptical in form and exquisitely harmonious, almost musical, a delightful work of genius. But delight seems to have possessed these masters.

Borromini builds S. Ivo in the Sapienza in the form of a bee to rejoice Urban VIII ; he tosses into the air the wonderful campanile of S. Andrea delle Fratte where Pope Urban stabled the winged angels Bernini had made for Ponte S. Angelo, because they were too beautiful to be exposed to the open air. He builds S. Carlino with its undulating façade, its honeycomb cupola, its charming sacristy, its double cloister. He builds the marvellous interior of S. Agnese in Piazza Navona beside Palazzo Pamphili where he constructs a gallery for the magnificent frescoes of the *Aeneid* by Pietro da Cortona ; and before the church Bernini sets his Fountain of the Four Rivers, the Nile shading his eyes, is it lest they be dazzled by the façade of the church, as baroque as the fountain ?

Meantime Bernini has created the lovely groups of sculpture in Villa Borghese, the Aeneas and Anchises (1617), the David (1618), the Rape of Proserpine (1622), the lovelier Apollo and Daphne (1623) and the unfinished Truth. He is now at work with Carlo Maderna on Palazzo Barberini for Cardinal Maffeo Barberini, afterwards Urban VIII, which was to be adorned by the masterpiece of Pietro da Cortona ; and before

LA CACCIA DI DIANA, by Domenichino (Borghese Gallery)

APOLLO AND DAPHNE, by Bernini (Borghese Gallery)

it he was to set his glorious Fontana del Tritone. Well might Urban say to him : *E gran fortuna la Vostra o Cavaliere, di veder papa il Cardinale Maffeo Barberini ; ma assai maggiore e la nostra, che il Cavalier Bernini viva nel nostro Pontificato.*[1] And it was Bernini who made in S. Peter's the tomb of Papa Barberini, where between them they had upreared under Michelangelo's dome, over the high altar, the unimaginable baldacchino of bronze with its twisted columns covered with gold and bees.

Then for Innocent X Bernini carved and arranged in Carlo Maderna's church of S. Maria della Vittoria the fantastic group of the Ecstasy of S. Teresa e Divino Amore, a scene for some unrealisable stage in a baroque theatre only matched by Crashaw's verses, *The Flaming Heart.* Finally for Alexander VII he enclosed the chair of S. Peter in a fabulous simulacrum of bronze, which seems to float there upheld by angels and supported by the four Doctors of the Church under the golden window of the Holy Spirit that only he could have imagined. To crown all he made the beautiful Scala Regia of the Vatican and that triumphant masterpiece the great Colonnade that encloses the Piazza di S. Pietro and stretches out as it were the arms of the Church herself to embrace the City and the world.

Others were busy too in those years of enthusiasm, Antonio Raggi carved the Berninesque *Noli Me Tangere* in SS. Domenico e Sisto ; Ercole Ferrata the Berninesque figure of S. Anastasia in the church of that name and Algardi the relief of Attila and the tomb of Leo XI in S. Peter's. Carlo Rainaldi builds the two churches at the head of the Corso in Piazza del Popolo and combines two Greek crosses in S. Maria in Campitelli (1656).

More various and perhaps therefore more interesting are the façades of these churches of the seventeenth century : Giacomo della Porta's simple design for S. Maria dei Monti (1579), the church itself interesting and typical of its period ; the same architect's very different façade of S. Luigi de' Francesi (1589), if indeed it be his. Then there is the curved façade of the

---

[1] Great fortune is yours, O Cavaliere, to see Pope the Cardinal Maffeo Barberini; but much greater our good fortune, that the Cavalier Bernini lives in our Pontificate. Baldinucci : *Notizie,* vol. IV, 284 ; V, 593 (Ed. Firenze, 1857).

Oratorio dei Filippini by Francesco Borromini, the undulating façade of S. Carlino by the same master and the outstandingly influential façade of S. Susanna (1603) by Carlo Maderna and the nobly satisfying façade by Giovanni Battista Soria of S. Gregorio Magno at the top of a flight of steps, with colonnade and forecourt, the upper storey once a magnificent library. The same master is responsible for the façade, in the same style, of Rosati's church of S. Carlo ai Catinari. The church dates 1612, the façade 1630, in which year Domenichino painted the four Cardinal Virtues below the dome and Pietro da Cortona a Procession with S. Charles Borromeo over the high altar. It is Pietro da Cortona who designs the charming façade of S. Maria in Via Lata. Again we have a façade above a flight of steps as in Soria's churches, only here the steps are delightfully curved in double flight, by Vincenzo della Greca before the church of SS. Domenico e Sisto (1623). Or there is the striking façade of SS. Vincenzo ed Anastasio, which, in Piazza Trevi with the most magnificent of great fountains, seems not to be too full of columns as it might do elsewhere.

The most original feature of the baroque church was the dome and there are very many of them from that over S. Peter's to that of S. Carlo al Corso, over the heart of S. Charles Borromeo and one of Carlo Maratta's finest works ; that of SS. Martina e Luca by Pietro da Cortona or those by Borromini over S. Andrea delle Fratte and over S. Agnese in Piazza Navona and the cupola of the Sapienza.

And then there are the pictures and frescoes of the period. The spirit of the Counter Reform which had created these magnificent and lovely churches demanded of the painters of the time an equal energy and an expression, a representation, of celestial splendour in those giddy and ample vaults together with a serenity and a grace of form, terrestrial and superterrestrial, which should be at once popular and seductive. Such is Baciccio's *Triumph of the Name of Jesus* on the vault of the Gesù.

In the first ten years of the seventeenth century Rome became a Mecca of Art : there arrived there artists not only from divers parts of Italy but from France, the Low Countries and Germany. Rome was thus the furnace in which were forged the immense talents that were to dominate European painting.

Already in the latter part of the sixteenth century, while inspiration was declining in painting, certain masters had appeared who interrupted the decline and became models for all European art in the seventeenth century ; Tintoretto and Veronese leap to the mind, but Correggio and Caravaggio are also of the company.

Federigo Barocci (1528–1612) seems to draw his technique from Correggio and to have been interested chiefly in a study of light and its play among various objects. He often seems to have created the forms Bernini was to use in sculpture as in the Angel of his Annunciation etching. He is full of delicacy and atmosphere, his colours are diffused all over his canvas ; he is full of grace and joy. His best works in Rome are, I think, his *Noli Me Tangere* in the Corsini Gallery, and the *Presentation in the Temple* in the Chiesa Nuova painted in 1594. His works in the Vatican and the Borghese Gallery are less remarkable. Barocci, as his best works show, is continually but not uninterruptedly inspired with tenderness, grace and truth.

Ludovico Carracci (1555–1619) also based himself on Correggio, but was not like Barocci constantly inspired ; more learned he and his cousins Agostino (1557–1602) and Annibale (1560–1609) are the real founders of the "Eclectic School". Ludovico is represented in Rome by his *Ecce Homo* in the Doria gallery. It was thanks to his cousins that their art triumphs in the official world in Rome and inspires and really sums up Italian monumental decoration. What could be lovelier as decoration, what more delightful in themselves, than the frescoes of Annibale and Agostino in the Palazzo Farnese ?

What could be more delightful, what more lovely with happiness, than the *Bacchus and Ariadne* of Annibale, the *Acis and Galatea* of Agostino in the Farnese Gallery, that gallery built for them in the Palace which Michelangelo had completed ? These works in all their vitality and accomplishment became the model for decorative painting in the Baroque period. Here in this gallery these decorations are as triumphant in their own way as Michelangelo's ceiling paintings in the Sistine Chapel. What could be more masterly than the drawing of the nude and of the draperies ; and the colours and light and shade are admirable—the poetical inspiration from the Classics perfectly expressed. Agostino and Annibale too, were learned men, but Annibale certainly is not without a riotous sense of humour as his *Mangiafagiuoli* in the Colonna Gallery proves ; and as a landscape painter he also excelled as may be seen in his historical pictures in the Louvre, though save in his *Flight into Egypt* scarcely evident in his works in Rome.

Out of the studio of the Carracci came Guido Reni (1575–1642) who in his clear chalky pictures as Venturi tells us " exalts an ideal of human nobility, feminine grace and sensitive religious feeling." He was certainly gifted with a feeling for beauty, but he is restrained by the conventions of his school and his age. His art is too calculated, too unspontaneous to delight us who do not, for better or worse, belong to a classical period. The name of Guido once so beloved leaves us as cold as does his *S. Michael Archangel* in the Cappuccini. And his *Martyrdom of S. Peter* in the Vatican Pinacoteca is surely without feeling, almost a *genre* piece. His best work is not of this kind, but such as we see in the pavilion of the Rospigliosi Palace here in Rome, *Aurora preceding Phoebus*, whose chariot is drawn by white horses, while the entrancing Hours advance in graceful flight ; and again his delightful *Andromeda* in the same pavilion. Or let us look at his work in the apse of the Cappella S. Silvia in S. Gregorio Magno, a fresco representing a Concert of Angels above a balustrade covered with drapery on which lie music books. In the centre are three *putti* singing and on either side charming figures of angels with trumpets, violoncellos, flutes and tabors ; some are whispering playfully together, others are looking curiously down. Above is God the Father in benediction, and the whole breathes an air of youthful happiness and beauty. In the neighbouring chapel of S. Andrea is another magnificent fresco of S. Andrew on his way to execution. He sees the cross, the instrument of his martyrdom, and, reminded of our Lord's Crucifixion, falls on his knees and adores the instrument of our redemption, before the astonished executioners. Another masterpiece by the same once adored but now too much depreciated master is in the Spada Gallery, his famous *Judith with the Head of Holofernes*. The so-called *Beatrice Cenci* in the Barberini Gallery is not among his best, though it has been among his most notorious works.

Another master from the school of the Carracci, Domenico Zampieri, was once famous as Domenichino (1581–1641). Such was once the reputation of this well-beloved master that both Poussin his contemporary and Stendhal in the early nineteenth century regarded him as the first of all painters after Raphael. Burckhardt notes his great sentiment but Venturi considers him " sincere and inspired but not a great painter." There can be no doubt, however, that led by Ruskin and the Romantic Movement we have neglected and depreciated Domenichino too much.[1] In the *Caccia di Diana* in the Borghese Gallery and in the equally unoriginal *Last Communion of S. Jerome* in the Vatican, if he is not a great painter, he has created two masterpieces. When Stendhal saw the *Caccia di Diana* he refused to look at any other picture in the Borghese Gallery, even the *Sacred and Profane Love* of Titian. In the *Communion of S. Jerome* he has been inspired by Agostino Carracci. He is more original perhaps and certainly extremely successful in his works in S. Andrea della Valle—the *Four Evangelists* in the pendentives of the cupola, very wonderful compositions, especially the S. John surrounded by angels, and below in the S. John Baptist revealing the Saviour to SS. Peter and Andrew. In the church of S. Luigi de' Francesi he has painted the frescoes of the story of S. Cecilia, where, if the saint disappoints us, the group of poor people struggling for the goods she is distributing are as masterly as they are moving.

With Guido Reni in competition he painted in the chapel of S. Andrew in S. Gregorio Magno the *Scourging of S. Andrew* in which again the emotion of the bystanders is what interests us and moves us—that group of women for instance thrust back by the carnifices is of great beauty.

---

[1] Ruskin, *Modern Painters*, vol. I, p. 93 : " palpably incapable of doing anything good ". Such a verdict seems as ridiculous to us as it would have seemed to Stendhal.

Giovanni Francesco Barbieri who is famous as Guercino (1591–1666), though he followed the same style, did not belong to the school of the Carracci. He is more lively than Guido Reni. His masterpiece in the Spada Gallery, the *Death of Dido*, is a magnificent work, passionate in its expression of sorrow and glorious in colour. If the *Incredulity of S. Thomas*, in the Vatican Pinacoteca is less moving, it is nevertheless a masterly work. Guercino is a fine, even brilliant, colourist, not above using crude tints and dramatic tricks of light. He often paints gloomy backgrounds with luminous reflections, but as often uses typically Emilian silvery light.

His gloomy backgrounds connect him if only in this with the Naturalists, the opponents of the Carracci school, and chief among them all with Michelangelo Caravaggio (1569–1609) whose wild, adventurous life was in keeping with his pictures. This great and stormy painter with his grand lines and falling lights, his carnation tints and coarseness is full of force, which sometimes even reminds us of his namesake. While the Carracci and their school were triumphant in Rome, Caravaggio from Lombardy comes down and, as Venturi describes it, " does away with the Florentine value of design as form, avoids all decorative adventure, simplifies his vision of objects by a clear demarcation between light and shade and so deepens and clarifies composition." His early pictures are full of a harmony of clear colours with a golden light and transparent shadows ; his last are gloomy, lighted by crude lights, yet always he proves himself to be the forerunner of the European masters of the century, Hals, Rembrandt, the young Velasquez. He it is more than any other individual painter who creates a new movement, a movement away from the imitation of Raphael and Michelangelo. If the Carracci sum up Italian monumental decoration, Caravaggio does the same for European realism.

The most characteristic works of Caravaggio in Rome are perhaps those in S. Luigi de' Francesi of the *Life of S. Matthew*, the *Calling of the Apostle* especially, with its grand and characteristic figures. One of his most famous works is the *Deposition* of the Vatican Pinacoteca. Its great overwhelming solemnity makes up for its lack of idealism: yet the figure of the sorrow-stricken Virgin with outstretched hands is as overwhelming as anything he ever painted. His pictures of single figures scattered through the many Roman galleries are always of high interest and charm us with their *genre* and in the so-called *Magdalen* of the Doria Gallery, just a girl playing with her jewels or in the *Boy with a basket of Flowers* in the Borghese gallery, he appears as the creator of " still life ".

In landscape the Baroque century expresses itself best in Claude and Poussin, foreign masters, yet Annibale Carracci may well represent Italy and his century and its wonderful style, more truly if with less romantic idealism, in those landscapes of his in Paris and Berlin which are not the least delight of his lovely and beloved art; while Salvator Rosa in his picture in the Colonna Gallery, a coast scene, is clearly fallen into Claude's mood.

Many another painter, often of importance, was at work at this time in Rome and in the full current of the *epoca barocca*. I have given a list, by no means complete, of their works in the appendix, for the use of the more curious reader. It would have been impossible in a work of this character to have discussed them and their works even with the brevity I have used above.

XXXI

THE PONTIFICAL NATIONAL COLLEGES IN ROME

ONE of the characteristic sights of Rome is the "crocodiles" of young ecclesiastics that in their various clerical dresses are continually to be met with in the streets, on the Pincio or in Villa Borghese, and never fail to rouse the curiosity of the most casual visitor.

These youthful clericals are the students of the various national Colleges or Seminaries for the training of priests in the Eternal City. Each College is distinguished by a special dress. The dress worn by the old foundations is the original collegiate dress : a black cassock and girdle or sash with long sleeveless coat (*soprana*) with two strings hanging from the arm holes (? leading strings). The clerical hat is worn by all. Here are a few of the various uniforms or student dresses familiar to every passer-by :—

Seminario Pontificio—Purple cassock and soprana, no sash.

Collegio Capranica—Black cassock and black soprana, no sash, silver buckles on shoes.

Propaganda Fide—Black double-breasted cassock, red pipings, and buttons, scarlet sash.

Austrian College—Scarlet cassock and black sash, scarlet soprana.

Greek College—Blue cassock with red sash, black soprana.

English College—Black cassock and soprana, no sash.

Scots College—Purple cassock, crimson sash, black soprana.

Irish College—Black cassock, red pipings, no sash, black soprana.

Canadian College—Priest's cassock, no sash.

North American College—Double black cassock, blue pipings, crimson sash.

French College—Priest's cassock, no soprana.

Belgian College—Priest's cassock, black sash, edged red.

Spanish College—Black cassock, blue sash, black cape, blue pipings.

The special education of youths for the Catholic priesthood
is of very great antiquity. A school for this purpose in Rome,
the Patriarchium, was attached to the Lateran by Gregory
the great and throughout the Middle Age such episcopal schools
existed side by side with the monastic schools and we may see
one of their children in Chaucer's " litel clergeon seven year
of age." The Council of Trent, as we might expect, established a stricter order with regard to these seminaries. The
Seminario Pontificio Romano was established at S. Apollinare
for the diocese of Rome. The Collegio Capranica which had
been founded in the fifteenth century and is thus reckoned the
oldest of all Pontifical seminaries was reformed, and the
Collegio for the Propaganda Fide which takes precedence of
the Capranica was founded by Gregory XV in 1622 and
established by Alexander VII in Piazza di Spagna in a palace
built by Bernini.

Of the National Colleges, the Austrian and the Greek are
reckoned the oldest, but their origins are parvenu beside
those of the English College, the *Venerabile*, which has been
established in one form or another in the Via Monserrato
since the fourteenth century and whose roots go back into the
eighth century or earlier, to the English Hospice founded in
727 by Ina, King of Wessex, according to Matthew of West-
minster.

" A.D. 727. Ina a prosperous and powerful King leaving
his Kingdom to his kinsman Ethelhard went to Rome in
order to exchange his temporal kingdom for an eternal one.
And when he arrived in that city he built a house in the
city with the consent and good will of Pope Gregory which
he called the school of the English, that the Kings of England and the royal family with the bishops and priests and
clergy might come to it to be instructed in the Catholic
doctrine and faith so as to prevent anything improper,
or contrary to the Catholic unity from being taught in the
English Church."

Under the year 816 the *Anglo-Saxon Chronicle* records
that " the English school in Rome was burned." This was the
fire in the Borgo represented in the fresco by Raphael in the
Stanze of the Vatican ; for the English school was situated
where the church of S. Spirito in Sassia still recalls the Schola

Saxonum or Anglorum, in the Borgo on the right bank of the Tiber. King Alfred obtained privileges for it from the Pope and it is said S. Thomas Becket dwelt there.

In the Jubilee of 1350 English pilgrims found it difficult to obtain hospitality and it was apparently this need that caused John Shepherd and Alice his wife and other English lay folk to buy property in the Via Monserrato which the Pope established as an English Hospice. This property was acquired in 1362. Here in the Hospice dedicated in honour of S. Thomas of Canterbury, which absorbed a hospice founded by an Englishman in Trastevere and dedicated in honour of S. Edmund, " every gentleman or well to do person if he desire was to be given bread wine and ware for three days free of charge and every commoner had the right to be received at the Hospice for eight days and nights with meat, drink and lodging." Here in 1415 Margery Kempe was received and given hospitality and then turned out :

> " Then was this creature received into the Hospital of Saint Thomas of Canterbury in Rome and she was houselled every Sunday with great weeping, boisterous sobbing and loud crying and was highly beloved by the Master of the Hospital and all his brethren. And then through the stirring of her ghostly enemy there came a priest that was held a holy man in the Hospital and also in other places of Rome, who was one of her fellows and one of her own countrymen. And not withstanding his holiness he spoke so evil of this creature and slandered so her name in the Hospital that through his evil language she was put out of the Hospital so that she might no longer be shriven or houselled therein." [1]

The numbers of English persons, rich and poor, who were able to make the pilgrimage to the Holy Places in the fifteenth and sixteenth centuries is very remarkable. In 1504–5, for instance, eighty-two persons were received at the Hospice, of whom 48 were poor people. In 1505–6 the guests were 212, of whom 157 were poor pilgrims ; in 1506–7 some 207 were received. Indeed until the quarrel of Henry VIII with the Pope the Hospice continually grew in usefulness, wealth and

[1] *The Book of Margery Kempe*, Ed. W. Butler-Bowdon (1936), pp. 123 *et seq.*

importance, and it was frequently the residence of the English Ambassador.

In 1412 the Hospice had been rebuilt and in 1445 a new church in honour of the Blessed Trinity and S. Thomas was consecrated and received among other papal privileges the extra parochial rights of a cemetery for the English which the old Schola Anglorum had possessed. It was the recognized centre of English influence in Rome, and in the time of Henry VII was officially controlled by the Crown, which in 1509 appointed Christopher Bainbridge, Archbishop of York, then in Rome, Custos of the English Hospice. In 1511 Bainbridge was created Cardinal, and dying in 1514, poisoned by his chaplain, was buried in the church of the Hospice and his beautiful monument with its effigy is still to be seen in the English College Chapel.

In 1527 the Hospice with the rest of the City suffered horrible outrage at the hands of the German mercenaries of the Constable Bourbon in the Sack of Rome. It lost all its plate and papers. From this blow the Hospice might have recovered, but not from the defection of the English King. Its source of revenue from England was cut off and its pilgrims were exiles seeking refuge from persecution. In 1538 the Pope appointed Cardinal Pole to be Custos. To this refuge of exiled priests in 1575 came Dr. Owen Lewis of New College, Oxford, an exile for his religion. He had been sent to Rome as his proctor by the Archbishop of Cambrai and having the confidence of the Pope and the Cardinal Protector of the English nation, persuaded His Holiness to turn the Hospice into a College for the training of English mission-priests and to use such revenues as remained to this end. In this project Dr. (afterwards Cardinal) Allen, also of Oxford, who had founded an English seminary in Flanders, concurred and agreed to send seminarists as a nucleus to the Roman seminary. Such was the inception of the *Venerabile*, this most famous English College whose children were designed to be martyrs for the Faith in the dreadful English Mission ; whose sons were greeted in the streets of Rome by S. Philip Neri with words from the hymn for the feast of Holy Innocents :

Salvete flores martyrum

so many they were who laid down their lives for the Faith and
the Supremacy of the Holy See.   Of these some have been
Beatified and many more declared Venerable.[1]

The hospitality of the College was not confined to Catholics.
John Milton was received here in 1648.   Richard Crashaw
too received its hospitality in 1646.   He was then a Catholic
and had been sent to the Pope by Queen Henrietta Maria.
He got little or nothing from His Holiness and is reported as
saying that if the Church was not founded on a rock, it was
founded on something as hard as a rock.

It would serve little purpose to go into the history of the
College thus founded which continued to flourish in Via
Monserrato under the Jesuit fathers and then under Secular
priests.   But a word may perhaps be said about its famous
title *il Venerabile*.

This was, it seems, conferred upon it by Pope Gregory XIII
(1572–1585) in honour of its martyrs.   The first document in
which we find the title is a broadsheet issued by Papal authority
publishing an Indulgence granted by Gregory XIII, for prayers
said for the conversion of England in the church of the Venerabile English College—" alla Chiesa del Ven.   Collegio degli Inglesi di Roma ".   This document is dated in manu-
script December 7, 1580.

In the following year Cardinal Cornelius writes in an official
document (*Ven. Arch. Chron.*, V, 319), " Venerabili Collegio
Anglicanae Nationis de Urbe " and thenceforth the notaries
of the Camera Apostolica all place the title " Venerabile "
before the name of the College and so it continued for 350
years.   When in 1918 the Constitutions of the College were
published in the official *Acta Apostolicae Sedis* the title was
" Constitutiones Ven. Collegii Anglici de Urbe."   Thus the
English College came by its unique, its most honourable and
its familiar title of " The Venerabile " which is borne by no
other seminary or college.[2]

The College has a beautiful villa at Palazzola on the Alban
Lake for summer residence.

---

[1] The College boasts forty-four martyrs in England.
[2] See article in *The Tablet*, Feb. 17, 1934, by Archbishop Godfrey, then Rector
of the Venerabile.

Among the more familiar names associated with the Venerabile are Blessed Robert Southwell, Fr. Persons, Cardinal Allen, Fr. Sherwin, Dr. Gradwell, Cardinal Wiseman, Cardinal Hinsley and Archbishop Godfrey, first Apostolic Delegate ln England.

THE SCOTS COLLEGE

The Scots also had a Hospice in Rome. It stood where S. Andrea delle Fratte now stands and no one can tell how old it was, but their College was founded by Clement VIII (1592–1605) in 1600. The Bull of December 5 of that year confers on the College thus founded all the privileges enjoyed by the Greek, Austrian and English colleges. At first the College was in Via del Tritone but in 1604 it was removed to its present site in Via delle Quattro Fontane. The country house of the College, where for nearly three hundred years the students have spent the summers, is in the Alban Hills near Grottaferrata.

THE IRISH COLLEGE

It was Gregory XIII who proposed to sanction an Irish College, but it is not till the following century that the project was carried out by Cardinal Ludovisi, Cardinal Protector of Ireland, at his own expense in 1625 under Urban VIII. A house was rented near S. Isodoro and opened on January 1, 1628. When Cardinal Ludovisi died in 1632 it was found he had made provision for the College in his will of an income of a thousand crowns a year, money to purchase a house, and a property at Castel Gandolfo for summer residence. At this time the famous Franciscan, Luke Wadding, was supervising the affairs of the College, but the Cardinal in his will directed that the College should be placed in the charge of the Jesuits. They governed it till 1772. It was at this time (1646) that Blessed Oliver Plunket was a student here. The College was attached to S. Agata dei Goti but in 1926 a new building in Via de' Santi Quattro was occupied, the College of S. Isidore.

All the other national colleges or seminaries are quite modern. The North American College dates from 1859, the French College from 1857, the Belgian from 1854, the South American College from 1858. The Spanish College in its present establishment dates from 1891.

THE BEDA COLLEGE

But the youngest of all is an English College, the Collegio Beda. Pope Leo XIII founded an institution in Rome for English-speaking students which he used to call " il mio collegio ". He dedicated it in honour of the Venerable Bede. Leo XIII realised the importance of providing a seminary for men of mature years who are called to the priesthood in middle life. It is the boast of the Beda that if S. Paul had lived in our time he would almost certainly have been sent to the Beda, that is of course had he been, as of course he would have been, an Anglo-Saxon.

There was already in existence the embryo of such an institution as the Beda under the name of the " Collegio Ecclesiastico " or, as it came to be known, the Collegio Pio. This had been established by Pius IX at the suggestion of Cardinal Wiseman when, as the result of the Oxford Move-ment and the conversion of Newman, after the re-establishment of the Catholic Hierarchy in England (1850) many Anglican clergy and laymen wished to enter the Catholic priesthood. This house of students was in Piazza Scossacavalli, near S. Peter's and was presently absorbed by the Venerabile. It was Cardinal Vaughan who approached Leo XIII with the suggestion of re-establishing the Collegio Pio as a separate College and this Leo determined to do, still within the Venerabile, in 1896, under the title Collegio Beda. In 1917 the Congregation responsible in Rome decided to separate the Beda from the Venerabile and a house was found for it in the Porta Castello near the Tiber. The Rector was the Rt. Rev. Mgr. H. K. Mann, the historian of the Popes of the Middle Ages. In 1922 the College removed to its present house in Via S. Nicolò da Tolentino. In 1928 Mgr. Mann died and the present Rector, Monsignor Charles

L. H. Duchemin, M.A., of Trinity College, Cambridge, himself an old student of the Beda, was appointed. The object of the College is the training for the priesthood of English converts and others of mature age and to enable English priests to pursue further studies in Rome. There are now (1950) more than fifty students ; the house is full and there is a waiting list.

XXXII

THE PINCIO—SANTA MARIA DEL POPOLO

THE Piazza di Spagna, that beautiful, irregular square, with its strange fountain by Pietro, father of Lorenzo Bernini, before the Palace of the Spanish Embassy at the foot of the Spanish steps, remains, for the English certainly, the very centre of Rome, though indeed it is but just within the Aurelian wall. It is, in fact, one of the most characteristic places in the modern city, Papal so long, the key, as it were, to all the strangers' quarter, which still forms so important and even so indispensable a part of the old capital of the world, for without it Rome might seem indeed something less than eternal. Here at least we may see daily under our eyes her old power of drawing all men to her still in action, in spite of every transformation, in spite even of the fact that she, to whom the whole world was once but an antechamber, has now become the plaything of the youngest of the nations.

From the Piazza the beautiful flight of steps, the Scala di Spagna built by Francesco de Sanctis in 1726, ascends to the famous church of the Santissima Trinità de' Monti and the convent of the Dames du Sacré-Cœur. On the right at the foot of the steps is the Keats-Shelley Memorial House. The Piazza opens on the south into the Piazza Mignatelli which is close by the Collegio di Propaganda Fide. There rises the lofty marble column of the Immaculate Conception crowned with a bronze statue of the Immacolata, erected in 1854 to commemorate the infallible definition of this dogma by the Pope.

Coming on a winter evening along the Via Condotti, which leaves the Piazza on the west and leads to the Corso, we see the real beauty of Rome, a beauty really of atmosphere, of colour in the splendour which the sunset has laid upon the whole Piazza, and not least upon that church of the SS.

HEAD OF THE APOLLO OF VEII (Museo di Villa Giulia)

APHRODITE (Museo delle Terme)

APOLLO (Museo delle Terme)

Trinità, whose twin towers seem to guard it from the summit of the Spanish steps. In that fortunate hour the whole place is an acropolis of ivory and precious moonstone, stained with delicate purple and red gold.

Eighteenth-century work though it be, on how many nights one is content to find that marvellous staircase the most beautiful thing in Rome. In the daytime, barricaded with flowers, noisy with the little people and old men who sit, as I suppose, to certain unthinkably romantic painters, the Scala della Trinità de' Monti seems as steep as the hill of Purgatory, but in the twilight and the darkness, when it is deserted by all, its grave, artificial lines, so cunningly sumptuous seem almost ascetic and very quiet in their ample beauty leading one slowly, with dignity, with many well-timed pauses, to the summit. And then, too, the mere stucco of the beautiful church to which it serves as a threshold or atrium is lost in the generous beauty of night. One might think it indeed to be of marble or some precious unheard of stone, chrysoprase or amber, jasper or chalcedony, or of ivory and pallid gold. Built in 1493 by that madman, Charles VIII of France, the SS. Trinità de' Monti has something of the ecstasy of a great French building restrained by the sanity of the sun. From its foundation till its partial destruction in 1798 it was in the possession of the Minimite friars, as their founder, the Calabrian, S. Francesco of Paola, wished his *frati* to be called —not the lesser friars like the Franciscans, but the least of all. Plundered and ruined during the French Revolution, the church was restored in 1816 by Louis XVIII and is now in the keeping of the little nuns of the Sacre Cuore, for whom Mendelssohn wrote the somewhat superficial music we may still hear at vespers, when, at the sound of their bell, the gardens of the Pincio so soon are empty, and all the City seems to pass suddenly from daylight into dusk under the iron cloud of sound that has burst over it, it seems at that signal.

Something of the fantastic beauty of that church which lends itself so readily to every aspect of the sky is to be found everywhere on the Pincio, which on certain afternoons is the one really gay and irresponsible place in the City. There, as it were, above the City, on a summer afternoon, amid

R

the languid fountains, under the evergreen trees whose sharp leaves seem to be all of bronze, the bourgeois world takes its ease, a little harshly and noisily perhaps, as Rome has always done, listening to music, or, cynically curious, watching the new Giulia Bella as she passes to and fro that small garden which takes on something of the aspect of a circus where the cars and a few horse-cabs pass continuously round and round. In the shadow and the sun run the children, little souls as gay as fairies, playing at hide-and-seek among their elders, or curiously watching one another, longing to be friends. Here and there struts an officer, in the shade under the trees a woman languishes beside her duenna, the little gay women pass alert, monotonously along the paths, the strangers yawn in their iron chairs or wander to the look-out ; round and round rush the motor cars, and the loud, self-conscious music of modern Italy plays the sun to its setting, boldly unaware of the tragic City which lies like a shadow on the hills, into which they will all pass so swiftly and so indifferently at the sound of the bells.

The seminarists in their various coloured uniforms, their frocks of scarlet, their cassocks of crude blue and orange, or purple, or black, mix with the indifferent crowd, or standing in a heap, as it were, unhealthy and listless and trooping away, company after company at the sound of the Ave Mary. One meets them often thus as one comes into the Pincian Gardens, as I love to do, from the Trinità de' Monti, at the close of the day, when the crowd is leaving it, past the beautiful Villa Medici with its cloister of ilex before it in which a fountain of a single jet plays all day long.

But it is not in the afternoon or at sunset alone that the Pincio has a charm, but early in the morning too, before the sun has southed. It is almost deserted then, and the fountains whisper together in the silence in the shadow and the sun. One wanders there under the trees or in Villa Borghese, always returning to the look-out over the City towards S. Peter's, lingering there for a time before descending to the Piazza del Popolo and the beautiful church of S. Maria del Popolo. Out of the gate Porta del Popolo passes the Flaminian way, and by that road our fathers came from England, S.

Maria del Popolo being indeed the first Roman church they would see.

Built at the end of the eleventh century by Pope Paschal II to exorcise those evil spirits which were supposed to haunt the tomb of Nero, buried hereabout, it was rebuilt in 1227 by Gregory IX and got its present name at that time, for the Pope brought thither a famous image of the Madonna from the Lateran, and it was built, it is said, from contributions made by the people. The church we now see, however, is not Gregory's, but that which Sixtus IV built after designs by Pintelli in 1472, re-decorated by Bernini and his pupils. It is strange that it has always been connected with people the most detested, for if it stands in Nero's burial place, it was the church of the Borgias, and Luther stayed in the adjacent convent of Augustinians when he came to Rome. The chief interest S. Maria del Popolo has for us to-day, however, is rather artistic than historical, for it possesses some fine frescoes by Pinturicchio, and the Chigi Chapel there was built after designs by Raphael, while the tombs of the founder, of the Rovere and of Marcantonio Albertoni are especially remarkable.

The church which Sixtus had restored was naturally a favourite with his family, the Rovere, and in 1480 Girolamo Riario, the Pope's nephew, became its chief warden. Nor were they alone in their love of it, for in 1473 Roderigo Borgia had given a marble altar for the service of the Madonna Gregory IX had brought from the Lateran. It is, however, chiefly to the Rovere family that we owe the frescoes of Pinturicchio that remain to us, those in the chapel painted to the order of Cardinal Innocenzo Cibò having perished.

For Domenico della Rovere, Cardinal of S. Clemente, Pinturicchio painted the first chapel on the left with the story of S. Jerome, while in the third chapel on the left he or his pupil painted, for the nephews of Cardinal Basso della Rovere, five lunettes of the life of the Madonna, and the vault of the choir above the tomb of Cardinal Basso is painted in his manner with the Redeemer and the Madonna, and beneath the four evangelists, the four sibyls, and the four doctors of the Church. Over the altar in the chapel of S. Jerome is the Nativity, that one might almost mistake for Perugino's Adoration at

Perugia, and there around it, as it were, five lunettes with scenes from the life of the saint.

On the opposite side of the church is the Chigi Chapel, which Raphael designed. In the form of an octagon, surmounted by a drum on which stands the beautiful cupola, it is worthy of that master, perfect in proportion and charming because it is absolutely in tune with itself. Decorated by Luigi della Pace from Raphael's designs, it is one of the few unspoiled works of art, carried out under the supervision of one man, left to us in Rome.

The Borgia, unlike the Rovere, have left in S. Maria del Popolo nothing but a memory, unless we remember that coat carved on the Tabernacle of Bregno in one of the chapels there. Nevertheless, the church was especially dear to them. There the Duke of Gandia was buried with his mother, Vanozza, there Lucrezia went to mourn her murdered husband, and later, September 1501, she there rejoiced when she learned that she was to marry Alfonso d'Este. She rode thither through the City in magnificent attire to offer thanks, escorted by four bishops and three hundred horsemen. Her robe, which cost some three hundred ducats, she gave to her court-buffoon who, putting it on, rode through Rome shouting, " Hurrah for the most illustrious Duchess of Ferrara ! Hurrah for Pope Alexander VI ! " In that spectacle Rome seemed once more to have expressed herself.

XXXIII

THE JANICULUM—SAN PIETRO IN MONTORIO —SANT' ONOFRIO

THE Janiculum, that golden hill of sand, Mons Aureus, Montorio, stands like a huge long bastion to the west of the City, between the City and the desert, the Campagna, the most beautiful desert in the world. Sacred to Janus of the sun, itself, as Pliny tells us, I know not with how much truth, the site of that old city of Janus Antipolis, where Numa, the Sabine king, was buried in the golden age, the books of his laws and ordinances being hidden with him in that sacred soil. For long the true bulwark of Rome, the key of Etruria, it was thence the great Etruscan leader, Tarquinius Priscus, the future king looked down on the City, as Lars Porsena did when that other Tarquin, surnamed the Proud, returned in vain after his deposing and expulsion, and Horatius kept the bridge. That is almost the last notable incident in the history of Rome which the Janiculum can claim : since then it has stood there a huge, disused bulwark between the City and the vast solitude which for so long has hemmed her in, that beautiful desert of which she has been the marvellous rose. And to-day the Janiculum still stands on guard : the wind that comes from the sea, like a white ghost across those low, inviolate downs, breaks first on this tremendous bastion which, scattered with gardens and flowers, hides the setting sun, casting at evening the first shadow over Rome. It keeps the gates of Latium and speaks with Soracte and the Alban Hills, the Monti Sabini and the sea. It is the look-out of the City, and just as the Tarquins and Porsena first gazed thence on Rome, so we too may look thence for the first time on what was once the capital of the world, and is still so beautiful and moving, full of the great and friendly shadows that people that immortal air.

Driving thither from the strangers' quarter by Trastevere

to S. Pietro in Montorio, or from S. Pietro in Vaticano by the gate of the Holy Spirit and S. Onofrio, by whatever way your approach may be, you come out of the City into a solitude, and it is in an almost absolute silence you will then look for the first time from the City to the Campagna, from the Campagna to the changeless hills. From that serene height Rome seems to lie beneath you spread out at your feet, a not too vast bewilderment of domes, towers, warm roofs and golden houses among the green oasis of her hills. Here and there some famous building shines like a planet in this vast constellation that has decided the fate of the world. Lonely, on the north, rises S. Peter's, thence to the east and southward stand, like seven stars, the seven domes, S. Agnese in Piazza Navona, S. Andrea della Valle, the Pantheon, S. Trinità de' Pellegrini, S. Carlo al Corso, Il Gesù, and S. Maria in Campitelli. Beyond these, eastward from north to south, rise Castel S. Angelo, the Villa Medici, the Villa Ludovisi, the Palazzo Quirinale, the Campidoglio, the Colosseum, the ruins of the Palatine, the Villa Mattei on the Coelian, S. Sabina in Aventino, S. Alessio in Aventino, and on the edge of the Campagna, scattered with the vast ruins of the acqueducts, stands the Pyramid of Cestius at the gate of S. Paul. Within this marvellous arc lies the City herself across which the Tiber is bound like an inviolate girdle of gold, sealed with the bridges whose names are household words.

Hinc septem dominos videre montes
Et totam licet æstimare Romam. . . .

One turns aside at last from that too dazzling spectacle to enter the church of S. Pietro in Montorio. Founded in the ninth century, but rebuilt in the fifteenth by the Catholic Kings after designs by Baccio Pintelli, the church consists of a single nave, fine and spacious, with four chapels on either side, the first and second on the south being decorated by Sebastiano del Piombo, and the pupils of Perugino. There is little else to see, but somewhere beside the high altar Beatrice Cenci sleeps in her nameless grave. Over the high altar Raphael's Transfiguration used to stand. The second chapel on the left was designed by Bernini. The fame of the church arose from the legend which was current in the fifteenth century, though apparently not earlier, that S. Peter was here crucified. For this cause Bramante designed the marvellously lovely Tempietto to the south of the church in the garden of the Franciscan convent that stands beside it.

Behind S. Pietro is the great Fontana Paolina in whose name you may find that of its architect and of the Pope, Paul V, who built it. Thence along the Passeggiata Margherita to S. Onofrio and Tasso's Oak, you have the City at your feet, and before you one of the most wonderful views in the world of the desert and the hills. And so it is always a little reluctantly that at evening or midday one descends at last to S. Onofrio.

Founded in the first half of the fifteenth century by a certain Niccolò da Forca Palena, a Gerolomite hermit, with the assistance of Eugenius IV, S. Onofrio became the last refuge of Tasso who, only a shadow of himself, came to die there in 1595. Half mad with disgrace, persecution and misfortune, the poet had come to Rome at the bidding of Clement VIII, Aldobrandini, who, thinking to honour him, wished to place on his head the crown of Petrarch. But as it happened, this consolation, and to Tasso certainly it would have been an infinite comfort, was denied him, for before the coronation took place he became ill with fever, and, retiring to S. Onofrio, he presently died there in a cell which we may still visit in the convent.

The church, certainly, has other claims on our notice than the presence there of Tasso. Approached by a fine portico, beneath which are certain lunettes painted by Domenichino, and the chapel of the Rosario, in which is the tomb of the founder of the order, Pietro Gambacorti of Pisa, it consists of a single wide nave with two chapels on either side, one of which contains an altarpiece by Carracci, another, the monument to Tasso, erected by Pius IX. It is, however, in the first chapel on the right are frescoes of the Annunciation by Melozzo da Forlì and in the tribune frescoes by Baldassare Peruzzi which, for all their repainting, still recall to us dimly the charming work of the school of Perugino. Below we see the Virgin and Child between S. Onofrio, S. Jerome, S. Mary

Magdalen, and Niccolò da Forca Palena, the founder of the church, while on one side is the Nativity, on the other the Flight into Egypt, and above, the Coronation of the Virgin, with the four Sibyls, and five angels in the lunettes. We come upon Peruzzi's work again in a lunette to the right of the high altar, where he has painted S. Anne and the Virgin, and indeed so charming a mannerist as he seems altogether in place in the church we have visited really for the sake of Tasso. But even Tasso's name might seem to be but an excuse for lingering where the world is so wide and fair, where, between the desert and the hills, Rome lies like some great flower in the sun, or at evening is lost in the twilight and built in our dreams.

XXXIV

THE GALLERIES OF SCULPTURE

MUSEO NAZIONALE

THE Museo Nazionale founded in the Baths of Diocletian in the monastery of the church of S. Maria degli Angeli chiefly for the reception of those antique works of art which, from time to time, are found within the Eternal City, and marvellously enriched by the inclusion of the Boncompagni Collection, and works from Cyrenaica, contains the most precious collection of sculptures in Rome, not only because of the rarity and beauty of the statues, but also because they are for the most part untouched by the restorer, and come to us with all, or nearly all, their original beauty of form and texture. In the Capitoline Museum, or the Galleries of the Vatican, we have a vast array of statues, Roman copies after lost Greek originals, compromised and spoiled for us by the restorer and polisher who, from the time of the Renaissance till our own day, have not hesitated to try to amend the destruction of time, only to confirm it and to hide from us what little beauty had escaped that inevitable vengeance. For this cause the Venus de' Medici moves us so little, the Venus of the Capitol seems to have lost its charm, the Apollo of the Belvedere fails to convince us of its nobility, the Apoxyomenos seems to have lost something of its perfection. In those famous galleries there is scarcely a statue that is not spoiled.

In the Museo Nazionale, however, another and a better fashion has been followed ; the works we see there, whatever their original beauty may have been, are not patched and smoothed out of all recognition, but remain, broken it is true, yet unspoiled by the narrow taste of the Renaissance, the vicious taste of the centuries since then. And so, although almost nothing is to be found there which may compare with the treasures of the museums of London, Paris, and Athens, we may find in those broken statues something of the delicacy and beauty which their creators gave to them, and which time alone has been powerless altogether to take away.

This at least would confer on the Museo Nazionale a distinction which no other museum in Rome possesses, and then, set as it is, about a garden of cypresses in a ruined monastery of which the beautiful church was designed by Michelangelo, within the Thermae, the building is in itself a work of art, romantic too and full of a peculiar charm which doubtless contributes to our enjoyment of the work that has been placed there—work that in its more precious examples at any rate has nothing to do with Rome, and remains as alien there as it is in the Louvre or the British Museum. All the art of the world is really a stranger in Rome ; crowded as it is with works of art, the Eternal City holds them all even to-day as spoil. Her art was government ; for the rest she had but contempt ; with her, art was a fashion that served to deck her triumphal progress or to commemorate what she had done.

Tu regere imperio populos, Romane, memento . . .
Excudent alii spirantia mollius aero . . .

Nor was this attitude towards beauty, beauty as a part of the moral nature of man, confined to the antique age. Her galleries to-day are full of the work of aliens, Florentines, Umbrians, Sienese and Neapolitans, while her museums are crowded with copies of the matchless work of the Greeks. Her materialism has always been almost transcendental. In her strange heart Aphrodite was born again as Venus, the goddess of animal pleasure and fecundity ; Ares was changed into Mars, the God, not of Virtue, but of War. She stole the world from us to give it us again in her own likeness. Well, that has always been her rôle in life. She conquered Greece like a barbarian, using the genius of the conquered to celebrate her own glory : and the most living things in Rome to-day are either Greek or imitations of them. It is this fact which places the Museo Nazionale so far above any other museum in Rome ; it possesses actual Greek work, while the others are full of the realistic, heavy, and imitative works of Rome.

Among the few precious fragments from the hands of the Greeks which are to be found in the Museo Nazionale, it is scarcely surprising that that should be the most beautiful which is furthest from the Roman understanding. I mean those reliefs of the fifth century B.C. which, carved about a throne, represent the Birth of Aphrodite. The goddess rises from the sea veiled, as it were, in the salt sea water, to be received by the Hours, two robust and supple girls whom she embraces half unconsciously, while they veil very sweetly her cold nudity. She rises to the sound of a pipe, to the sharp yet languid odour of incense in the nimble morning air, that seems to have sent a delicious shiver along her virginal body. Passionate and noble in her divine innocence, she turns towards one of the Hours almost as maidenly as herself, with a look, is it of welcome? Her hair, caught by a narrow band, falls on her shoulders heavily, and under her dripping tunic, delicate and light, one sees the tender body, the virginal breasts, the long throat, and girlish limbs. The emotion we receive is as profoundly religious as it is human.

It is into another and less real if more actual world that we come when we stand before the Apollo, carved after an early work by Pheidias. It is not a god who has here put on humanity, but man who is become a god and is about to return to the world.

Nothing, however, of that great age expressed in the work of Pheidias is to be found in Rome, unless we accept the magnificent statue of a Kneeling Youth, really a fragment but superb alike in its marvellous texture, its delicate *nuances*, and its finish, or the Juno Ludovisi as examples of it ; and indeed that head is one of the most majestic and beautiful fragments left in the City. " It is like a poem of Homer," wrote Goethe in his enthusiasm. Yes, it is like a poem of Homer translated by Virgil.

That Aphrodite who came into the world so innocently in the fifth century might seem to be but the elder sister, or just to have grown up perhaps and to have passed into the sunlight, losing something, it is true, of the beautiful severity that was part of her youth and her godhead, in the draped statue which passes under her name. She stands before us like some exquisite vision clothed from head to foot in a long, clinging veil that only reveals the wonder of her loveliness. The influence of the fifth century is there, as it is though more subtly in the Dionysus from Hadrian's Villa, a fine copy of a Greek original in bronze, cast probably in the early years of the fourth century.

The superb Aphrodite of Cyrene, an Hellenistic work of the second century B.C., is now one of the outstanding glories of the Museum and might seem to justify the Italian annexation of Cyrenaica now so tragically ended. In all its sensual beauty it conjures up for us in a vision that fair Greek city on the plateau above the African shore :

> Where the shoals hide and ceaseless south winds blow,
> Between Great Syrtes and the Egyptian sand,
> Fearful, the Grecian galleys sought thy strand,
> Cyrene, child of Thera, long ago.
> And where Apollo's murmuring sources flow,
> And whispering pines and whispering poplars stand,
> They built thee, lovely in a stony land,
> Nor dreamed what end their templed streets should know.
> Young Sophists crowded Aristippus' school,
> And Lais' beauty gilded many a tale,
> And where the plane tree shadows Cyre's pool
> Callimachus first heard the nightingale.
> All, all forgot, and thou ! Yea, all but one
> Simon, thy envied, thy compassionate son.

Those adorable figures of Ariadne sleeping and of Sappho are copies of works by some pupil of Praxiteles, and with them, lovely as they are, we are already come to the decadence. With the Pugilist at Rest we are in the midst of the realism that Rome could so well understand and that was to take refuge from itself in the sensuality of such a figure as the Hermaphrodite. But perhaps the happiest and certainly the most charming examples we find here of Roman work are the stucco reliefs which once decorated the walls of a Roman house that stood close to the Farnesina in the time of the early Empire. They represent scenes of country life, and of certain religious mysteries in which we see women dancing and sacrificing to Priapus on the feast of Dionysus. Nothing more exquisite than those three lithe and charming figures who, clothed in supple draperies, sacrifice to the god, is to be found in Rome. And indeed we may only compare with them their sister, she, who from the height of a great rock, turns to her companions with I know not what welcome or encouragement in a gesture altogether naïve and lovely. It is as though suddenly, amid all this dead beauty, one had heard in the still sunshine some secret and youthful voice chanting in a garden the verses of Theocritus.

II. THE CAPITOLINE MUSEUMS

It is an emotion less fresh and less spontaneous that we experience in the Museum of the Capitol. One of the first of those Roman galleries which later became so famous, it was founded by Innocent X, and is indeed only of later foundation than the collection in the Palazzo dei Conservatori which was established by Sixtus IV in 1471. But if it be less precious than the Museo Nazionale, it is far more famous, being indeed the most famous museum in Rome, since it possesses the " Dying Gaul," the " Wounded Amazon," the " Faun," after Praxiteles, and the " Aphrodite." But what need can there be to speak of such things as these, or what joy in remembering them ? They have become the commonplaces of the schools, and great as they are, their fame has consumed them.

For long called the " Gladiator "[1] the nationality of the figure which we know as the " Dying Gaul " is to be recognised by the necklace, the hair brushed back from the forehead, the moustache, and the shield, and trumpet beside him. No Roman sculptor was ever capable of creating a figure so wonderful in its vitality, dignity, and modelling. At Pergamum, however, Attalus had set up statues in bronze to commemorate his victories over the Gauls, and this figure is probably a contemporary copy of one of those Greek works, the material being of a local marble of Asia Minor and the execution genuine Pergamene work.

The origin of the " Wounded Amazon " is more doubtful ; one hesitates whether to attribute it to Pheidias or Polycleitus.

[1] Among others by Byron in the well-known verses in *Childe Harold*.

There are at least three types of this subject, the first of which, after Polycleitus as it is thought, is represented in the Vatican ; the second, of which a statue is also to be found in the Vatican, is best represented by the Capitoline statue ; and the third, the so-called Mattei type, also in the Vatican, which does not represent a wounded Amazon at all, but one using her spear to mount her horse. All these types probably go back to the statues of the Amazons in the Temple at Ephesus of which Pliny speaks. The first type is generally attributed to Polycleitus ; but with the second no decision seems possible. We see an Amazon with her right arm raised, leaning probably on a spear. Her head is bent and her *chiton*, fastened on the left shoulder, has been slipped from her right by her left hand, which still holds the drapery at her waist, so as to keep it away from a wound under the right breast. The second type is softer and more sentimental than the first, and may well have been a sort of protest against its inconsistencies.

In the " Aphrodite " of the Capitol, we come for the first time upon a copy or adaptation of the most famous work of Praxiteles, the " Aprodite " of Cnidus. The best and most beautiful copy at present known to us is, we are told, that in the Vatican which has been covered from the waist down with a hideous petticoat of stucco. But since that is hidden from us, we must be content with the " Aphrodite " of the Capitol.

The story runs that when Phryne, whose glorified beauty we may see perhaps in the " Aphrodite," tricked Praxiteles into naming his finest statues by telling him his studio was on fire, he exclaimed that all his labour was lost if the " Satyr " and the " Eros " were destroyed. She chose the " Eros " and dedicated it at Thespiae, but the " Satyr " was set up in the street of Tripods in Athens. It was copied many times ; the most famous replica that has come down to us being the " Faun " of the Capitol. Soulless, happy as a bird is happy in the sunshine and the wind, the " Satyr " of Praxiteles appears to us as altogether human in bodily form save for his pointed ears. Leaning on the trunk of a tree, a leopard skin across his shoulders, he is resting for a little while in the genial heat, a pipe in his right hand, smiling faintly for joy of the long afternoon to come. Here again, as so often, before Greek work, in our hearts we find a subtle music, as though all their thought and effort had been, as indeed it was, to evoke a harmony in the soul, between body and spirit.

But after all what is perhaps the most satisfying, because the most original, of the works of art to be found in the Capitoline Museum is the vast series of portrait busts of the Emperors, the most perfect, I suppose, and certainly the most complete in existence. Lingering there, we seem for a moment to understand what this was which we call the Roman Empire ; we are able to apprehend its common virtues, its sense of order, at least of the need of order, as well as its materialism and blindness to the necessities of the hearts of men. No one, as it seems to me, can pass through that hall without a certain shrinking and disgust, yes, at our very selves, our own civilisation which we see so surely mirrored there. This is the bureaucracy, blatant, assured, and never to be shamed from which we too are suffering. And as we look into the sad, disillusioned face of Aurelius, so indifferent and defeated, or into the eager countenance of Julian, we seem to understand that even such men, even the best of them, as Trajan or Aurelius, were prisoners who had lost all thought or desire of freedom, and were indeed incapable of anything but a sort of domination in which all has been surrendered but a fond assurance of their own omnipotence.

In the Palazzo dei Conservatori, and the Palazzo Caffarelli once the German Embassy adjoining it, opposite the Capitoline Museum, a number of collections of works of art, sculpture and pictures have been brought together including the New Capitoline Collection, the Museo Mussolini and the old collection assembled here in Papal times.

In the New Capitoline Collection one's attention is arrested by the colossal statue of the Emperor Constantius, son of Constantine the great : the head and limbs of a similar statue of his mighty father are in the entrance courtyard. The best things here are the Head of an Amazon, the relief of a Maenad and the Marsyas, a Hellenistic work of the second century B.C.

The Museo Mussolini was arranged here in 1925. It consists of fragmentary works, for the most part in marble, from the recent excavations and those once assembled in the Antiquarium.

But the most beautiful things here belong to the old collections, the archaic Greek works of the fifth century and earlier, the draped Female statues, the Tomb-stele of a girl with a dove, the Hermae. And then there are the famous Capitoline bronze She Wolf which was preserved in the Lateran already in the tenth century ; the Boy taking a thorn from his foot, a made-up work with its lovely Archaic head and Hellenistic body ; the magnificent Roman bust of a bearded man of the Consular period, perhaps Junius Brutus. Further in the Sala degli Orazi there is the baroque bust of Urban VIII by Bernini.

The Picture Gallery founded by Benedict XIV has some important works of the seventeenth century by Annibale Carracci, Domenichino, Guido Reni, Salvator Rosa, Caravaggio, Pietro da Cortona, Luca Cambiaso and a portrait by Van Dyck.

III. MUSEO DI VILLA GIULIA

In the Valle Giulia beyond the Borghese gardens is the Villa of Pope Julius III, built by Vignola in 1550, not without advice both of Michelangelo and Vasari. This beautiful building has been arranged as a Museum chiefly for the magnificent Etruscan antiquities from Palestrina, Veii, Falerii, and so forth, and because of at least of two of its treasures should not on any account be missed.

The work that particularly delights me here is the wonderful Apollo of Veii, a life-size terracotta statue discovered in 1916. It dates from the sixth century B.C. and is, we are told, a figure from a group consisting of Heracles and Apollo fighting for a hind in the presence of Hermes and Artemis. Parts of this group may still be seen in the garden on the south of the Capitol; where, in the Palazzo dei Conservatori, the Capitoline She Wolf the work of the same artists, is kennelled.[1]

The Apollo is perhaps the finest extant work of Etruscan

---

[1] Fine as this Wolf is, it is completely put in the shade by the bronze Chimaera of Arezzo in Florence, a magnificent work of creative imagination.

FOUNTAIN OF THE TRITON, by Bernini (Piazza Barberini)

SACRED AND PROFANE LOVE, by Titian (Borghese Gallery)

sculpture. It is of terracotta painted in polychrome and its attitude suggests that it formed part of a group as it did, though all we have of the other figures save tiny fragments is a beautiful head, said to be that of the Hermes. But these are the mere facts about it. The aesthetic impression this wonderful figure makes as a work of art is absolutely overwhelming. No one who has looked on this masterpiece, terrible and ruthless in its beauty, can ever forget it again.

The other work here which moves and delights me is that sarcophagus from Cervetri (Caere) with its figures, a noble and his wife half sitting, half reclining on a bed or a couch, at a feast is it? beautifully decorated. The man is noble of countenance, dignified, grave, with long hair and clipped and tended beard and shaven lips. His consort wears a round close-fitting cap under which her hair arranged in plaits falls on her shoulders. This work is of the same age as the Apollo.

A visit to the Museo di Villa Giulia is, on account of these two works of art, not to be omitted, but the Museum has many other fine things, including on the upper floor the objects found at Falerii near Città Castellana, that ancient and powerful city of Etruria which gave so much trouble to Republican Rome. But like Stendhal with the Caccia di Diana of Domenichino I have no eyes for anything here save the Apollo and the sarcophagus on any one day.

IV. THE VATICAN MUSEUM

If the Capitoline Museum comes at last to be full of disappointment, incapable of giving us any profound emotion by reason of the materialism, as we say, of the Roman work to be found there, copies of the exquisite and serious work of the Greeks from which all that was really living has unaccountably vanished, what are we to say of the Vatican galleries which are filled with works of far less account, and without, or almost without, an original statue, are crowded with reproductions of classical models? Indeed it is as though we had come into a vast necropolis. For these strange caricatures of statues that once were living in the world are a part of the ostentation of Rome, they were made, not for love, but for pride, that some

S

wealthy senator or favourite might hear the echo of an immortal fame and read the names of Polycleitus, of Scopas, of Praxiteles, of Lysippus on the statues that decorated his house. The only possible value of such works for us consists in the material truthfulness with which they have been copied from the original. Not that we can hope to find in them even a shadow of the beauty of the Greek work that is lost for ever, but that we may perhaps hope to know—if that be of any value in itself—something of the gesture, attitude, and shape of things which were once part of the most beautiful treasure in the world. We shall assuredly get but little further satisfaction out of a collection, which, renovated and repaired, as it has been again and again, no longer represents even the work of the Romans in its integrity, but is now the caricature of a caricature. For, if the Roman work was originally dull and heavy and base, what are we to think of it now that it has passed through the hands of the sixteenth, seventeenth, and eighteenth centuries, which restored and repolished what even at first had been a sort of grimace, a mere imitation ?

This being so, we shall be inclined to pass by, for all its immense fame, the " Apollo Belvedere," and concentrate our attention on such realistic work as the great " Torso " or the "Apoxyomenos " or the " Antinous " among the statues, and to such busts as that of the " Young Augustus."

The " Torso" is obviously the work of an Hellenistic artist for a Roman patron, and like all the work of that school is full of exaggeration. It is, of course, but a fragment of a once perfect work which is generally supposed to have represented the Cyclops Polyphemus seated on a rock by the seashore, shading his eyes with his hand and looking for Galatea. There can be but little doubt that the original work of which this was a copy was of the period after Lysippus. And however fine that original may have been, we have here, in spite of the admiration of Michelangelo, a representation of the human form at once decadent and conventional. Who knows how far the minute and hard realism of such a thing as this might not have led the great Florentine in his admiration of it, had he not cared too greatly for the beauty of his material to do more than allow it to express itself ?

We come upon the work of Lysippus himself, though only, as it were, in a translation, in the "Apoxyomenos," which is perhaps the most precious statue in the gallery. Lysippus, we are told, was an impressionist, that is to say he was not concerned so much with the actual imitation of nature, as with the correctness and vividness of his expression of it. In the statue of an Athlete scraping the oil and sand of the palaestra from his right arm with a strigil held in his left hand, he seems by no means to have made a portrait statue, but to have summed up his impressions of the Athlete generally, to have made in fact an ideal statue, or rather not to have imitated life, but to have expressed it. The pose is exquisite and vigorous and almost momentary in its lightness. The gesture is noble and free, and the whole statue of which this is a copy must have been of a splendid beauty. Pliny tells us that when Agrippa brought it from Greece to adorn the baths, Tiberius admired it so much that he carried it away to his own palace, but was compelled to restore it by the people, who mobbed him when he next appeared among them.

What the general Roman taste really was, even among the most cultivated, we may understand from the praise Pliny gives to the Laocoon group which stands to-day in the beautiful Cortile del Belvedere which Bramante made for Julius II. " . . . The Laocoon," he tells us, " . . . which stands in the palace of the Emperor Titus . . . may be considered superior to all other works both in painting and sculpture. The whole group, the father—the boys and the awful folds of the serpents—were formed out of a single block in accordance with a vote of the Senate by Agesander, Polydorus, and Athenodorus, Rhodian sculptors of the highest merit." In accordance with a vote of the Senate ! It is almost as though we heard the voice of one of our own countrymen. But the finest things in the world are not achieved by the vote of an assembly but by the genius of a man, for whom the " vote of the Senate " must always be an impertinence. And as a matter of fact the Laocoon, far from being " superior to all other works both in painting and sculpture," is just an example of what sculpture should not attempt. That it is falsely restored goes for nothing or very little. And we feel that this ecstasy of pain is invoked not for any high purpose or on its own account, but that the sculptor may seize the opportunity of producing a decorative effect while, at the same time, he shows us how realistic his work can be. One cannot deny a certain technical achievement to the group, but it is displayed at the expense of every other beauty and truth.

As for the " Apollo Belvedere," it will be enough to place beside it a single slab from the frieze or a mutilated torso from the pediment of the Parthenon to expose it for what it is. Beside a genuine work of Hellenic art it cannot live for an instant. That this sentimental figure can ever have deceived the world might seem impossible, but that the words of Winckelmann, the verse of Byron remain to prove how infinitely man may deceive himself.

Perhaps the best statue in the Vatican is that which the authorities will not allow us to see, the " Aphrodite " called of Cnidus, though it is but a free copy of that lost glory. There does not seem to me to be a single statue or relief here that could for a moment be placed beside the work of Donatello or Luca della Robbia without exposing its want of spontaneity and life.

XXXV

THE FOUNTAINS

HORACE tells us somewhere that he is the friend of fountains, and, indeed, no true Roman, whether of the ancient or the modern world, can ever have been without some sentiment for them, since, in fact, they are the joy of Rome, her voice, as it were, a pleasant and a joyful voice ; for no city in Europe is so truly a city of running waters. All day long they waken in the heart some mystery of delight and refreshment ;—the slender jets of water wavering between the cypresses in the shadow, flashing in the sun, splashing among the statues on the cold marble. And their song in the cool, diaphanous mornings of spring is a song of life, of joy, of the brief joy of life.

And like most of that which is eternal in Rome, which is wholly characteristic of her and her own, the fountains, the song of the fountains, come to us hardly changed from the Rome which, in the splendour of its pride, conceived this luxury ; for it was Agrippa, the son-in-law of Augustus, who first dreamed of this beauty and refreshment, and endowed the city with a song. To Agrippa Rome owed much, but among his marvellous and enormous works nothing was at once so original, so noble, and so enduring as this which he contrived during the three years of his aedileship, building at his own cost two aqueducts, a hundred and thirty reservoirs, a naumachia, several baths and piscinae, and more than two hundred fountains, which, in many disguises, for the most part remain to us, they and their children.

The splendid gift of Agrippa was added to again and again. Caligula and Claudius, not to be outdone, built two new aqueducts, which brought to the city as much water, indeed, as all those that were before them, till in Trajan's time Rome had more than ten aqueducts feeding some thirteen hundred fountains.

And these joyful and pleasant waters, flashing and singing in the hot streets, the quiet piazzas, the shady gardens, were the pride of the people of Rome, and, in some sort, their most precious possession, so that at last some mystery seems to have passed into them, even the life of the City itself, and we find Rome defending her waters when she could scarcely hold her walls, with all the fierceness of a last hope. Were they not her life, her last luxury, her last joy ? Nor was she robbed of them till in 537 Vitiges and his Goths, masters of the Campagna, broke the long lines of the aqueducts, and left them as we now see them, more wonderful still than anything else within or without the City, lending their beauty to the tragic grandeur and solitude of the Campagna, the Latin plain ; and Rome was silenced. That blow seems to have been fatal. From that day the City gradually became the appalling ruin that she remained through all the Middle Age : till in the fifteenth century the Popes of the Renaissance, wishing to restore to her the leadership of the world, gave her back her waters, and suddenly, in a moment, as though by enchantment, she arose once more out of the wilderness and the ruins, healed and whole at the sound of that song.

Often very early in those spring mornings, which are so fair in Rome, or maybe on a summer evening, under a moon great and golden as the sun, I have wandered through the city of fountains for the sake of their song. It begins with the strange artificial voice of Pietro Bernini's Barcaccia in the Piazza di Spagna, where the Acqua Vergine falls humbly at the feet of the Madonna, that galley of war shooting forth from her guns, not death, but refreshment. Then, as I pass into the silence up the beautiful Scala di Spagna, and turn towards the Pincio, presently, still far off, I hear the most beautiful voice in Rome, the single aria, languid, and full of mystery and all enchantment, of the fountain before the Villa Medici, where, under the primeval ilex, a single jet of water towers like some exquisite slender lily, to droop, to fall in unimagined loveliness into the brimming vase of marble, so admirably simple and in place under those sacred trees, before that lofty villa, which, in some sort, dominates the whole City, and whence one may look across the towers and domes to the Capitol, to S. Peter's, to the Campagna stretching away to the sea.

No other fountain in Rome is at once so simple and so beautiful as this, nor is there another which commands so wide and so majestic a prospect. And yet, if one passes down the slope of the Pincio into the Piazza del Popolo, and so crossing the Ponte Margherita, and passing at last under the height of the Vatican, comes at last into the Piazza di S. Pietro, one finds there, in one of the holiest and most famous places in the world, two fountains, more beautiful in their way, though truly less simple, singing ever before the threshold of the shrine of the Apostle. Rising in the shape, as it were, of *fleurs de lys*, the water harmonises perfectly, not only with the fountains themselves, but with the beautiful piazza in which they are so marvellously placed, forming together with it the masterpiece of Bernini. Here, indeed, we have a beauty wholly artificial and architectural, perhaps the one perfect thing that the seventeenth century contrived in that art. We shall find an early effort of that period more romantic, both in its situation and contrivance, if we climb the Janiculum, and passing along its height through the Passeggiata Margherita, come at last, above the church of S. Pietro in Montorio, on the immense Acqua Paolina, the ancient Acqua Trajana, which draws its water from Lago di Bracciano, more than thirty miles away. The fountain, a huge façade, the work of Fontana and Maderna, under Paul V, in 1611, was built out of the materials of older buildings, the marble is from the Temple of Minerva in the Forum of Nerva, the granite pillars from the vestibule of old S. Peter's. Its grandiose beauty harmonises well with the site.

From the Acqua Paolina, in my early morning pilgrimage, I like to pass down to the Ponte Sisto where is the Fontana Paolo Quinto, built by Giovanni Fontana in 1617, but at the other end of the bridge ; and so crossing the Tiber I make my way into the Piazza Mattei, where, before the palace, stands the delicate and lovely Fountain of the Tortoises, built in 1585 by Giacomo della Porta and Taddeo Landini. Nothing in Rome is more alluring in a certain lightness and finesse than this fountain, where four slim youths, hold each a tortoise, grouped round a vase of water, which drains the upper basin.

From here, it is but a step back into Piazza Benedetto Cairoli, and so through Via di Giubbonari to the Campo de' Fiori and Piazza Farnese, whose two fountains remind us in their spacious setting of those in the Piazza di S. Pietro. Then crossing the Corso between the palaces we come to the perfect Piazza Navona, with its three fountains; that in the middle among the more extraordinary of all Bernini's works (1647), the brilliant and bizarre fountain with its obelisk and statues personifying the four great rivers of the world. The fountain at the south end of the Piazza is also by Bernini. The third is modern.

It is again to a work of Bernini we come, as, passing on through the City, we stand at last before the great fountain of Trevi, which resembles the Acqua Paolina, and which may be heard above all the noise of the Piazza. And it is fitting that, since Rome is the city of fountains, to make sure of one's return to her, it should be necessary to make an offering, not at the grave of Romulus, nor at the shrine of S. Peter, but to the greatest and most famous of her fountains, for it is said, whoever, at the hour of departure, drinks a cup of the water of Trevi and pays for it, has not looked on Rome for the last time.

The hour of departure, if indeed you keep it in the time-honoured way, and make your offering there in Piazza Trevi, will lead you by the way of my morning pilgrimage, first into Piazza Barberini, where another of Bernini's fountains, the beautiful Fountain of the Triton, still stands though now deprived of its quiet and charming background; and his Bee fountain re-erected in 1925. Then by the Via Quattro Fontane, past the four fountains, and so turning to the left there, past the Acqua Felice by Domenico Fontana, you may come into the Piazza delle Terme and the Railway Station. And it is well that your last thought in Rome, as indeed your first has been, should be one of astonishment, your last spectacle the sight of a fountain. For, as it happens, the modern Romans are not less in love with the sound and sight of running water than were their fathers of old. And while all the other fountains in Rome are restorations or works of the sixteenth and seventeenth centuries, here, for our encouragement, to greet us when we enter, to greet us when we depart, our Rome too has set up a great fountain of splashing water. It is true that it is vulgar, flamboyant, and eccentric, full, indeed, of every sort of astonishment. But in the luxury of its design, in the extraordinary gesture of its figures, in the splendour and gladness of its waters, it is to me a sign and a symbol of the new Rome, which, though she be indeed less noble and less strong than of old, is yet living and ready to entertain us : and we too may hear in her streets, as Horace did so long ago " the splash of fountains with jets of water clear."

XXXVI

SOME PALACES AND VILLAS

IN passing through almost all the cities of Italy—those cities which alone in the world might seem truly to vie in beauty with the country itself—really the first thing the traveller searches out is the great mediaeval palace, Palazzo della Signoria, Palazzo del Municipio, Palazzo Comunale, which is often the oldest and almost certainly the most splendid building remaining in the city to this day. It is so in such places as, for instance, Florence, Siena, and Perugia—but in Rome it is not so. In other cities of Italy the Middle Age has left plenty of secular memorials, but in Rome, too little : it was full of disturbance, and then when indeed, though late, it might have flowered with all the beauty we find in Florence, in Siena, in Pistoia, in Assisi, the Popes went into exile in Avignon, and the City was desolate. Thus, in looking at the secular buildings of the City, the earliest work we find that is not merely ruin is work of the Renaissance. The earliest palace is Palazzo Colonna, which was built by Pope Martin V in 1430, when peace, though not yet actually achieved, had been assured ; but it has suffered from rebuilding and restoration. Its best claim on our notice to-day is probably its fine gallery of pictures. At the end of the same Piazza SS. Apostoli is the Palazzo Muti, the Roman home of the Pretender.

A happier example of the art of the fifteenth century is to be found in the Palazzo Venezia, which Pope Paul II, Barbo of Venice, built in the Florentine style about 1455, while he was still a Cardinal, with stones he had brought from the ruin of the Colosseum. Vasari attributes the design to Giuliano da Maiano, but he seems to have had no hand in it. One is in fact altogether at a loss to say to whom it is due. The most picturesque and massive of Roman palaces, it was

presented in 1560 by Pius IV, Medici, to the Republic of
Venice, and so, in 1797, came into the hands of Austria,
whose embassy it remained till 1915. An interesting gallery
of pictures and furniture has been arranged in a wing of the
palace.

The church of San Marco at the back of the palace is
older than the Palace whose chapel it in some sort became when
the Venetian Pope Paul II enclosed the church in the palace
he had founded as a Cardinal. The church is, however, one
of the oldest in Rome, dating from the time of Constantine
when Pope Marcus the successor of Pope Sylvester dedicated it
in honour of S. Mark Evangelist. It was rebuilt in the ninth
century and it is from that time the tribune dates with its rather
disappointing mosaic. The Campanile too remains from an
early time and the ciborium, but the rest was demolished
when the church was rebuilt as part of the palace in the middle
of the fifteenth century.

The pavement of the church is far below the level of the
piazza and one descends to it by nine steps, to find oneself in
a small, well proportioned basilica of three aisles and now completely transformed in a baroque dress. The ceiling, however,
remains a magnificent piece of coloured and gilded coffering
of the fifteenth century. The mosaic, which is very much
restored, was once of the ninth century. In the apse is the full
length figure of Christ in benediction surrounded by SS.
Mark and Felicianus, Pope Gregory IV who rebuilt the church
and erected this mosaic, SS. Agapitus and Agnes. Above on
the arch are a bust of Christ and the symbols of the
four evangelists and below are the sheep of His pasture. The
pavement here is a work of the Cosmati.

If we follow the Corso Vittorio Emanuele (now Plebiscito)
downwards towards the Tiber, we shall presently come to the
immense pile of the Cancelleria, which was begun in 1486
by some Tuscan architect for Cardinal Raffaele Riario. It
is one of the noblest buildings in Rome, its beautiful arcaded
court, partly built from old materials, being perhaps its most
original feature. It has always remained the property of the Pope.

So with the end of the fifteenth century Rome began to
be once more the city of palaces under the Renaissance Popes

as under the Roman emperors. It was the time of Julius II
and of Leo X, of Raphael, of Michelangelo, of Bramante, of
Peruzzi, and Sangallo. Peruzzi built, in 1508, for the Sienese
banker, Agostino Chigi, the Farnesina, which Raphael, Giulio
Romano, and Giovanni da Udine decorated for him with the
Story of Psyche, in twelve scenes enclosed with garlands.
The ceiling alone is covered, the scenes being confined to that
part of the story which took place on Olympus. It was probably intended to cover the walls with the more human part
of the story. Unhappily this was never achieved, and what we
have has been spoiled by the unhappy restoration of Maratta.
In another apartment Raphael has painted, with more charm
too, Galatea borne across the sea in a sea-shell surrounded
by Nymphs, Tritons, and Loves ; while to the left Sebastiano
del Piombo has painted Polyphemus trying in vain to move
her with love songs.

> *Huc ades, o Galatea, quis est nam ludus in undis?*
> *hic ver purpureum, varios hic flumina circum*
> *fundit humus flores, hic candida populus antro*
> *imminet et lentae texunt umbracula vites :*
> *huc ades, insani feriant sine litora fluctus . . .*

The ceiling in this room is the work of Peruzzi.

The Farnesina passed from the Chigi in 1580 to Cardinal
Alessandro Farnese by inheritance. This family, which
became extinct in 1731, had already built, in 1516, by the
hand of Antonio da Sangallo, the magnificent Palazzo Farnese,
perhaps the most splendid palace in Rome, which Michelangelo, Vignola, and Giacomo della Porta decorated and
finished, and which the Carracci decorated with the lovely
pictures of Bacchus and Ariadne, Pan and Diana, Aurora and
Cephalus, Galatea and Acis and such. When the Farnese
became extinct in the eighteenth century, this palace, which
since 1874 has been the French Embassy, passed with the
Farnesina to the Kings of Naples.

We come upon Sangallo's work again in the Palazzo
Sacchetti, but indeed the palaces of the sixteenth and seventeenth centuries are innumerable, among the more famous

being the Palazzo Corsini, Palazzo Borghese, Palazzo Chigi, and Palazzo Barberini, which is a work of Maderna and Bernini and perhaps the finest of these buildings of the Baroque period, full of faults of construction, but sumptuous and splendid. The Palazzo Doria-Pamphili, built in 1655, one may examine within to some extent, for it contains a gallery of pictures, among them being the most splendid portrait in Rome, Velasquez' Innocent X, and an early work by Titian, a Salome.

But if the palaces are, in spite of their size and splendour, a little dull, a little lacking in interest and beauty, so that nowhere in Rome may we find one that moves us as the Palazzo Pubblico in Siena does, or as a few of the wonderful buildings in Florence or on the Grand Canal in Venice do, it is otherwise with the Villas. Rome is unique among the cities of the world in possessing them, and they are unique in their loveliness and charm. They have nothing in common with anything in England, but one might feel something of their charm if Hampton Court Palace with its gardens were suddenly to be found in the midst of London. And yet, even then, there would be something too much, and a certain artificiality would be lacking, an artificiality that makes of the gardens and parks of the Roman villa only a continuation as it were of the saloons, which makes of the saloons only a cooler and more private part of the garden. Such were those villas, almost numberless, of the seventeenth and eighteenth centuries, Albani, Colonna, Medici, Mattei, Corsini, Ludovisi, Negroni, Borghese, Pamphili. If to-day, in those which remain to us after the awful vandalism of the nineteenth century, neglect has sometimes allowed nature so free a hand that they have changed their character, it is always with regret we see it, and yet who can deny the mysterious charm of lichen-grown statues, tangled woods, grass-grown paths and silent fountains, among which in spring the wildflowers run unchecked?

But Italy is not England. Nature, here in Italy, is very surely master or servant, and might seem never able to be our friend as in England. Here the sun is god, and your garden must be artificial if you would have a garden at all. Flowers are an affair of pots and careful tending, and save in spring, one must in fact do without them on any other terms. Nor does one need their colour, when earth and sky, two blinding jewels, make all invisible but their own splendour. One thinks only of the shadow, of the shade, and so, instead of a lawn, one plants a bosco of ilex, instead of walks between the flowers, alley-ways of cypresses, of laurel, of sacred ilex, while, for a flower-bed, one builds a fountain.

The Roman villa garden is just that ; it has an air of the eighteenth century ; it is full of silence. The cypresses are set thickly in a half-circle about a statue, or in long alley-ways that lead to a fountain ; vista passes into vista, till you are led to lose yourself in the twilight of the bosco, in the midst of which you find yourself suddenly at the foot of a magical staircase of stone, wide and spacious and beautiful, and passing up it, you come at last to a little summer house of marble, just above the tree-tops, and there, far below you, is Rome.

Or again, you pass from terrace to terrace, between the trees, half in fear, while fountain calls to fountain, and the cypresses burn ever in the sun, and the air is heavy with their incense.

And everywhere there are fountains—at the end of every way, at the turning of every path, in the midst of every cloister, at the end of every terrace. And these are the Roman gardens —only we miss the flowers.

This spaciousness, these silences, these lines that are indeed architectural and contrived with a profound art, are Roman, are classic. Ancient Rome must have conceived of a garden, one may think, somewhat in this fashion : on these lines the gardens of Lucullus were planted and built. Is that why they appealed so strongly to the Renaissance ?

But of all these villas with their marvellous gardens which were once the glory of Rome, but few remain. Of those which are still left to us, perhaps the best known are the Villa Pamphili, the Villa Medici, and the Villa Borghese. The first is of an incomparable loveliness, the second of an incomparable mystery, the third is less rare, and of late has become one of the playgrounds of Rome, larger and more spaciously beautiful and less crowded than the Pincio. But in truth the Villa Borghese, with its gardens and park, is still one of the

most enchanting things in the City. Yes, it remains to con-
sole us, since we have seen so much that was perfect turned into
building sites by rascals for rascals. And then it adds to its
other delights a treasure of art, a collection of pictures that is
the finest in the City.

The Villa was built in the early years of the seventeenth
century by Cardinal Scipione Borghese, nephew of Pope Paul
V ; and was bought, with its magnificent collection of pictures,
and beautiful gardens and parks, by the Italian government for
£144,000, much less than its real value, in 1901.

On entering the Villa we find that the spacious saloons on
the ground floor are devoted to the collection of sculpture
which was so unfortunately depleted by Prince Camillo
Borghese, who sold more than two hundred pieces to Napoleon
for the Louvre. There remain here, however, perhaps the
most famous works of Bernini and of Canova—four works
by Bernini among them the exquisite group of Apollo and
Daphne, and by Canova the portrait statue as Venus of Pauline
Buonaparte, the wife of Prince Camillo, which he allowed no
one to look on but himself. As to the Venus, it is said that when
the Princess was asked whether she did not feel uncomfortable
when sitting to Canova, she replied : " Oh no, there was a
fire."

But it is really the Gallery of Pictures which calls for our
wonder and admiration, since it is, perhaps, the finest general
collection of the Italian masterpieces of the sixteenth and
seventeenth centuries anywhere to be found. A few pictures
by the Florentines of the fifteenth century serve, as it were, as
introduction. Among these are a fine Madonna and Child
with S. John and Angels of the school of Botticelli, and a
Madonna and Child with S. John, by Lorenzo di Credi.
The Florentine school of the sixteenth century is represented
by a good portrait of a Cardinal and a picture of Tobias and
the Angel, by Pontormo. As for the Umbrians, we find there a
Crucifixion with SS. Christopher and Jerome, an early work
by Fiorenzo di Lorenzo ; a portrait of Perugino, an early
work by Raphael ; and the celebrated Entombment, painted
in 1507 by the same master, as well as a Venus by Baldassare
Peruzzi.

But the true glory of the gallery consists not only, or even chiefly, in the work of Raphael, but in four works by the greatest master of that or any other period, Titian, the first belonging to his youth, the others to his old age.

The Sacred and Profane Love, painted about 1512 for Niccolò Aurelio, Grand Chancellor of Venice, is the highest achievement of Titian's art at the end of his Giorgionesque period. It has been in this collection since 1613, when it was called " Beltà diornata e Beltà ornata "—" Beauty unadorned and Beauty adorned." In fact, the name it now bears, which has so puzzled the world, does not occur till the end of the eighteenth century, when it seems to have been given it by the Germans. For us, at least, it can have no authority, the subject of the picture being merely a moment of beauty— a moment gone, but for Titian's genius, while we try to apprehend it, in the golden summer heat, under the trees by a fountain of water. Its only fellow is the Three Ages by the same master in the Ellesmere collection.

In the Education of Cupid we see a work of Titian's late period, full of mastery and a wonderful originality, but certainly without the sheer lyrical and mysterious beauty of that early masterpiece. And yet each picture is in its own mood unapproachable. In the first we see all the brilliance and poetry of youth, in the second, the absolute triumph of an art which has been immensely successful, and has paid the price of triumph.

The third picture here by Titian, the S. Dominic, is also a work of his later period, though scarcely so late as the Education of Cupid. It seems to have been painted about 1565. It is a very noble and impressive picture, full of all those intellectual qualities which we find in his work of this time, and by no means without a profound spiritual power. He seems to have set himself a problem in colour of the most difficult and intricate sort, and to have solved it with his usual ease and harmony.

The fourth picture from his hand is the Christ at the Column, also a late work.

From Titian we pass to the work of his pupils, Paris Bordone in a Jupiter and Antiope, and Jacopo Bassano in a Last Supper,

ACIS AND GALATEA, by A. Carracci (Palazzo Farnese)

THE SABINE HILLS

and a picture of the Trinity ; to the work of his contemporaries in the Lucrece and the Madonna with SS. Francis and Jerome of Palma Vecchio, and the Madonna with S. Onofrio and a Bishop, and the Portrait of a Man, by Lorenzo Lotto ; while the work of his predecessors is represented by the Portrait of a Man, by Antonello da Messina.

Nor are the North Italian schools of Ferrara, Bologna, and Parma unrepresented. Of the first we have the fine and magical Circe, by Dosso Dossi, and the Holy Family and the Landscape by his brother, Battista di Dosso, the Descent from the Cross, by Ortolano. Of the second, the exquisite S. Stephen, by Francia, the academic Caccia di Diana, by Domenichino, which Stendhal so much admired that he refused to look at any other picture on the same day. Of the third, the splendid Danae, by Correggio, the fine Portrait by Parmigianino.

But, after all, what we have come here to see is the Sacred and Profane Love, by Titian, and that will lead us, not from picture to picture in a sudden enthusiasm for painting, but most certainly back again into the gardens, where the world is so sleepily golden in the heat, and the shade so cool and grateful. There we shall linger till, from the far-away city, the Ave Mary rings from all the cupolas, and we must return down the long alleys in the softly fading light, stealing softly, half reluctantly, out of the world of dreams back into the streets and the ways of men.

T

XXXVII

THE CAMPAGNA

ROME possesses nothing half so lovely, half so precious, half so venerable, as the Campagna, in which she lies like a ship in the midst of the sea, now just visible over the billows, now lost altogether in that vast solitude of which, for the most part, she is oblivious. My happiest hours during all my sojourns in Rome have been spent in the Campagna, at all hours of the day, at every season of the year.

This immense and universal thing which lies unregarded at the gates of the Eternal City is the one Roman possession to be loved without reserve or any afterthought. One loves it at first sight, and to leave it still brings tears to the eyes. And yet one feels no intimacy with it, as one does with the Umbrian valleys and the Tuscan hillsides. It is too vast and too silent for intimacy : but it has our fear and love as God has them, because it is more enduring than we, and in some sort has produced us. It has, too, the indefinite beauty of all supernatural things. One may find there always all that is in one's heart, and each will find what he brings and the reward of which he is worthy. It is too beautiful to praise and too mysterious to explain or to describe. You may map all its roads and name all its ruins, number the arches of its aqueducts, and call all its towns and villages by name, and when you have finished, you are aware you have done nothing, and you find yourself at last speaking of it as every one must do, as it were in images, with vague words of beauty and mystery and love, as of a place seen in a vision, as the English speak of the sea. For, as the sea is the secret of England, so the Campagna is the secret of Rome ; it haunts the City, and the majesty and largeness of its silence are the springs of her immortality. Nor may you long escape it, for all the great ways lead to it at last, and it surges against every gate.

All unaware of this world of involate silence which guards the Eternal City as no other city was ever guarded, you catch sight of it first, perhaps, at evening from the Pincio, or in the early morning from the Janiculum, or at sunset from the quietness of the Aventine. From wherever you first see it, it calls you instantly in its solemn immensity, its vast indwelling strength, its ruined splendour, across which the broken arches of the aqueducts stagger still, and the vague white roads, lined with empty and rifled tombs, wander aimlessly, losing themselves in the silence and vastness that only the mountains may contain. And it is the mountains which hem in the Campagna, the most beautiful mountains in the world.

Wherever you may go in Rome, after that first revelation, whatever you may see, before whatever shrine you may kneel, it is the Campagna which is in your heart, for you have discovered Rome, the soul of Rome. Did you think, then, it was this trumpery ruin or that, the Colosseum, a heap of cruel bricks, S. Peter's and its tomb, that had captured the world? But it is Rome that is eternal, and you will find her in the Campagna.

You will come to it first, doubtless, half unaware, toward the end of the day, perhaps after visiting S. Sebastiano, on the Via Appia. You will think to venture only so far as the tomb of Caecilia Metella, but if you go so far you will never really come back; evening will find you still following that marvellous ruined road between the tombs that never ends, with the gaunt ruins of the broken aqueducts going along with you, and when at last the sunset finds you far from home, and after sunset night, you will return changed for ever by those few short hours, and the whole world will have for you, as for me, a new and more mysterious meaning.

And you will return, often you will return; hours, days, weeks, months will be consumed on that most ancient way, where the broken marble lies upon the stones that Caesar trod, and the dead are more alive than the living.

Though it were without history or renown, and man had given it no name, this unbroken wilderness would yet hold us by reason of the splendour of its form, its vastness, and silence, the breadth of its undulations, the transparency of its light, the beauty of its colour, the nobility of the mountains that contain it. But seeing that it is the cradle of our history, and that its name is Latium, to look upon it rouses within us much the same emotion as that with which, after long absence, we look upon our home. Nothing that man has dared to do or to think, no sorrow he has suffered, nor passion he has endured or conquered, his profoundest desires, his most tenacious hate, his most splendid domination, his most marvellous love, nothing that is his is a stranger there. Of all those forces it is a monument, the grandest and the most terrible, the monument of man—a vast graveyard.

It is this one comes to realise at last, as day after day, week after week, one passes along that ancient Appian Way, between the crumbling tombs. Here and there we may find them still, the likeness of our brother carved in relief, some thought of his about it all, a few Latin words, part of an inscription, half hidden with the grass and the flowers. And as night overtakes us on that marvellous road, when the splendour of sunset is faded, and the stars one by one have scattered the heavens with hope, in the immense silence that nothing may break our imagination sinks beneath the lonely majesty of that desert, littered with the monsters of old forgotten religions, full of the dead things of Paganism and Christianity, the bones of saints, the mighty trunks of forgotten gods.

What more is there to come out of that vast grave, that marvellous solitude ?

APPENDIX I

LIST OF CHRISTIAN MOSAICS IN ROME

Santa Costanza : mosaics in roof of ambulatory (IV century) —mosaics in niches (VII–VIII century).

San Giovanni in Laterano : Baptistery mosaic in apse of Atrium (IV century)—mosaic of Cappella di S. Giovanni (V century)—mosaic of S. Venanzio (VII century) —mosaic of apse of the Basilica (XIII century), entirely restored.

Santa Pudentiana : mosaic of apse (V century).

Santa Maria Maggiore : mosaics of nave and of triumphal arch (III, IV, V century ?)—mosaic of apse (Torriti, XIII century)—mosaic in loggia of façade (Rusuti, XIII century)—mosaic in tomb of Rodriquez (XIII century).

Santa Sabina : inscription with two figures (V century).

San Paolo fuori le Mura : mosaic of triumphal arch (V century)—mosaic of apse (XIII century).

Santi Cosma e Damiano : mosaics of apse and triumphal arch (VI century).

San Lorenzo fuori le Mura : mosaic of triumphal arch (VI century).

San Teodoro : mosaic of apse (VII century).

Sant' Agnese : mosaic of apse (VII century).

Santo Stefano Rotondo : mosaic of apse (VII century).

San Pietro in Vincoli : mosaic panel of S. Sebastiano (VII century).

Santa Maria in Cosmedin : mosaic panel of Adoration of Magi (VIII century).

Santi Nereo ed Achilleo : mosaic on triumphal arch (VIII century).

Santa Maria in Domnica : mosaics of apse and triumphal arch (IX century).

Santa Prassede : mosaics of arch and apse (IX century) —
mosaic of Cappella di S. Zenone (IX century).

Santa Cecilia in Trastevere : mosaic of apse (IX century).

San Marco : mosaic of apse (IX century).

Santa Francesca Romana : mosaic of apse (XII century).

San Clemente : mosaic of apse (XII century).

Santa Maria in Trastevere : mosaics of apse and triumphal
arch (XIII century)—mosaic of façade (Cavallini,
XIII century).

Cappella di Sancta Sanctorum : mosaic over the altar
(XIII century).

San Tommaso in Formis : mosaic of façade (XIII century).

Santa Maria in Aracoeli : mosaic over side door (XIII
century).

San Crisogono : mosaic of Virgin enthroned (XIV century).

APPENDIX II

LIST OF CHIEF BAROQUE ARCHITECTURAL WORKS IN ROME

BY

CARLO MADERNA, BERNINI, BORROMINI AND PIETRO DA CORTONA

CARLO MADERNA (1556–1629)

1603—S. Susanna (especially façade)).
—S. Gregorio Magno : Salviati chapel (with Volterra).
—S. Maria della Vittoria.
1607–1629—S. Pietro : prolongation of nave, façade, and one fountain in the Piazza.
—S. Giovanni de' Fiorentini : cupola.
1623—S. Andrea della Valle.

GIOVANNI LORENZO BERNINI (1598–1680)

1624–33—S. Pietro : baldacchino.
1626—S. Bibiana : façade.
1627—Palazzo di Propaganda : façade.
1630—Palazzo Barberini.
1635—S. Pietro : tomb of Contessa Matilda.
1640—Fontana del Tritone.
1643—Fontana delle Api.
1647—S. Pietro : tomb of Urban VIII.
1647—S. Maria della Vittoria : Cornaro chapel.
1647–1652—Fontana della Piazza Navona.
1648—S. Pietro in Montorio : Raimondi chapel.
1650—Palazzo di Montecitorio.
1656—S. Maria del Popolo : decoration.
1658—S. Andrea al Quirinale.
1663—S. Pietro : Colonnades.

1665—S. Pietro : Cattedra di S. Pietro.
1666—Palace of the Vatican : Scala Regia.
1667—Ponte S. Angelo : statues and decoration. Two angels
in S. Andrea delle Fratte.
1672—S. Pietro : tomb of Alexander VII.
1674—S. Pietro : Ciborio of Blessed Sacrament chapel.

FRANCESCO BORROMINI (1599–1667)

1624–1634—Palazzo Barberini (with Maderna).
1632–1660—Palazzo della Sapienza with cupola and lantern.
1638–1667—S. Carlino.
1637–1642—Oratory and Convent of the Oratorians
1638—Palazzo Spada.
1640—S. Ivo della Sapienza.
1647–1650—Rebuilding of S. Giovanni in Laterano.
1653–1657—S. Agnese in Piazza Navona.
1654—S. Andrea delle Fratte : campanile and cupola.
1660—S. Girolamo di Carità : Spada chapel.
1664—S. Giovanni de' Fiorentini : cappella maggiore.
1667—S. Carlino : (façade completed 1682).

PIETRO DA CORTONA (1596–1669)

1629—Palazza Barberini.
1625—SS. Luca e Martina.
1656—S. Maria della Pace : façade and interior decoration.
1658—S. Maria in Via Lata : façade and portico.
1665—S. Carlo al Corso : cupola.

APPENDIX III
LIST OF PICTURES OF THE SEVENTEENTH CENTURY IN ROME

ALBANI, FRANCESCO (1578–1660) :

Albani gallery : Repose in Egypt.

Borghese gallery : Toilette of Venus—Mars Jealous—Venus—Diana Triumphant.

Colonna gallery : Ecce Homo—Rape of Europa.

Capitoline gallery : The Magdalen.

Corsini gallery : Mercury, Apollo and the Muses—Venus sleeping—Venus and Amorini—Virgin and Child.

Doria-Pamphili gallery : Assumption.

BACICCIO (GAULLI, G.-B., 1639–1709) :

S. Agnese : Four Cardinal Virtues.

S. Andrea al Quirinale : Death of S. Francis Xavier.

S. Francesco a Ripa : S. Anne kneeling before the Virgin and Child.

Il Gesù : Vault of Nave, Adoration of the Name of Jesus—Left transept vault, Apotheosis of S. Francis Xavier—Dome : Assumption—Apotheosis : Four Prophets—Apse : Adoration of the Lamb.

Spada Gallery : Sketch for Adoration of the Name of Jesus.

BAROCCI, FEDERIGO (1528–1612) :

S. Maria in Vallicella : Presentation in the Temple.

Accademia di S. Luca : Repose in Egypt.

Borghese gallery : Aeneas fleeing from Troy.—S Girolamo.

Corsini gallery : Noli me Tangere.—Holy Family.

Doria-Pamphili gallery : Head of a Youth (drawing).

Vatican Pinacoteca : Flight into Egypt—Annunciation—Ecstasy of S. Michelina.

CARAVAGGIO IL (1569–1609) :

S. Agostino : Madonna del Popolo.

S. Luigi de' Francesi : S. Matthew and the Angel—Vocation of S. Matthew—Martyrdom of S. Matthew.

S. Maria della Concezione (S. Cappuccini) : S. Francis.
S. Maria del Popolo : Martyrdom of S. Peter—Conversion of S. Paul.
Barberini gallery : Portrait of Sister of Beatrice Cenci.
Borghese gallery : David with head of Goliath—La Vergine dal serpente—S. John Baptist—S. Jerome —Boy with a basket of Flowers.
Colonna gallery : Il Gaudente.
Corsini gallery : Narcissus.
Doria-Pamphili gallery : S. John Baptist—the Magdalen —Repose in Egypt.
Sciarra gallery : Dishonest Gamester.
Spada gallery : The Drinkers—The Virgin and S. Anne—S. Cecilia—David with head of Goliath —Geometry.
Vatican Pinacoteca : Deposition—Denial of S. Peter.
CARRACCI, ANNIBALE (1560–1609) ; AGOSTINO (1557–1602).
S. Caterina de' Funari : S. Margherita.
S. Maria del Popolo : Assumption.
Capitoline gallery : S. Sebastian.
Colonna gallery : Il Mangiafagiuoli.
Doria-Pamphili gallery : Deposition—Visitation—Nativity—Adoration of Magi—Flight into Egypt (landscape)-Assumption–Pietà–S. Mary Magdalen.
Farnese gallery : Mythological frescoes : Triumph of Bacchus and Ariadne—Mercury and Paris—Pan and Diana—Diana and Endymion—Venus and Anchises—Polyphemus, Acis and Galatea—Aurora and Cephalus, etc.
Spada gallery : Pietà.
CAVALIER D'ARPINO (1560–1640) :
S. Maria in Vallicella : Coronation of the Virgin.
S. Prassede : Ascension—Prophets and Sibyls—Moses— Jeremiah.
Borghese gallery : Judgment of Paris.
Vatican Pinacoteca : Annunciation.
CAVALLINO, BERNARDO (1622–58).
Corsini gallery : S. Peter and Cornelius—Tobiolo si congeda dal padre.

CLAUDE LORRAINE (1600–1682) :
Accademia di S. Luca : Seaport.
Colonna gallery : Landscape.
Doria-Pamphili gallery : Landscape with Hippolytus
and the Arician Artemis—Landscape with Mer-
cury and the kine of Apollo—Sacrifice in Delphi
—Landscape : the Mill—Landscape with Return
of Holy Family from Egypt.

DOLCI, CARLO (1616–1686) :
Borghese gallery : Virgin and Child (2 pictures)—The
Saviour.
Corsini gallery : S. Apollonia.

DOMENICHINO (DOMENICO ZAMPIERI, 1581–1641) :
S. Andrea della Valle : Frescoes, Ecce Agnus Dei, in
Apse—Four Evangelists under cupola—and in
choir, Life of S. Andrew—Virtues.
S. Carlo ai Catinari : Frescoes under Cupola.
S. Cecilia : Angel crowning SS. Cecilia and Valerian.
S. Gregorio Magno : Chapel of S. Andrew : Martyrdom
of S. Andrew.
S. Luigi de' Francesi : Life of S. Cecilia.
S. Maria degli Angeli : Martyrdom of S. Sebastian.
S. Maria in Trastevere : Vault of Nave : Assumption.
S. Maria della Vittoria : Virgin and Child with S. Francis.
S. Onofrio : Three frescoes of life of S. Jerome.
S. Pietro in Vincoli : Sacristy : Deliverance of S. Peter.
S. Silvestro al Quirinale : Four Scenes from the Old
Testament.
Barberini gallery : Expulsion from Paradise.
Borghese gallery : Caccia di Diana.
Costaguti gallery : The Chariot of Apollo.
Doria-Pamphili gallery : Landscape—The Ford.
Vatican Pinacoteca : Communion of S. Jerome (1614).

FETI, DOMENICO (1589–1624) :
Borghese gallery : Madonna and Child.
Doria-Pamphili gallery : The Magdalen.

GENTILESCHI, ORAZIO (1597–1651) :

S. Adriano : S. Pietro Nolasco.
S. Cecilia : Madonna and Child.
Corsini gallery : S. Francis.

GHERARDO DELLA NOTTE (1590–1656) :

S. Maria della Scala : Beheading of St. John Baptist.
Borghese gallery :—Susanna and the Elders—Concert.
Doria-Pamphili gallery : Head of a Youth in the light of
    a candle—Youth with lantern—Young woman
    pouring oil on to a lamp and four others.

GIORDANO, LUCA (1632–1705) :

Albani gallery : Bacchanal (2 pictures)—Roman Charity.
Borghese gallery : Death of S. Ignatius.
Capitoline gallery : The Golden Fleece.

GIOVANNI DA S. GIOVANNI (1592–1636) :

S. Maria del Popolo : Frescoes in vault of third chapel
    on left.
SS. Quattro Coronati : Fresco in apse.

GUERCINO, IL (1591–1666) :

S. Pietro in Vincoli : S. Margherita.
Accademia di S. Luca : Venus and Cupid.
Barberini gallery : S. Matthew.
Borghese gallery : Return of Prodigal Son.
Capitoline gallery : S. John Baptist—S. Petronilla—
    Sibilla Persica—Cleopatra and Octavius.
Colonna gallery : Angel and Tobias.
Corsini gallery : Ecce Homo—Christ and the Woman of
    Samaria—Annunciation (2 pictures)—S. Jerome—
    Il Presepio.
Ludovisi Casino : Aurora—Notte.
Spada gallery : Portrait of Cardinal Spada—Death of
    Dido.
Vatican Pinacoteca : Incredulity of S. Thomas—S.
    Margaret of Cortona—The Magdalen.

LANFRANCO, GIOVANNI (1581–1647) :
S Andrea della Valle : Assumption (in cupola).
S. Carlo ai Catinari : Fresco in apse : Apotheosis of
S. Carlo—Virgin with Saints.
Doria-Pamphili gallery : Polyphemus and Galatea—
Deliverance of S. Peter.
Corsini gallery : S. Agatha.

MARATTA, CARLO (1625–1713) :
Chiesa dei Sette Dolori : S. Augustine.
S. Isidoro : Dream of S. Joseph.
S. Maria degli Angeli : Baptism.
S. Maria del Popolo : Second chapel on right : Im-
maculate Conception.
S. Maria in Vallicella : Madonna with Saints (altarpiece
of Spada Chapel).
S. Pietro in Vincoli : Annunciation.
Albani gallery : Portrait of Clement XI (Albani)—
Election of Cardinal Albani as Pope—Resurrection
of Lazarus—Death of the Virgin.
Barberini gallery : Portrait of Taddeo Barberini.
Borghese gallery : Madonna with S. Giovanni.
Corsini gallery : Portrait—Portrait of the painter's
daughter, Faustina—The Virgin—Virgin and Child
with Saints—Holy Family.
Quirinale Palace : Adoration of the Shepherds.
Vatican Pinacoteca : Holy Family.

MOLA, PIER FRANCESCO (1612–1668) :
SS. Domenico e Sisto : Apparition of S. Domenico.
Borghese gallery : Portrait of a Youth—Deliverance of
S. Peter.
Capitoline gallery : Hagar and Ishmael.
Corsini gallery : Portrait of Fulvia Testi.
Doria-Pamphili gallery : Head of a Young Woman—
Ecstasy of S. Bruno.

PADOVANINO, IL (1590–1650) :
Doria-Pamphili gallery : Entombment.
Corsini gallery : Portrait of a Lady.
Rospigliosi-Pallavicini gallery : Vanity.

PASSIGNANO, IL (1560–1638) :
S. Maria Maggiore : Sacristy : The vault frescoes.
Doria-Pamphili gallery : Nativity.

PIETRO DA CORTONA (1596–1669) :
S. Maria in Vallicella : Decorations : Apse, Assumption ;
Sacristy vault : Camera of S. Philip, vault : Life
of the Saint.
S. Maria della Concezione(Cappuccini): Healing of S. Paul.
Barberini Palace : Ceiling paintings—Glory of Urban VIII.
Barberini gallery : Sacrifice to Diana.
Borghese gallery : Portrait of Giuseppe Ghislieri.
Conservatori gallery : Portrait of Urban VIII—Rape of
Sabines.
Doria-Pamphili gallery : Sacrifice of Noah—Erminia
among the Shepherds.
Palazzo Doria-Pamphili : Frescoes of the Aeneid.

POUSSIN, GASPARD (1613–1675) :
S. Martino ai Monti : Story of Prophet Elias.
Colonna gallery : Six landscapes.
Doria-Pamphili gallery : Flight into Egypt—St. Augus-
tine and Angel—Two Landscapes.

POUSSIN, NICOLAS (1594–1665) :
Barberini gallery : Death of Germanicus.
Colonna gallery : Shepherds' dream.
Corsini gallery : Triumph of David.
Doria-Pamphili gallery : Landscape.
Vatican Pinacoteca : Martyrdom of S. Erasmus.

POZZO, ANDREA (1642–1709) :
S. Maria Maggiore : Sacristy : the Presepio.
Il Gesù : Corridor leading to Camera of S. Ignatius :
two paintings of Life of Ignatius.
S. Ignazio : Fresco of vault of nave : Glorification of the
Company of Jesus—Entry of S. Ignatius into
Paradise ;—Apse : Vision of S. Ignatius.
Accademia di S. Luca : Death of S. Cecilia.

RENI, GUIDO (1575–1642) :
S. Carlo ai Catinari : Fresco in choir : S. Charles in
ecstasy.

S. Gregorio Magno : S. Andrew on his way to Martyrdom, fresco.—Chapel of S. Silvia : A Concert of Angels, fresco.

S. Lorenzo in Lucina : Crucifixion.

S. Maria della Concezione (Cappuccini) : S. Michael Archangel.

S. Maria in Vallicella : Camera of S. Philip—Apparition of the Madonna to S. Philip.

Accademia di S. Luca : Fortune—Putto with dove—The Addolorata.

Albani gallery : Bacchus and Ariadne—The Virgin of Sorrows—Ecce Homo.

Barberini gallery : Portrait of Beatrice Cenci(?)—S. S. Andrea Corsini.

Capitoline gallery : S. Sebastian—The Magdalen.

Colonna gallery : S. Agnes.

Corsini gallery : Ecce Homo—L'Addolorata—S. John Baptist—The Young S. John Baptist—Portrait of Vittoria Albani—Salome with head of Baptist—S. Joseph.

Doria-Pamphili gallery : Virgin in Adoration—Putti at play.

Quirinal Palace Chapel : Annunciation and frescoes.

Rospigliosi-Pallavicini gallery : Aurora and the Hours—Perseus and Andromeda.

Spada gallery : Portrait of Cardinal Bernardino Spada—Judith with the head of Holofernes—Rape of Helen—Lucrece.

Vatican Biblioteca : Vault of Sala Aldobrandini : Story of Samson.

Vatican Pinacoteca: Martyrdom of S. Peter–Virgin in glory.

ROMANELLI, GIOV. FRANCESCO (1610–1662) :

S. Maria degli Angeli : Presentation in Temple.

Barberini gallery : Bacchus and Ariadne.

Capitoline gallery : S. Cecilia.

ROSA, SALVATOR (1615–1673) :

S. Giovanni de' Fiorentini : Martyrdom of SS. Cosma and Damiano.

Colonna gallery : Coast Scene.

Corsini gallery : Battle piece.

Doria-Pamphili gallery : Landscape—Gruppi di Bravi (2 pictures).

Quirinale Palace : Fresco : Gideon's Fleece.

Spada gallery : Cain and Abel—Several Landscapes.

SACCHI, ANDREA (1598–1661) :
S. Carlo ai Catinari : Death of S. Anne.
S. Paolo fuori le Mura : Pinacoteca : Vision of Blessed Thomas of Celano.
Barberini Palace : Celestial Wisdom.
Borghese gallery : Portrait of Orazio Giustiniani—Portrait of G. L. Bernini—Portrait of M. Merlini.
Corsini gallery : Portrait of S. Philip Neri.
Vatican Pinacoteca : Miracle of S. Gregory—Vision of S. Romuald.

SARACENI, CARLO (1585–1625) :
S. Adriano : S. Raimondo.
S. Maria dell' Anima : Miracle of San Benone.
Barberini gallery : Suonatrice di Liuto.
Corsini gallery : Vanity.

SASSOFERRANTO, IL (1609–1685) :
S. Sabina : Madonna of the Rosary.
Accademia di S. Luca : Virgin and Child.
Borghese gallery : Virgin and Child—Three Ages of Man (copy of Titian).
Doria-Pamphili gallery : Holy Family—Adoration of the Child.
Vatican Pinacoteca : Virgin in Glory—Portrait of a Cardinal.

SPAGNOLETTO, IL (RIBERA) (1588–1656) :
Accademia di S. Luca : S. Jerome disputing with the Jews.
Borghese gallery : S. Mary of Egypt—S. Jerome.
Doria-Pamphili gallery : S. Jerome in Wilderness.
Vatican Pinacoteca : Martyrdom of S. Laurence.

STROZZI, BERNARDO (1581–1644) :
Corsini gallery : The Beggar.

VELASQUEZ, DIEGO (1599–1660) :
Capitoline gallery : Self Portrait.
Doria-Pamphili gallery : Portrait of Innocent X.

INDEX